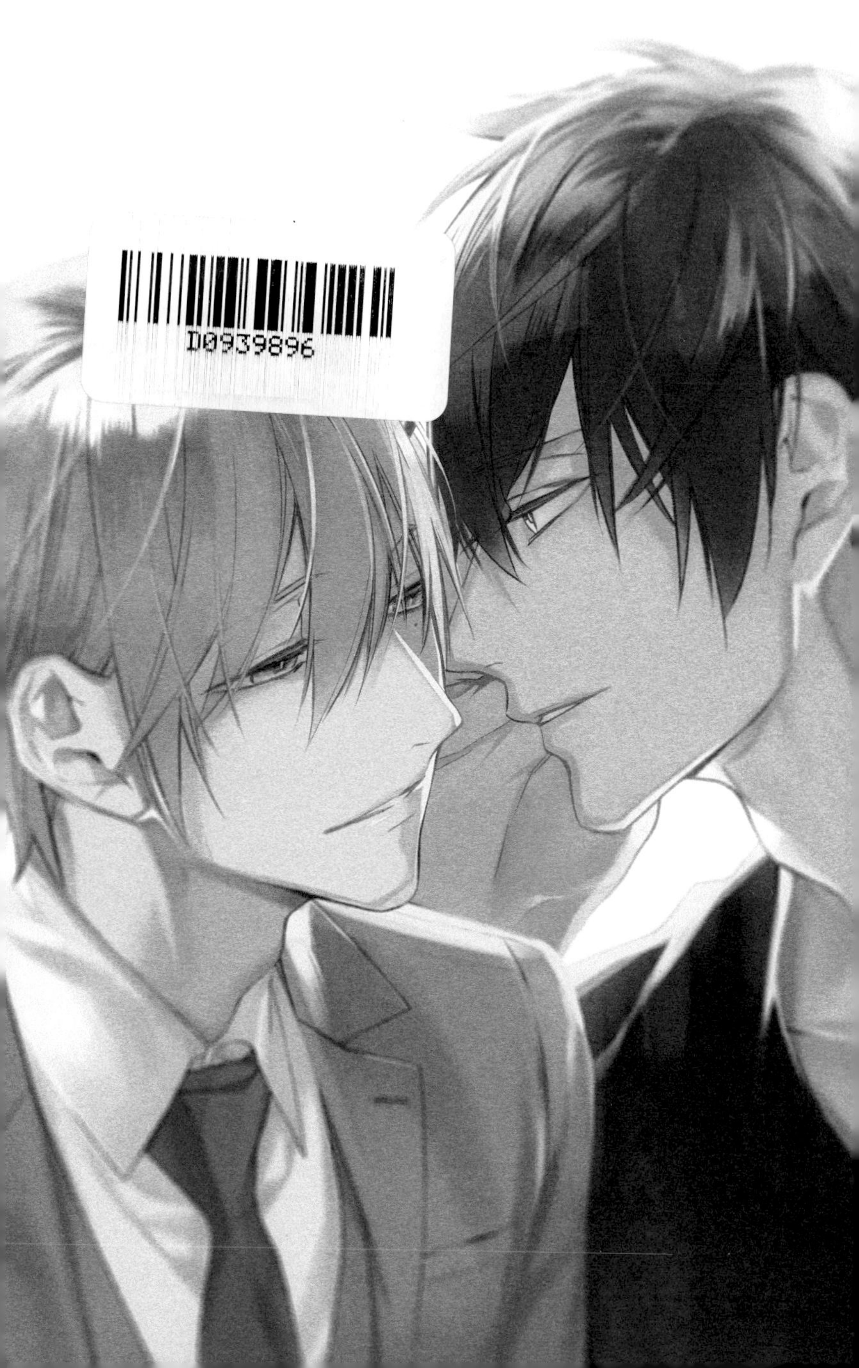

Ten Count

Story and Art by **Rihito Takarai** volume **4**

CONTENTS

SUBLIME
SuBLime Manga Edition

0 1 2 3 4 5 6 7 8 9

TEN COUNT

4

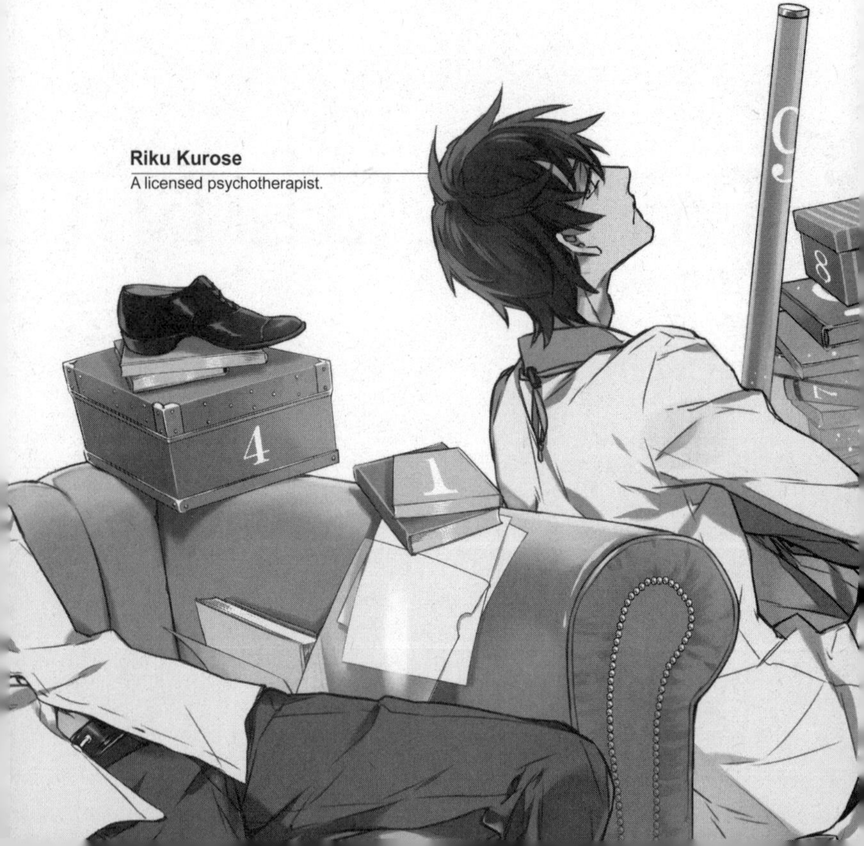
Riku Kurose
A licensed psychotherapist.

s t o r y

After meeting through sheer happenstance, psychotherapist Kurose offers to give Shirotani free personal counseling on how to overcome his germophobia. Shirotani agrees, and once a week, the two meet at a café close to Kurose's office for an exposure and response prevention (ERP) therapy session. Realizing he is developing feelings for his client, Kurose attempts to stop their sessions, telling Shirotani that he wants to touch him whenever he is near. But Shirotani counters by saying he can't stand the idea of not seeing Kurose again, so their counseling continues. And just as he predicted, Kurose ends up touching Shirotani…intimately and repeatedly. Though he knows he should dislike it, for some reason Shirotani can't seem to bring himself to say no to Kurose's advances. And when Shirotani goes to Kurose's apartment to watch a movie, he soon finds himself at the mercy of Kurose's persuasive hands…

Exposure and Response Prevention Therapy

ERP therapy is a behavioral response therapy designed to treat anxiety disorders, especially obsessive-compulsive disorder. Its purpose is to first expose the patient to their trigger stimulus and then encourage them to not do their familiar escape response until their desire to do so passes. It is similar to but not the same as exposure therapy, a behavioral therapy for sufferers of PTSD. Given the varied forms OCD can take, there is no one specific procedure for ERP therapy. In Shirotani's case, Kurose suggested he create a list from one to ten of tasks he had an aversion to, with one being the least averse. Together they would attempt to perform the tasks and overcome them, starting with number one.

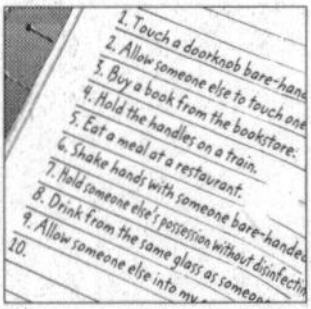
1. Touch a doorknob bare-
2. Allow someone else to touch
3. Buy a book from the bookstore.
4. Hold the handles on a train.
5. Eat a meal at a restaurant.
6. Shake hands with someone bare-
7. Hold someone else's possession without
8. Drink from the same glass as
9. Allow someone else into
10.
Shirotani's list

c h a r a c t e r s

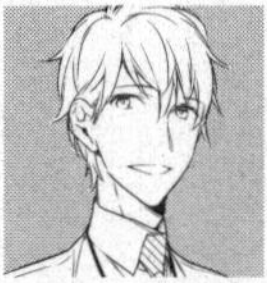

Mikami

Shirotani's coworker and friend who works in Sales.

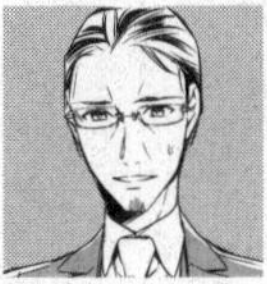

Kuramoto

Shirotani's boss and CEO of the company.

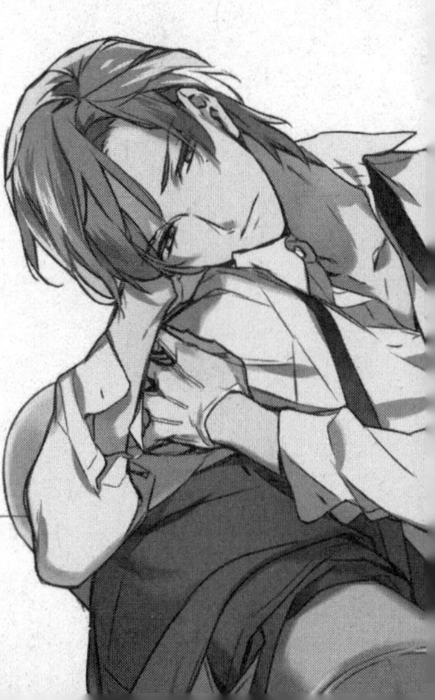

Tadaomi Shirotani

A corporate secretary with acute germophobia.

ten count by rihito takarai

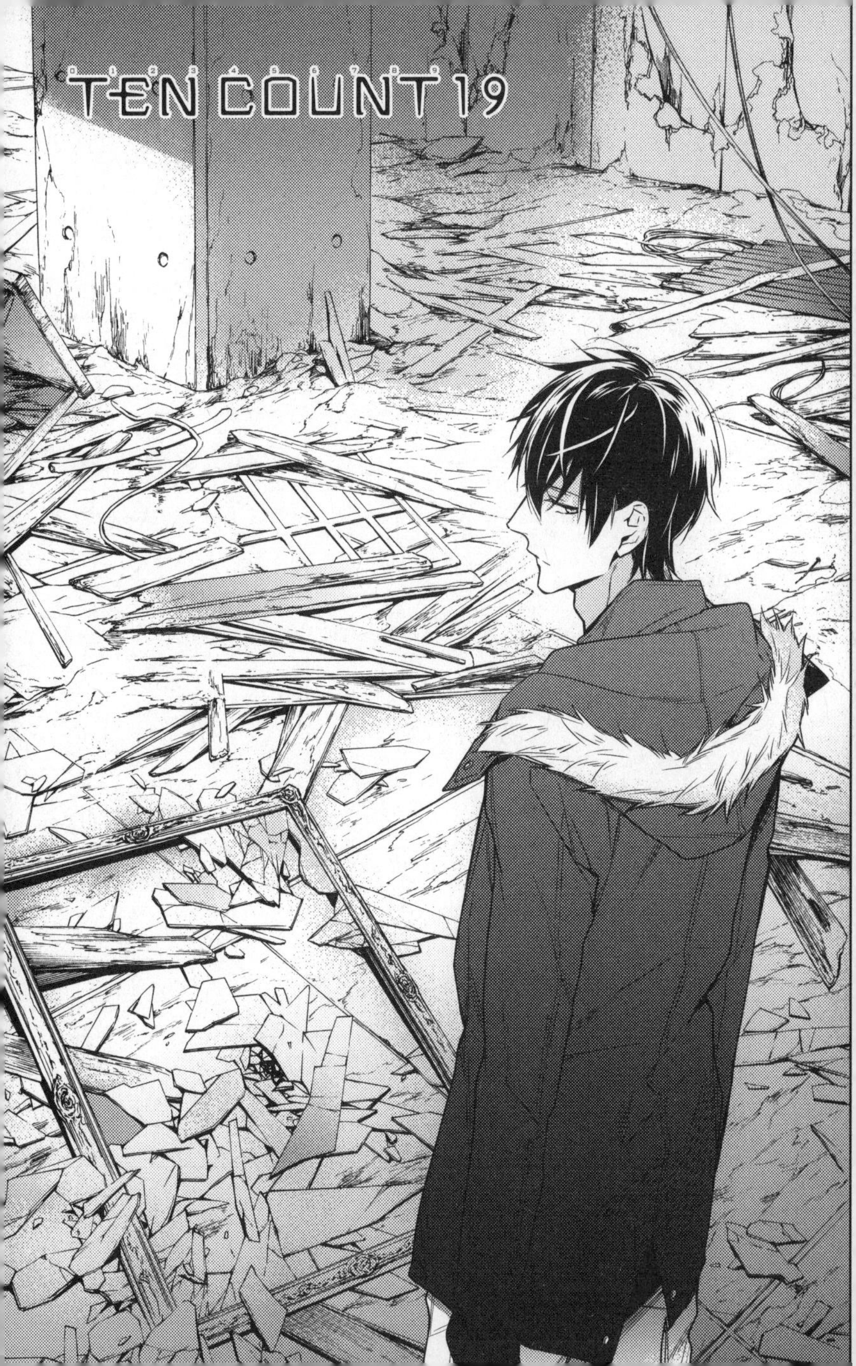
TEN COUNT 19

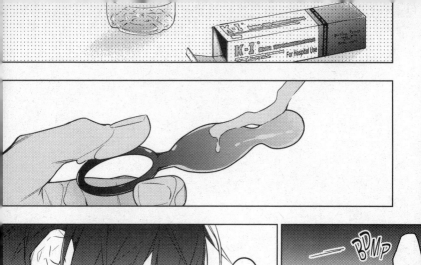

YES.

I'LL TAKE IT SLOW.

TRY NOT TO JERK.

BDMP

AH!

UM!

A-ALREADY ?!

...!

FLINCH

NUDGE

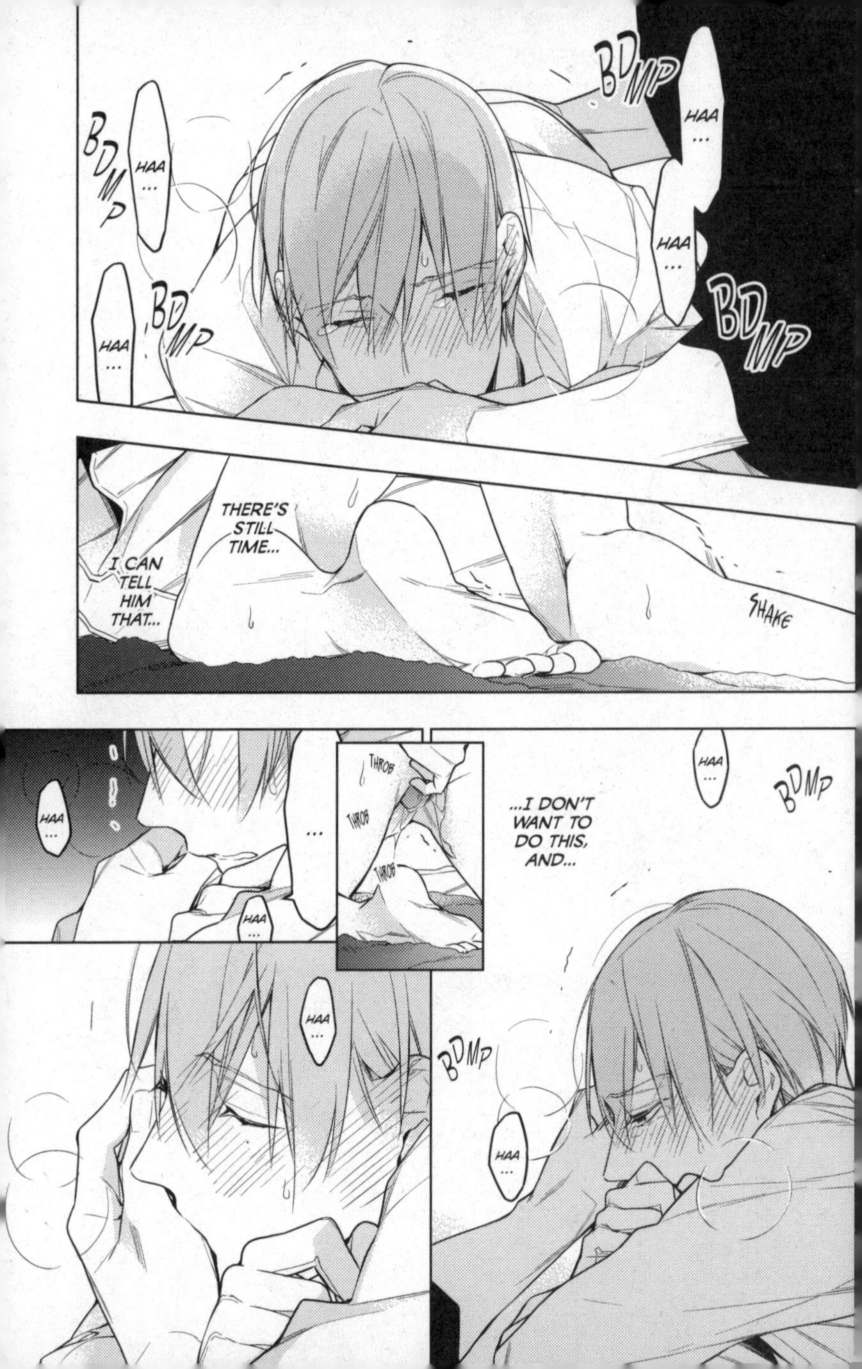
BDMP
HAA...
HAA...
BDMP
HAA...
BDMP
HAA...
BDMP
SHAKE
THERE'S STILL TIME...
I CAN TELL HIM THAT...
HAA...
BDMP
...I DON'T WANT TO DO THIS, AND...
BDMP
HAA...
THROB
THROB
THROB
...
HAA...
HAA...
HAA...

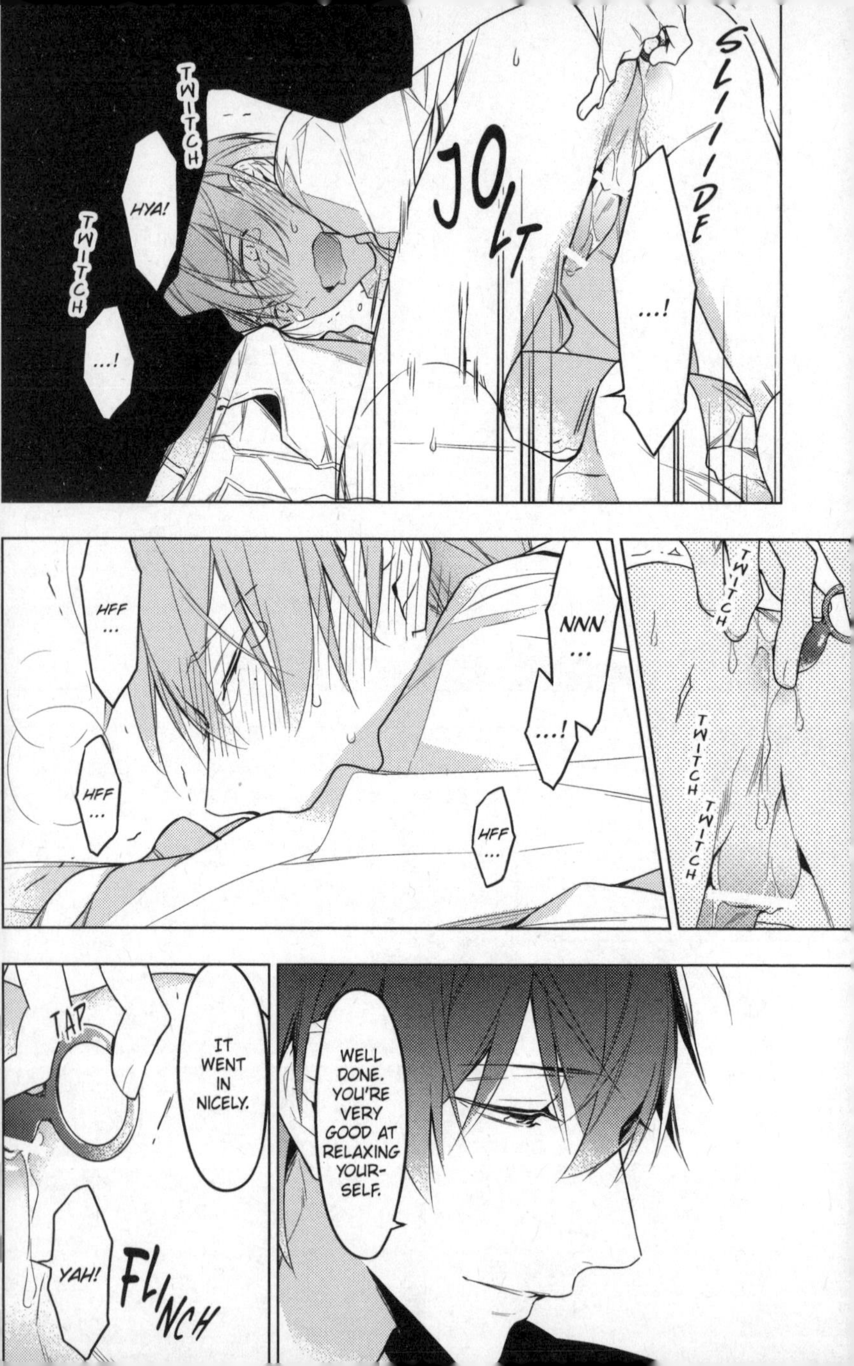
SLIIIIDE
...!
JOLT
TWITCH
HYA!
TWITCH
...!
TWITCH
TWITCH TWITCH
NNN ...
...!
HFF ...
HFF ...
HFF ...
WELL DONE. YOU'RE VERY GOOD AT RELAXING YOUR-SELF.
IT WENT IN NICELY.
TAP
YAH!
FLINCH

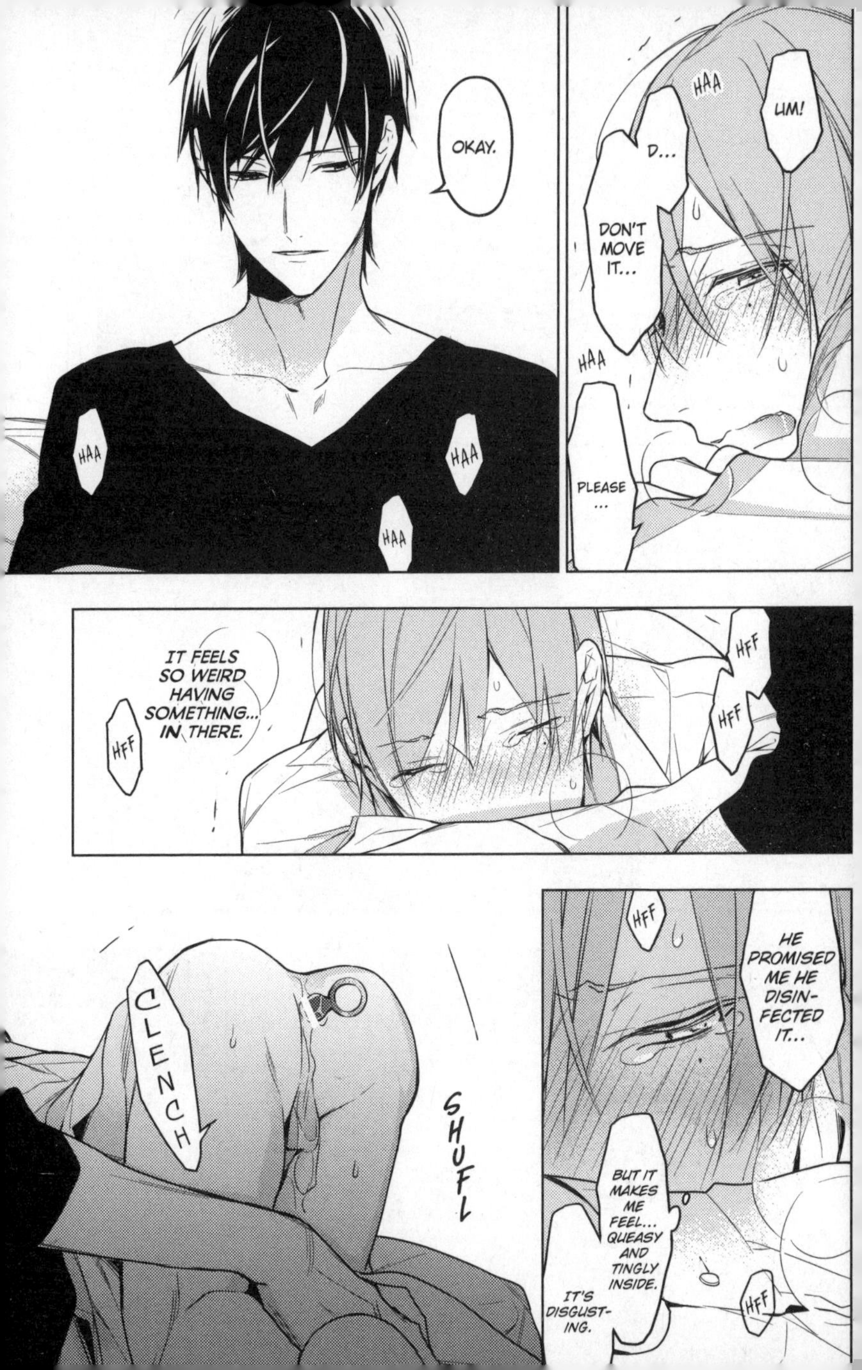
HAA
UM!
D...
DON'T MOVE IT...
HAA
PLEASE ...
OKAY.
HAA
HAA
HAA
HFF
HFF
IT FEELS SO WEIRD HAVING SOMETHING... IN THERE.
HFF
HFF
HE PROMISED ME HE DISIN-FECTED IT...
BUT IT MAKES ME FEEL... QUEASY AND TINGLY INSIDE.
IT'S DISGUST-ING.
HFF
CLENCH
SHUFL

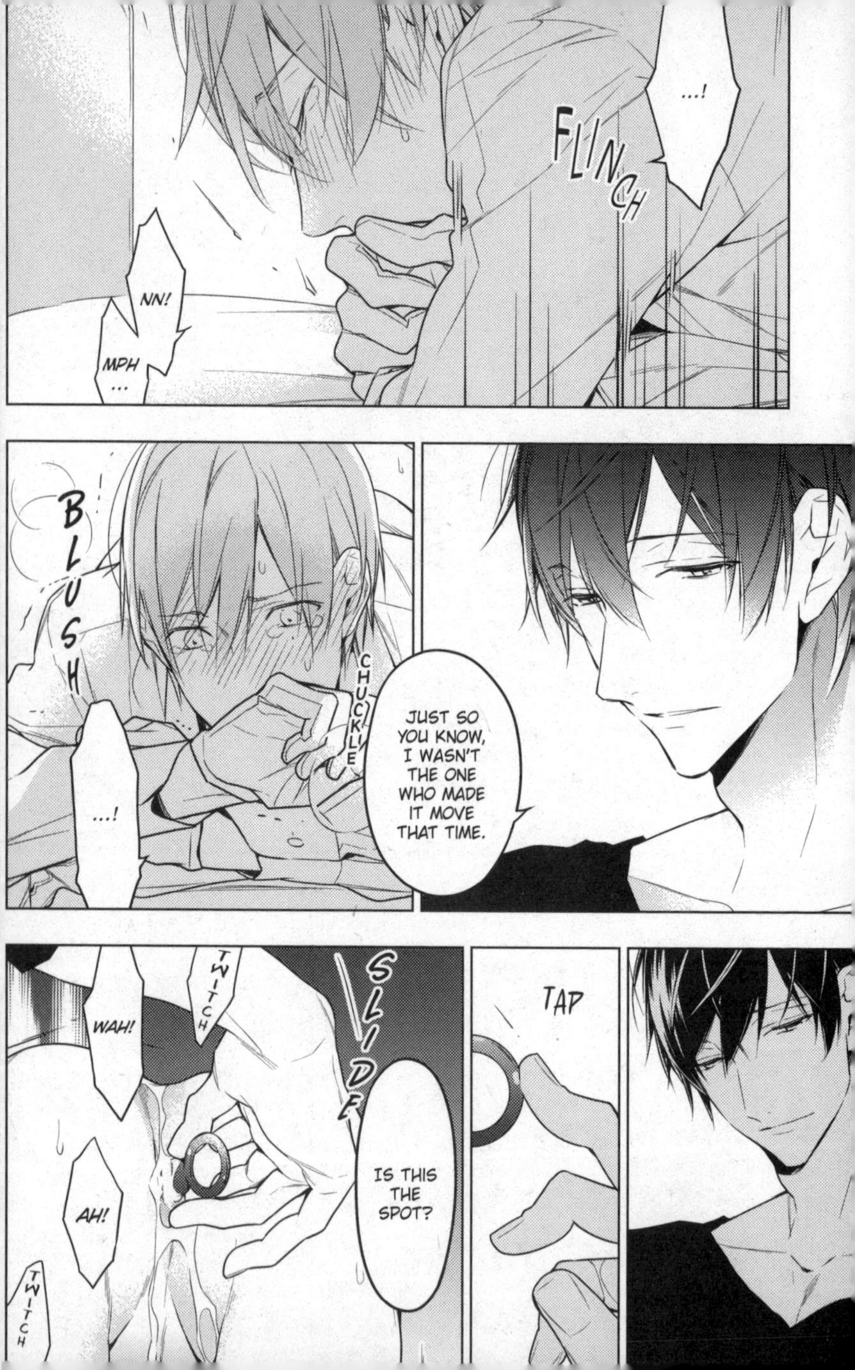

...!
FLINCH
NN!
MPH...
JUST SO YOU KNOW, I WASN'T THE ONE WHO MADE IT MOVE THAT TIME.
CHUCKLE
!
BLUSH
...!
TAP
SLIDE
IS THIS THE SPOT?
TWITCH
WAH!
AH!
TWITCH

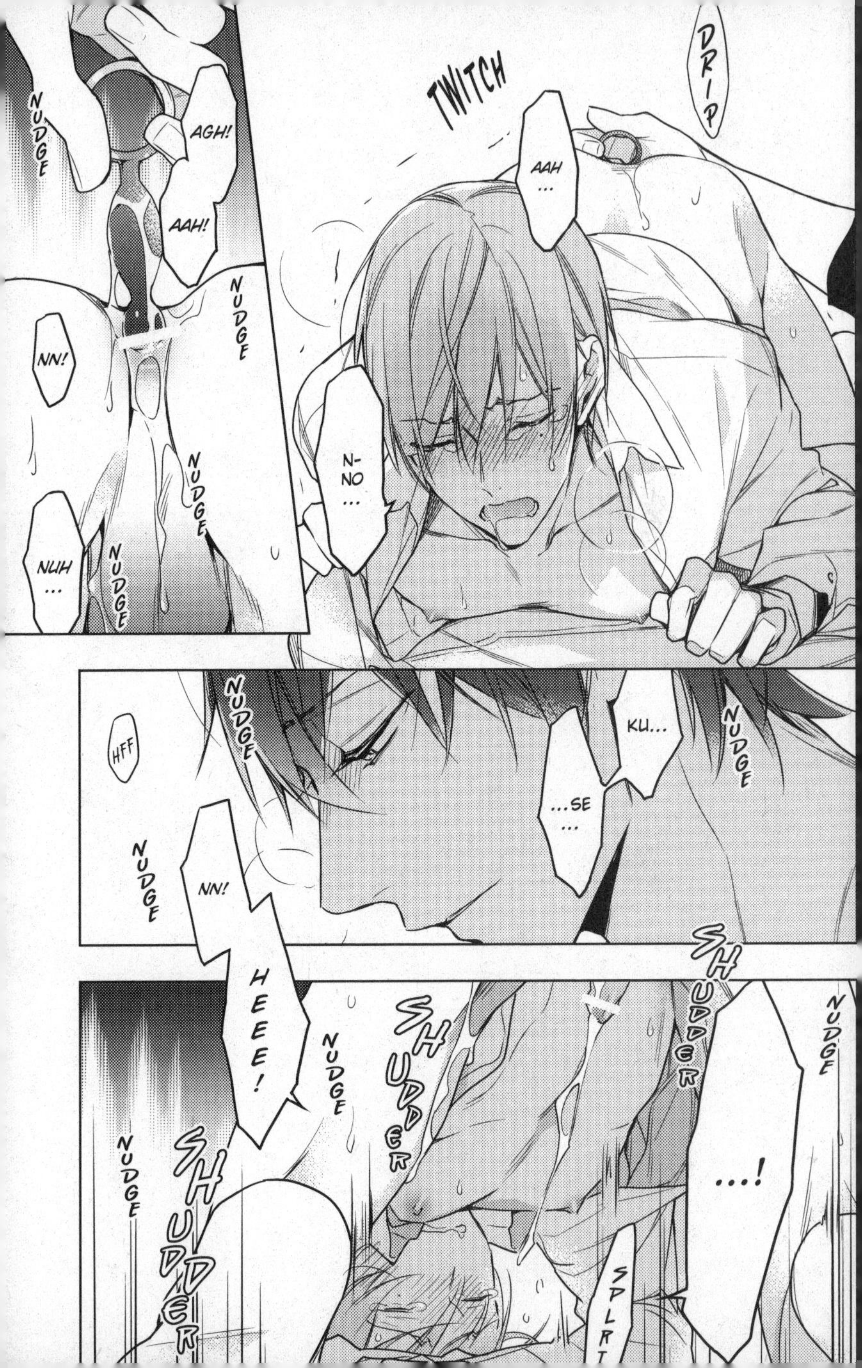
DRIP
TWITCH
AAH ...
N-NO ...
AGH!
NUDGE
AAH!
NUDGE
NN!
NUDGE
NUDGE
NUH ...
NUDGE
KU...
...SE ...
NUDGE
HFF
NUDGE
NN!
HEEEE!
NUDGE
SHUDDER
...!
SPLRT
SHUDDER
NUDGE
NUDGE
SHUDDER

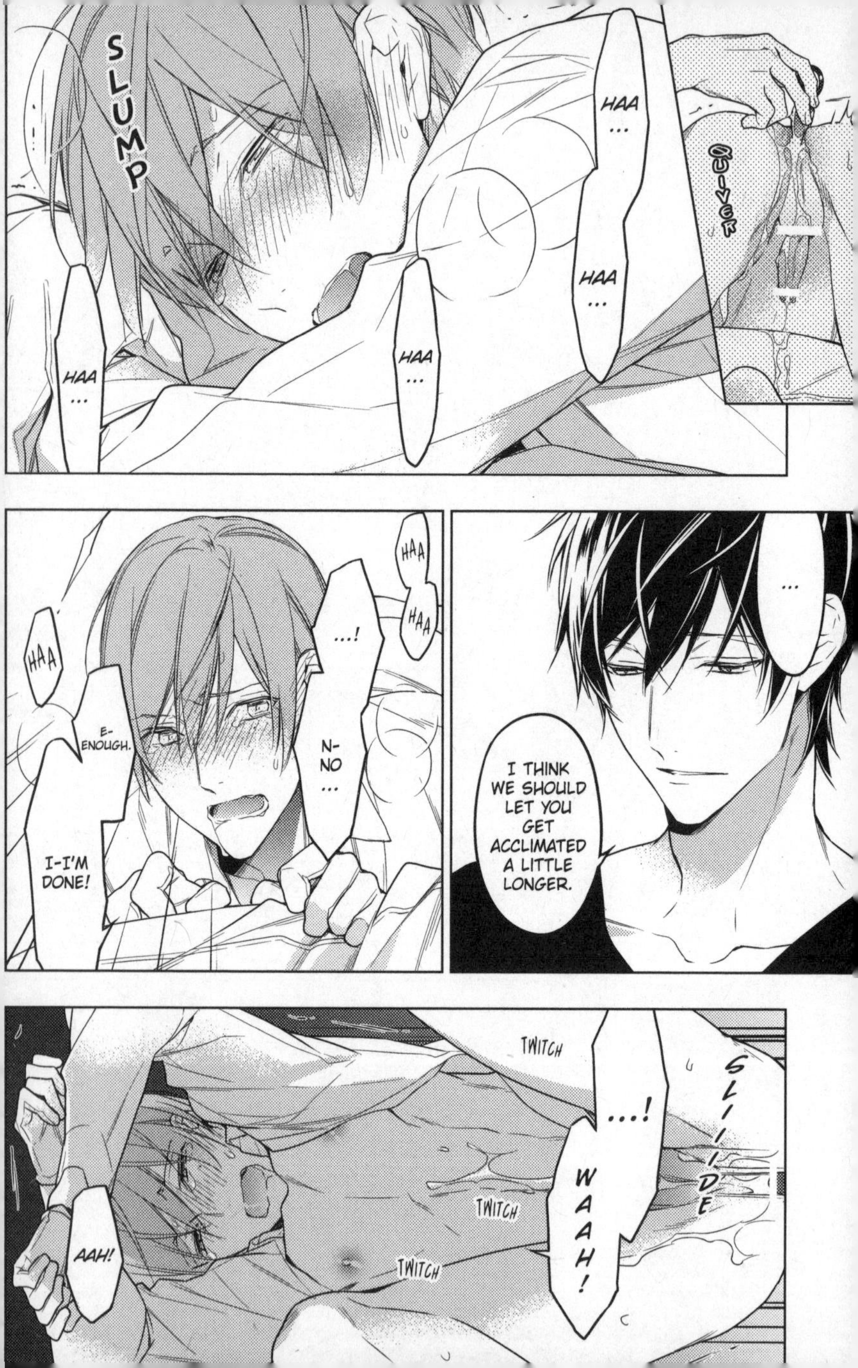
QUIVER
HAA...
HAA...
HAA...
SLUMP
HAA...
...
I THINK WE SHOULD LET YOU GET ACCLIMATED A LITTLE LONGER.
HAA HAA
...!
N-NO...
HAA
E-ENOUGH.
I-I'M DONE!
SLIIIDE
...!
WAAH!
TWITCH
TWITCH
TWITCH
AAH!

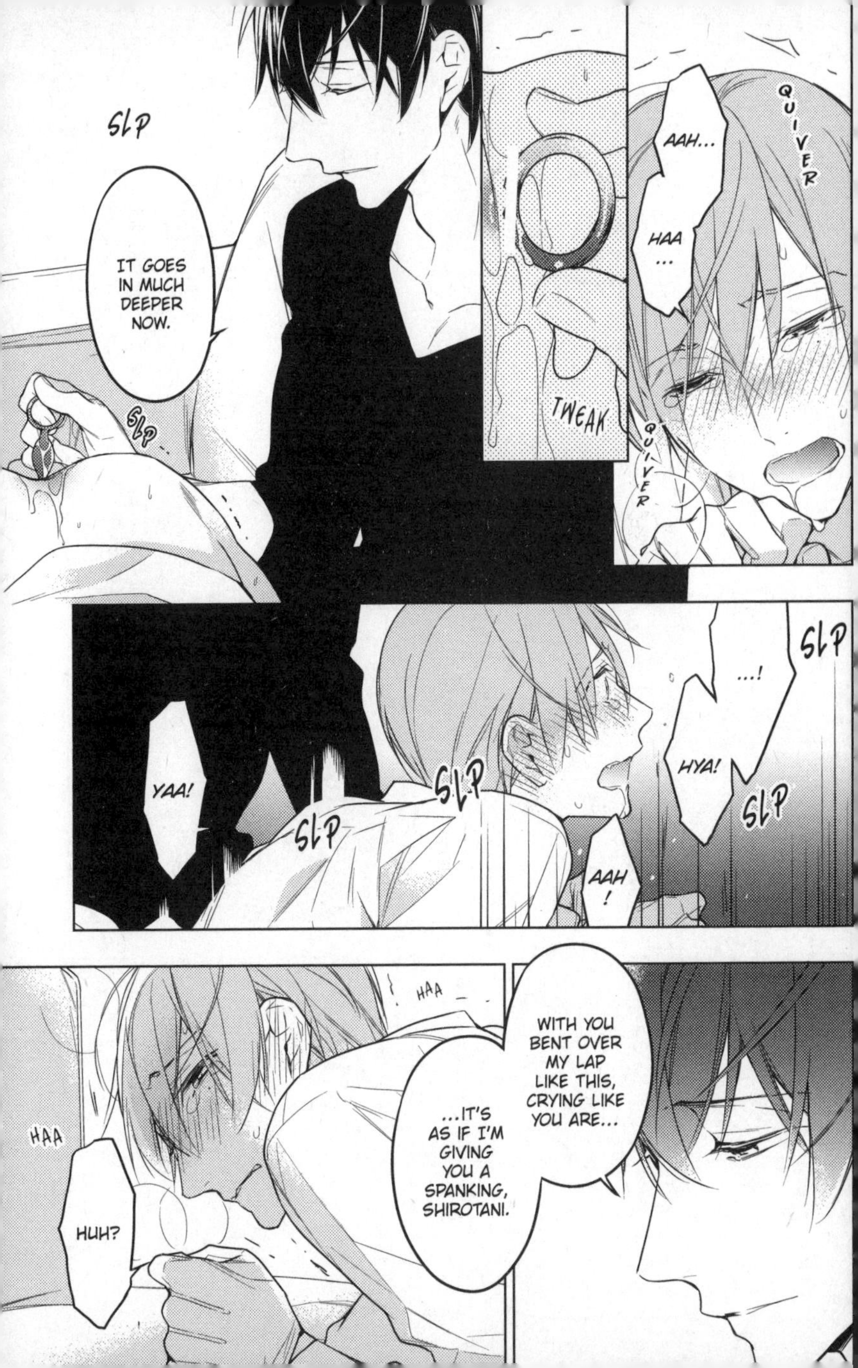
AAH...
QUIVER
HAA ...
QUIVER
TWEAK
SLP
IT GOES IN MUCH DEEPER NOW.
SLP...
SLP
...!
HYA!
SLP
AAH!
SLP
SLP
YAA!
WITH YOU BENT OVER MY LAP LIKE THIS, CRYING LIKE YOU ARE...
...IT'S AS IF I'M GIVING YOU A SPANKING, SHIROTANI.
HAA
HAA
HUH?

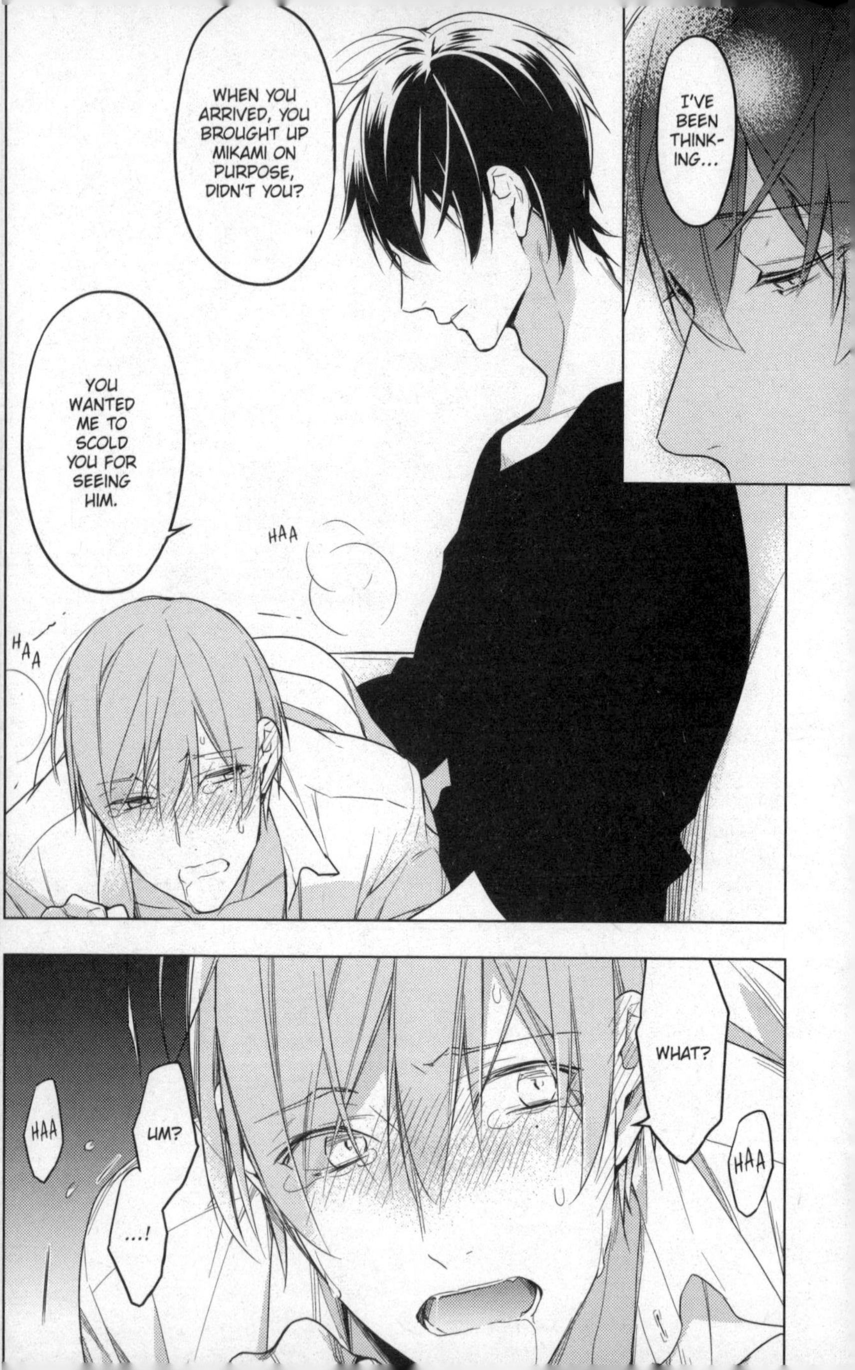
I'VE BEEN THINKING...
WHEN YOU ARRIVED, YOU BROUGHT UP MIKAMI ON PURPOSE, DIDN'T YOU?
YOU WANTED ME TO SCOLD YOU FOR SEEING HIM.
HAA
HAA
WHAT?
HAA
UM?
HAA
...!

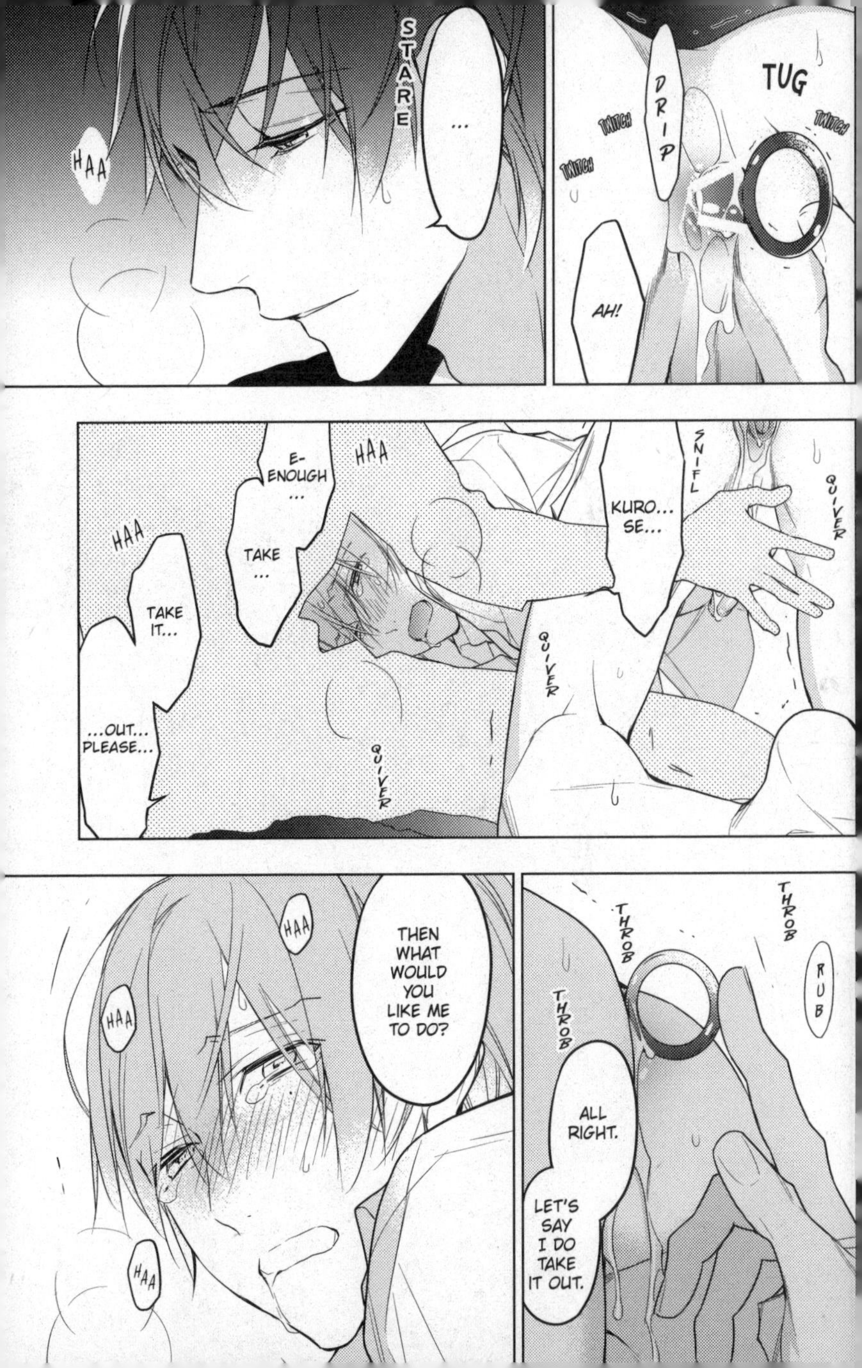
TUG
TWITCH
DRIP
TWITCH
TWITCH
AH!
STARE
...
HAA
SNIFL
QUIVER
KURO... SE...
HAA
E- ENOUGH ...
TAKE ...
HAA
TAKE IT...
...OUT... PLEASE...
QUIVER
QUIVER
THROB
RUB
THROB
THROB
ALL RIGHT.
LET'S SAY I DO TAKE IT OUT.
HAA
THEN WHAT WOULD YOU LIKE ME TO DO?
HAA
HAA

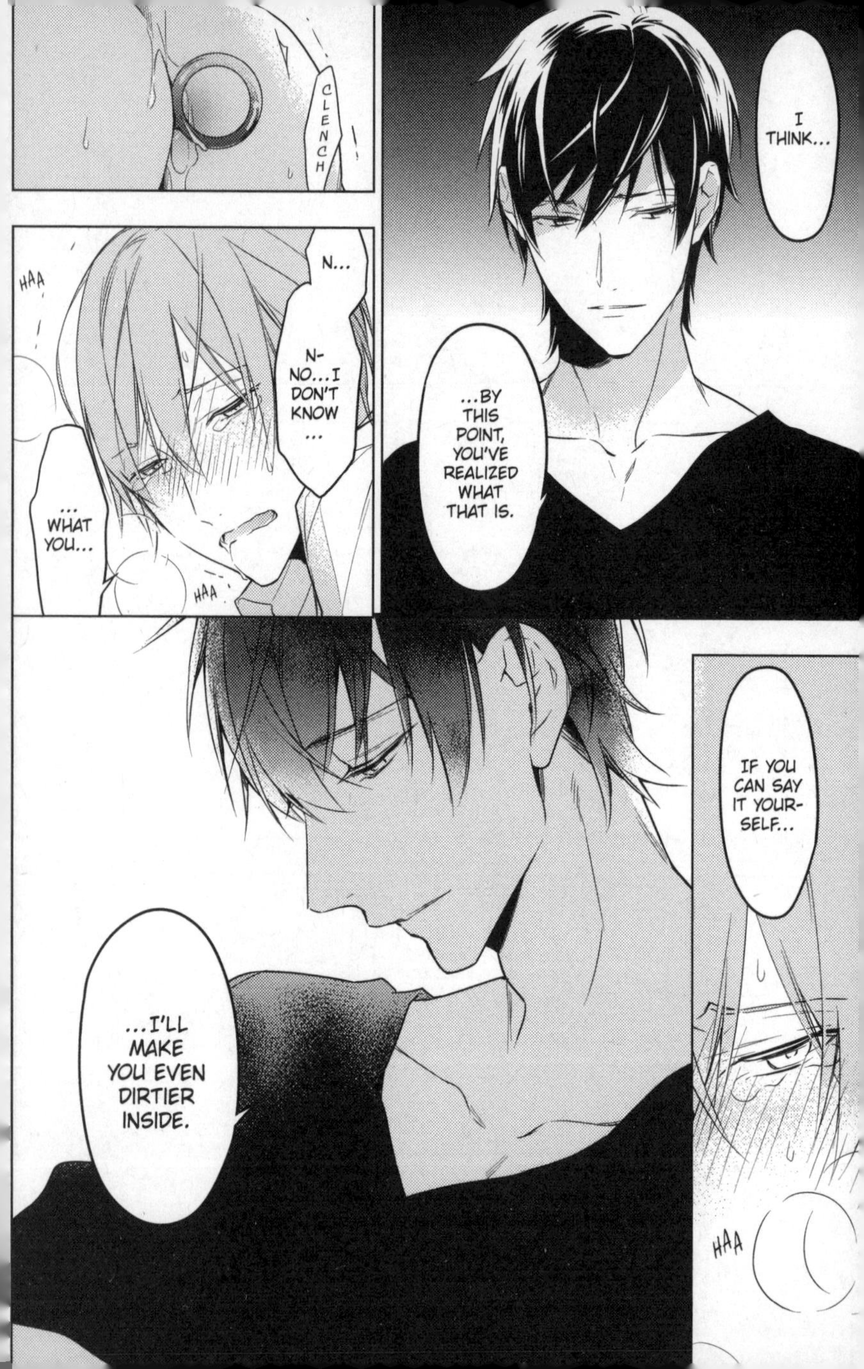
I THINK...
...BY THIS POINT, YOU'VE REALIZED WHAT THAT IS.
CLENCH
N...
N-NO...I DON'T KNOW...
HAA
...WHAT YOU...
HAA
IF YOU CAN SAY IT YOUR-SELF...
HAA
...I'LL MAKE YOU EVEN DIRTIER INSIDE.

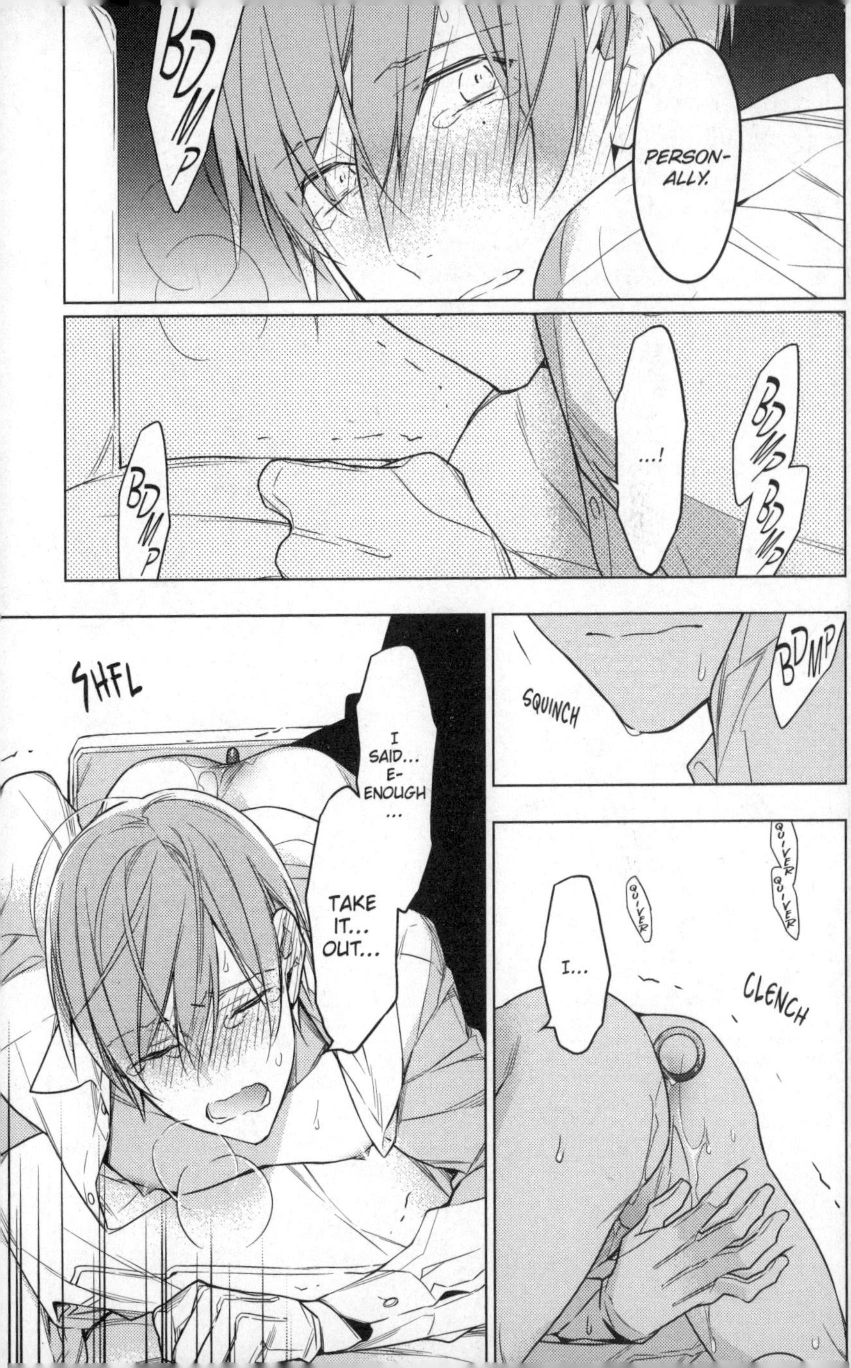
BDMP
PERSON-
ALLY.
BDMP
BDMP
...!
BDMP
BDMP
SQUINCH
QUIVER
QUIVER
QUIVER
I...
CLENCH
SHFL
I SAID... E-ENOUGH...
TAKE IT... OUT...

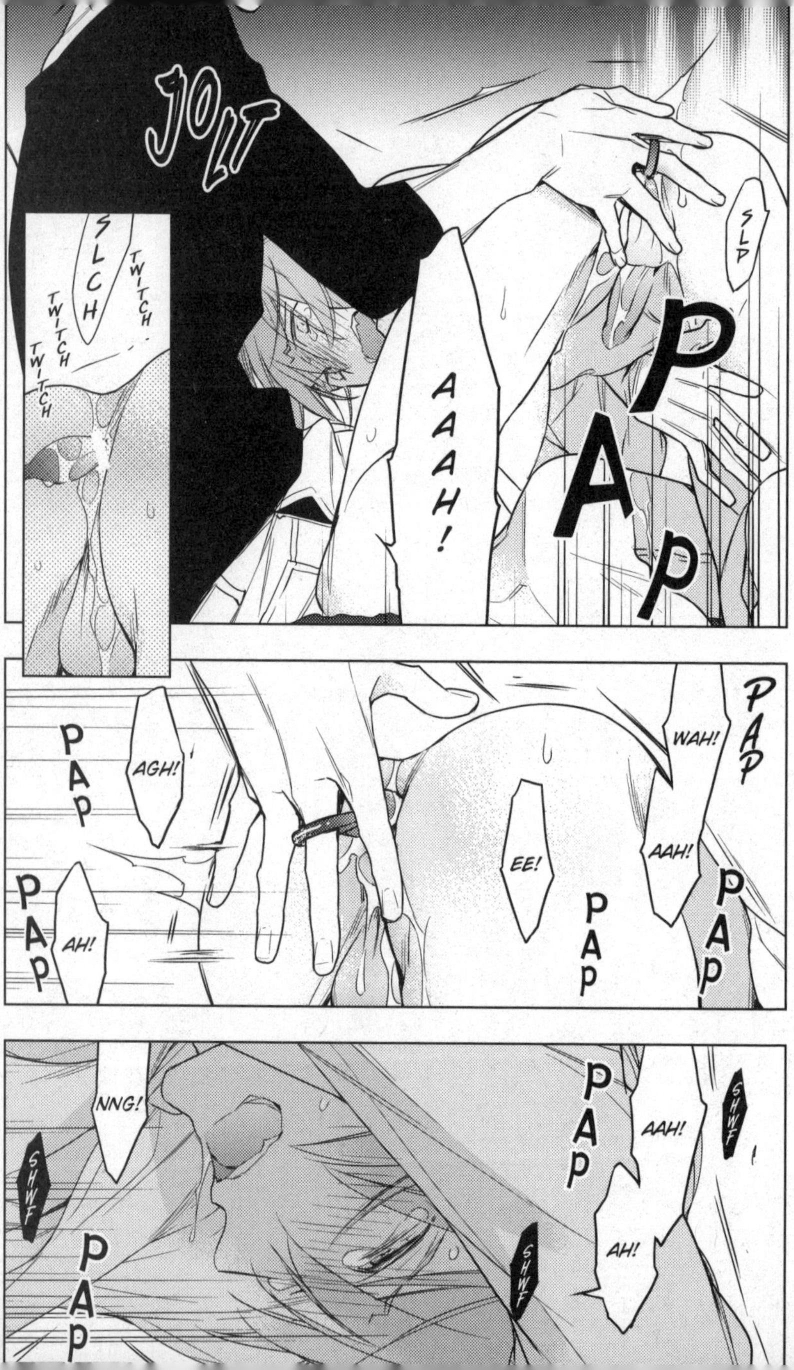
SLP
PAP
JOLT
AAAAH!
SLCH
TWITCH
TWITCH
TWITCH
PAP
PAP
WAH!
PAP
PAP
AAH!
PAP
PAP
EE!
AGH!
PAP
PAP
AH!
PAP
PAP
SHWF
PAP
PAP
AAH!
AH!
SHWF
NNG!
SHWF
PAP
PAP

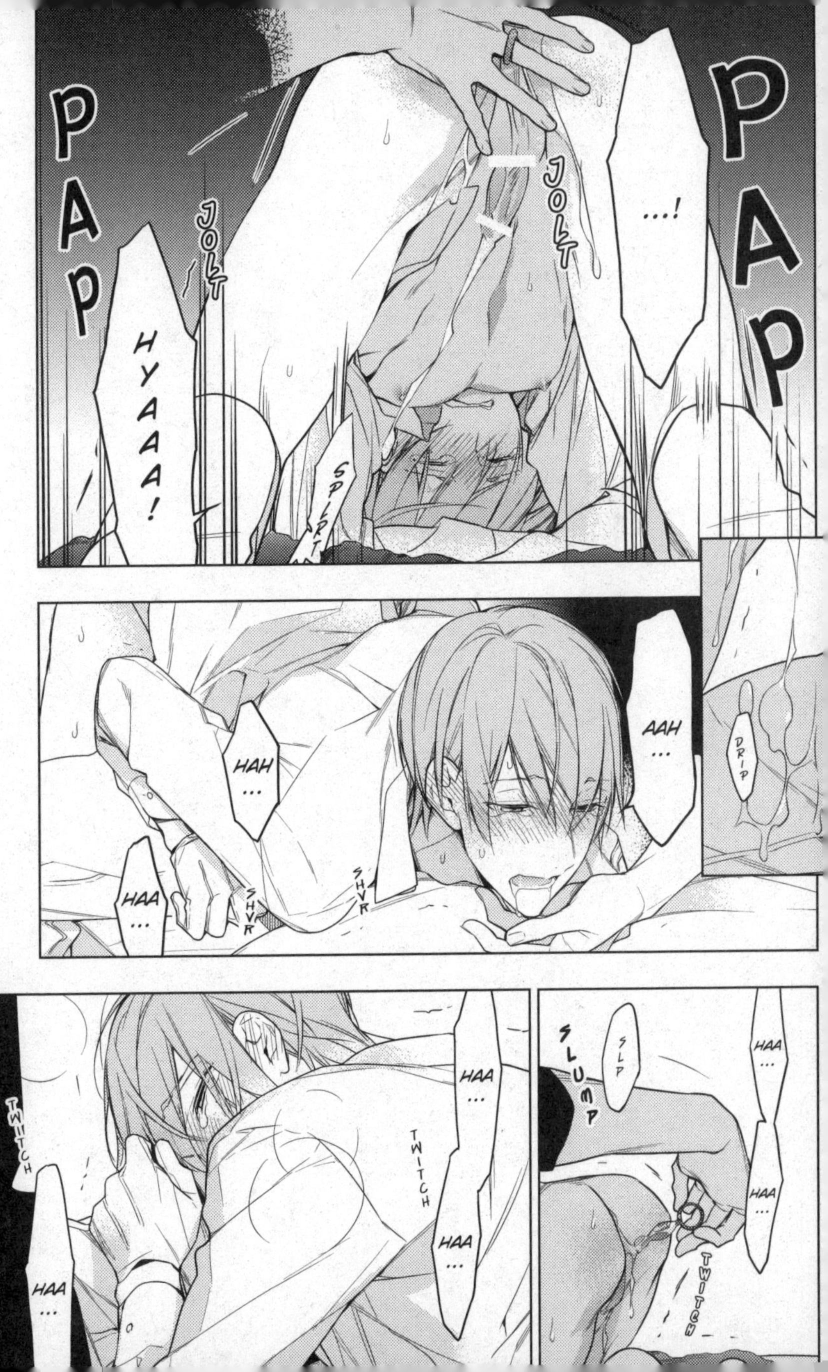
PAP
PAP
...!
JOLT
JOLT
PAP
PAP
HYAAAA!
SPLRT
DRIP
AAH...
SHVR
HAH...
SHVR
HAA...
HAA...
HAA...
SLP
SLUMP
TWITCH
HAA...
TWITCH
HAA...
TWITCH
HAA...

ten count

by

rihito takarai

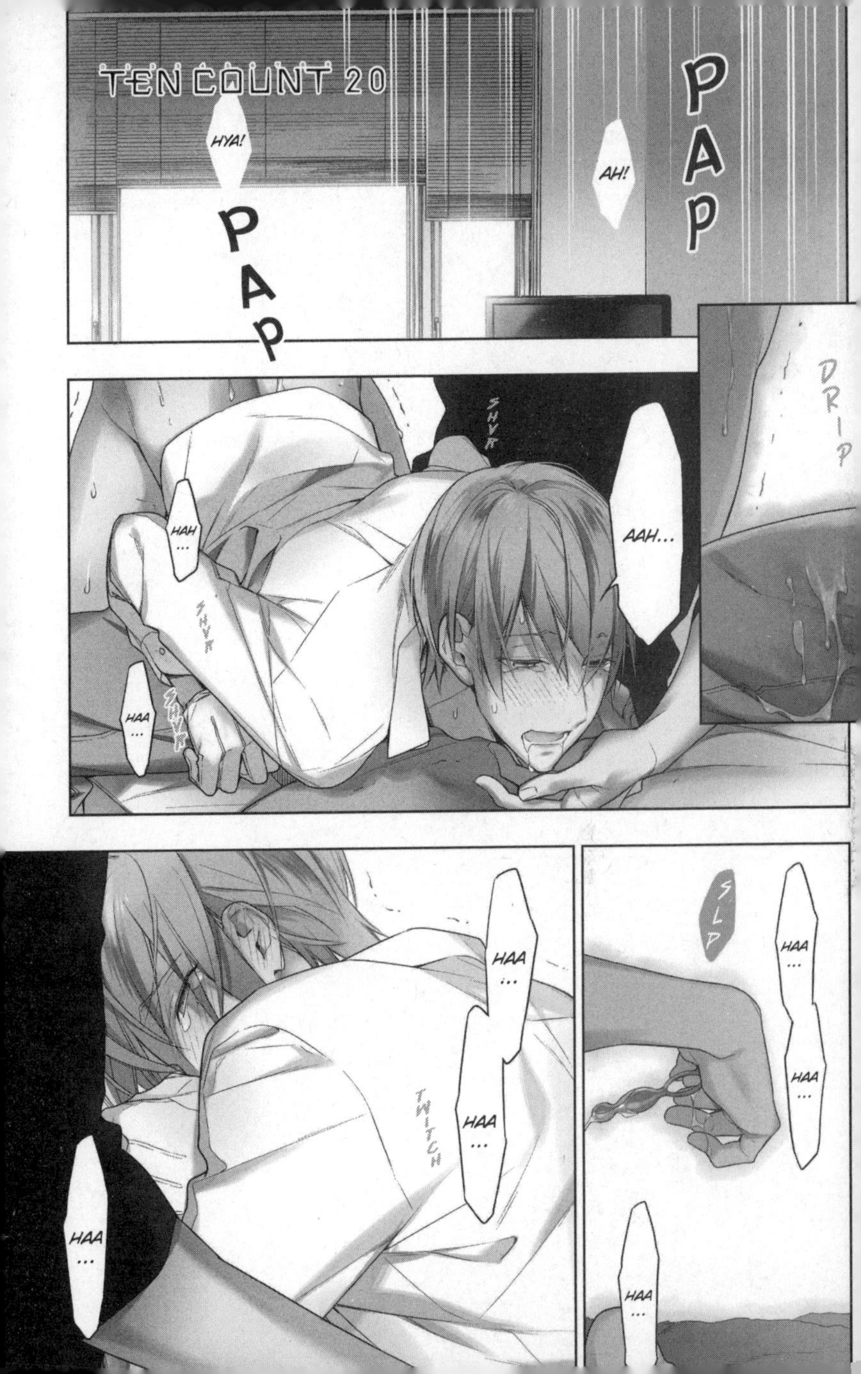
TEN COUNT 20
PAP
AH!
HYA!
PAP
DRIP
AAH...
SHVR
HAH...
SHVR
HAA...
SHVR
SLP
HAA...
HAA...
HAA...
HAA...
TWITCH
HAA...
HAA...

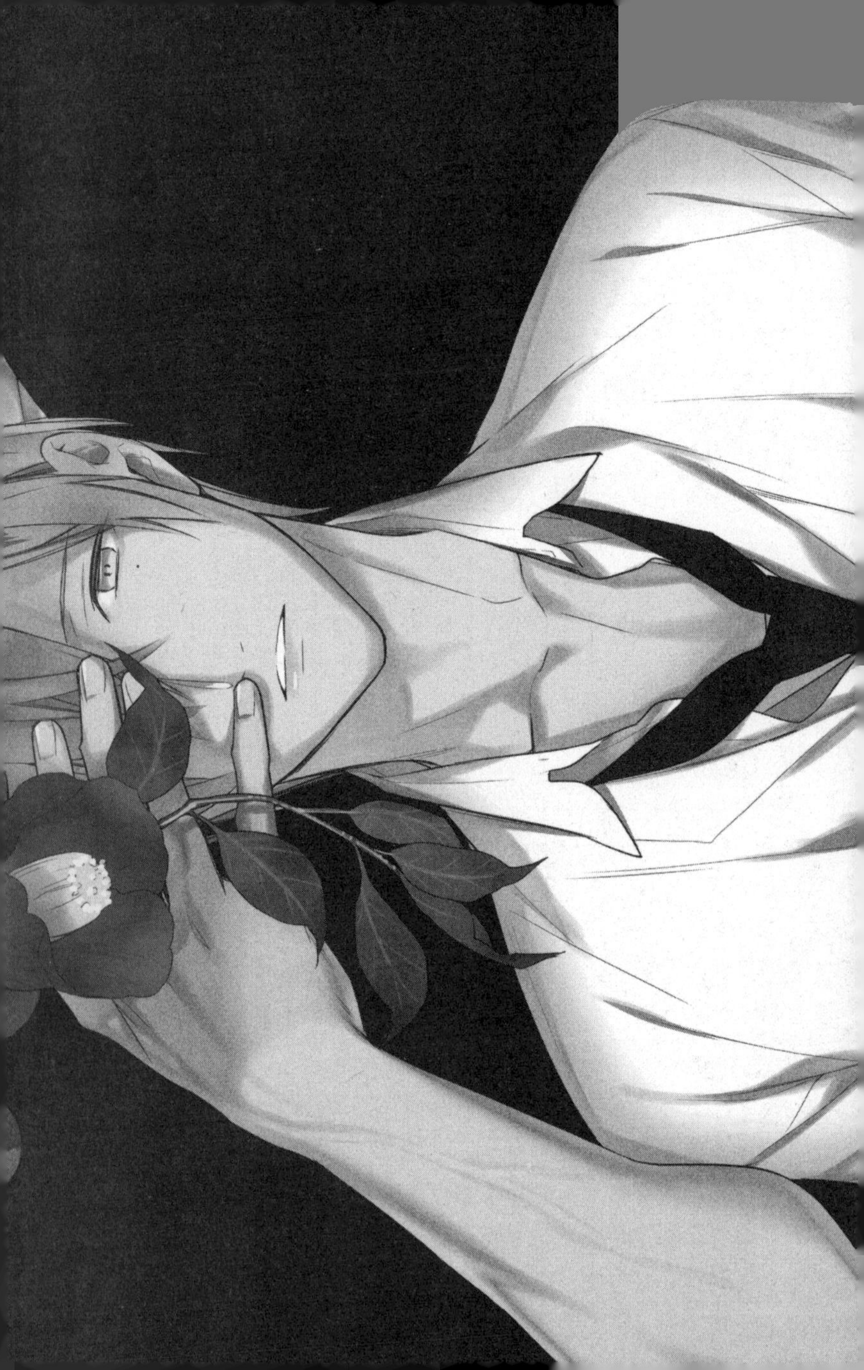

TEN COUNT 20

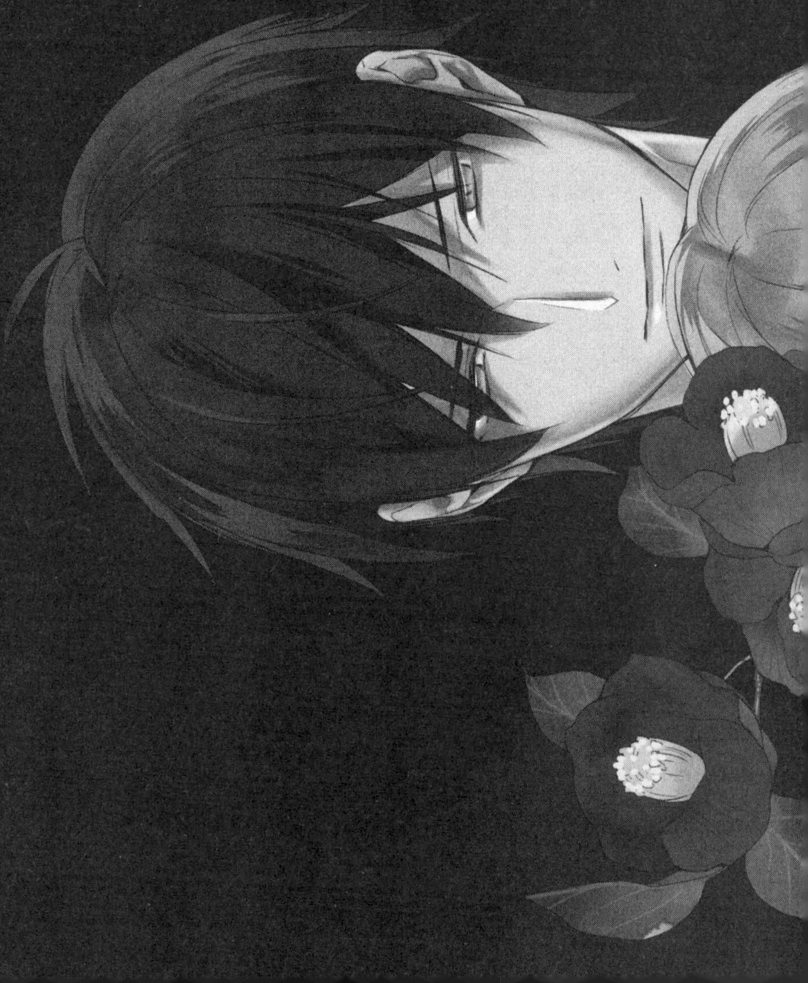

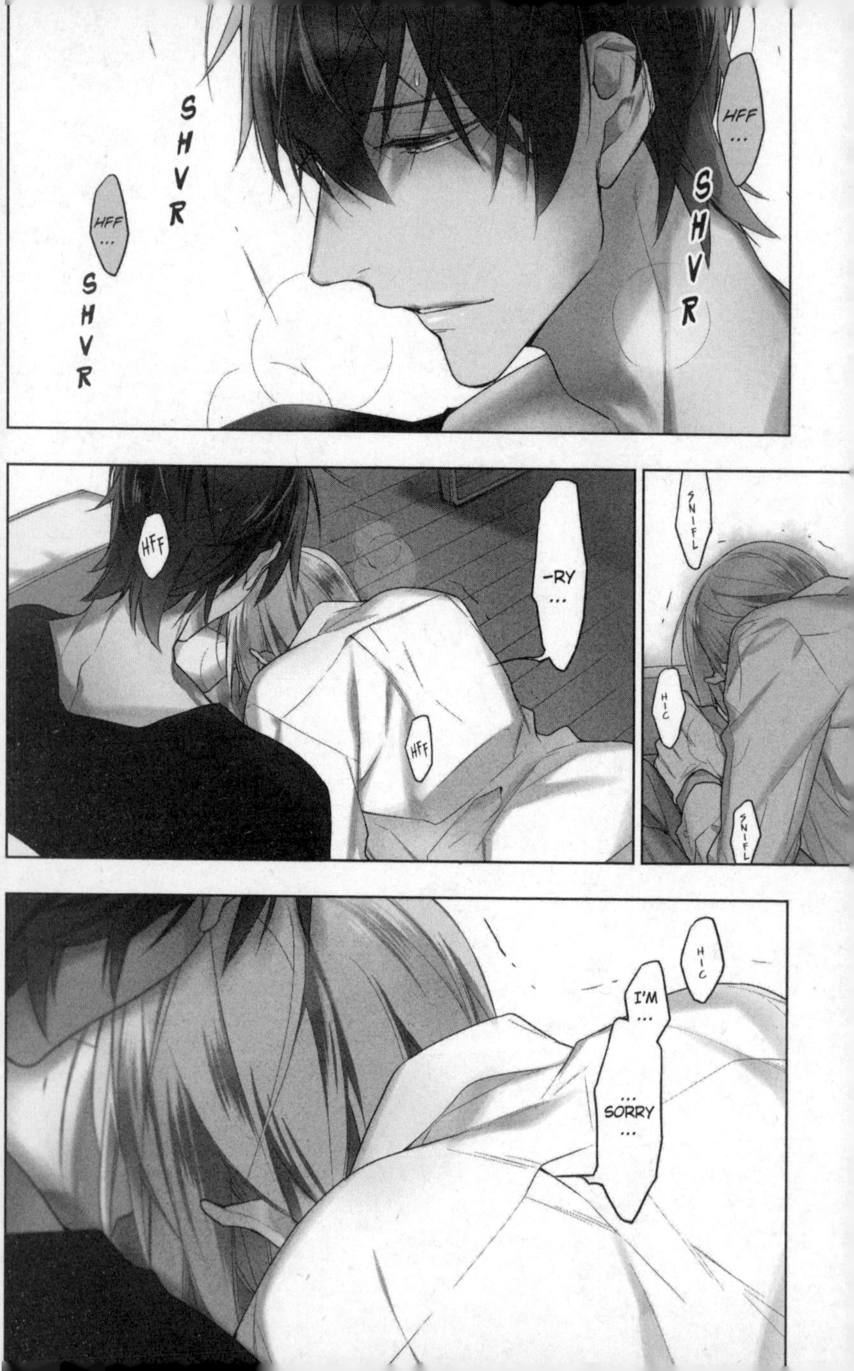
HFF...
SHVR
SHVR
HFF...
SHVR
SNIFL
HIC
SNIFL
-RY...
HFF
HFF
HIC
I'M...
...SORRY...

... DADDY ...

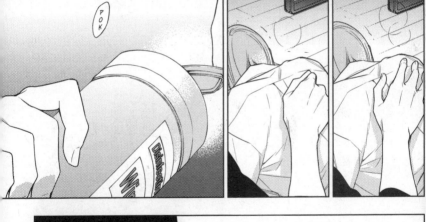

POK

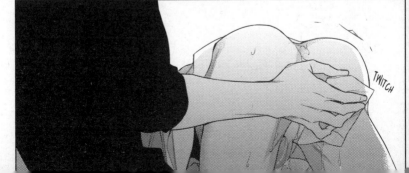

TWITCH

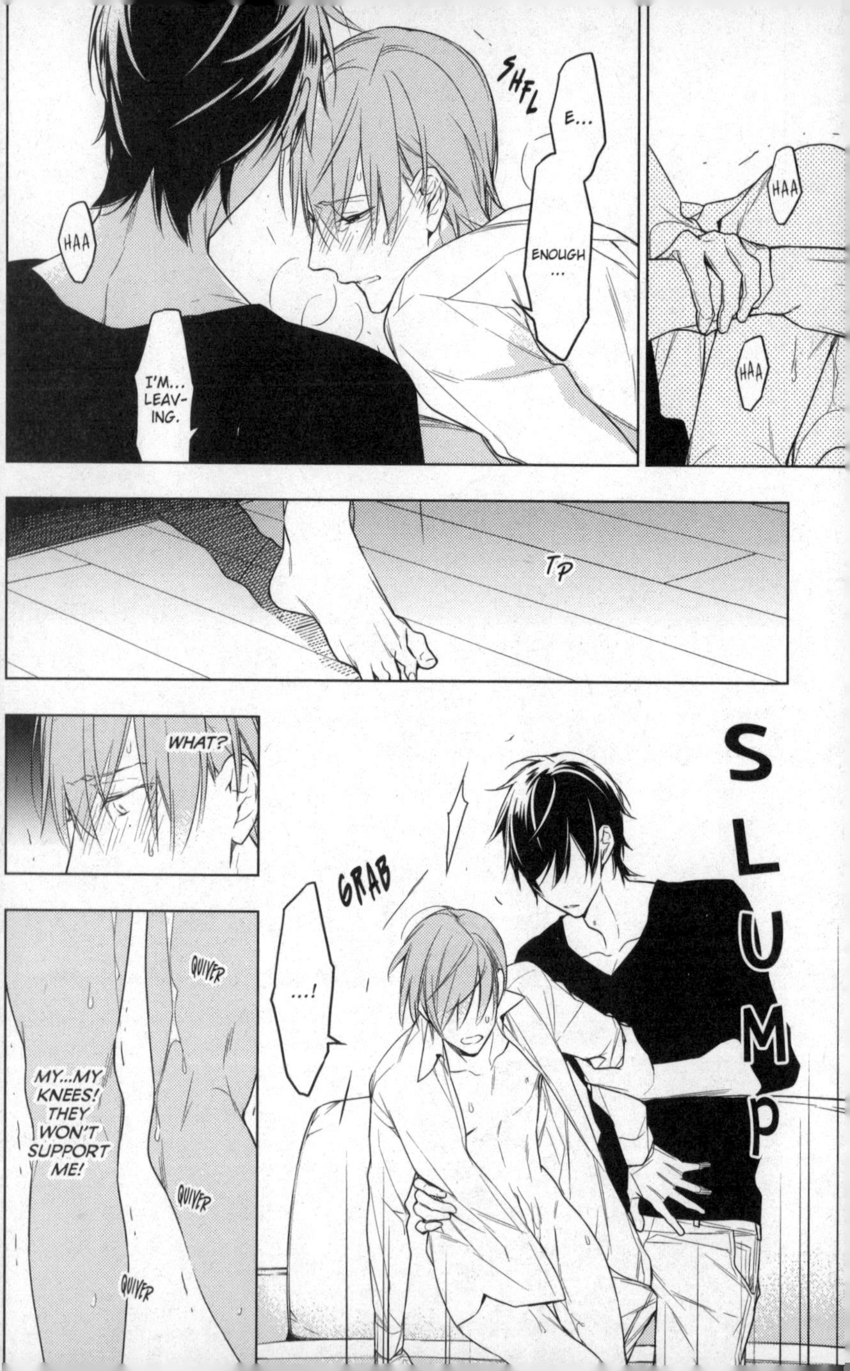
HAA
HAA
SHFL
E...
ENOUGH...
HAA
I'M... LEAVING.
TP
SLUMP
GRAB
...!
WHAT?
QUIVER
MY...MY KNEES! THEY WON'T SUPPORT ME!
QUIVER
QUIVER

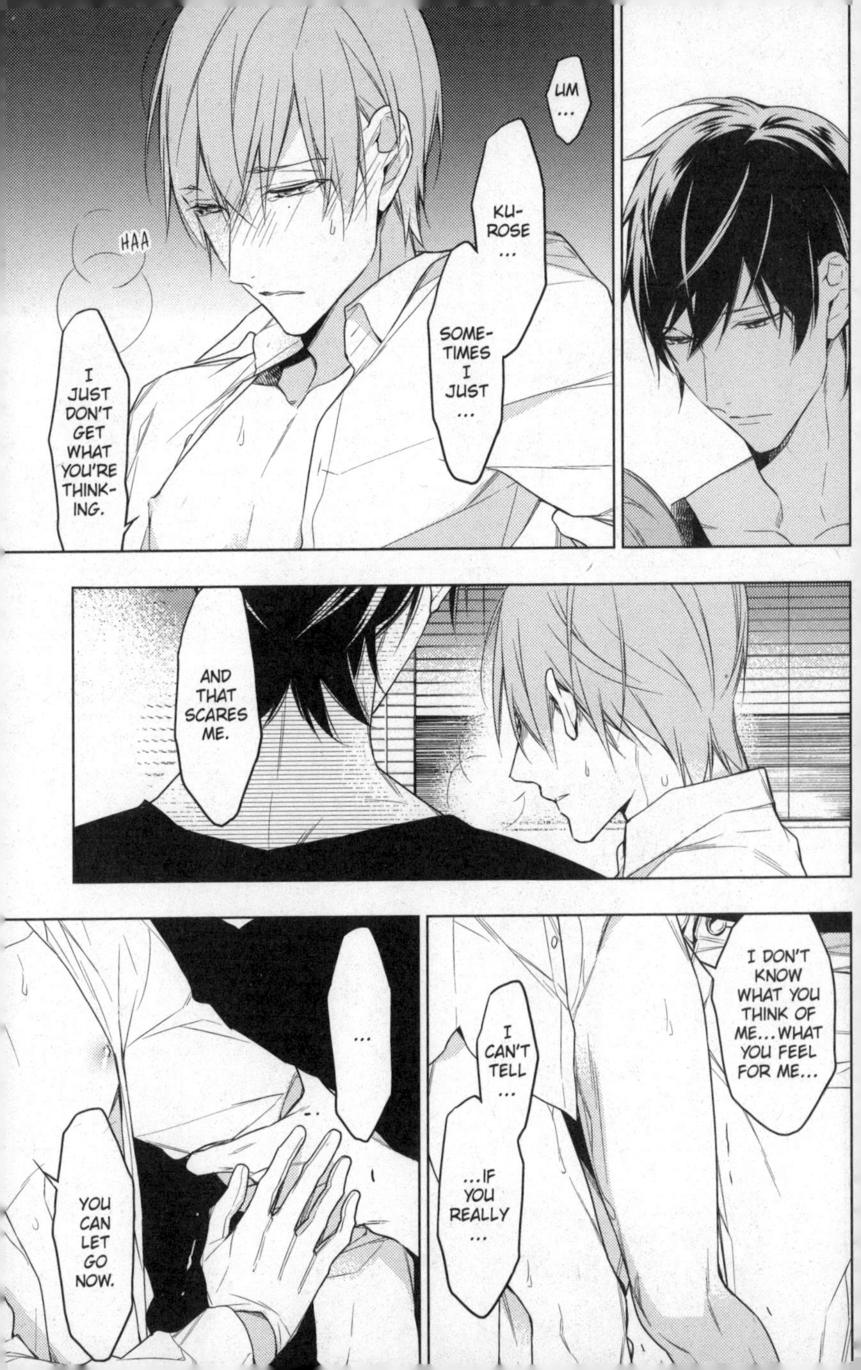
UM...
KU-ROSE...
SOME-TIMES I JUST...
HAA
I JUST DON'T GET WHAT YOU'RE THINK-ING.
AND THAT SCARES ME.
I DON'T KNOW WHAT YOU THINK OF ME...WHAT YOU FEEL FOR ME...
I CAN'T TELL...
...IF YOU REALLY...
...
YOU CAN LET GO NOW.

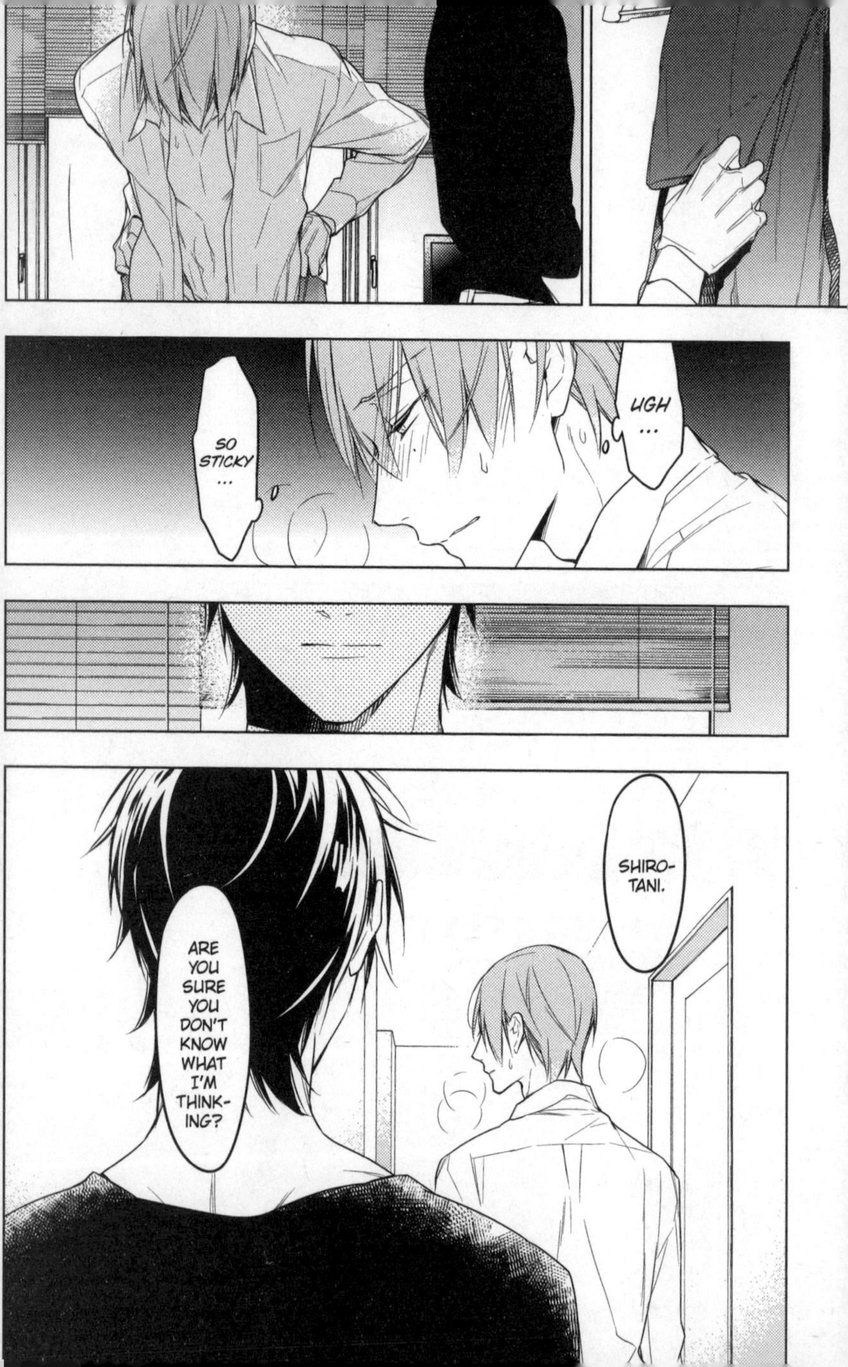
UGH ...
SO STICKY ...
SHIRO-TANI.
ARE YOU SURE YOU DON'T KNOW WHAT I'M THINKING?

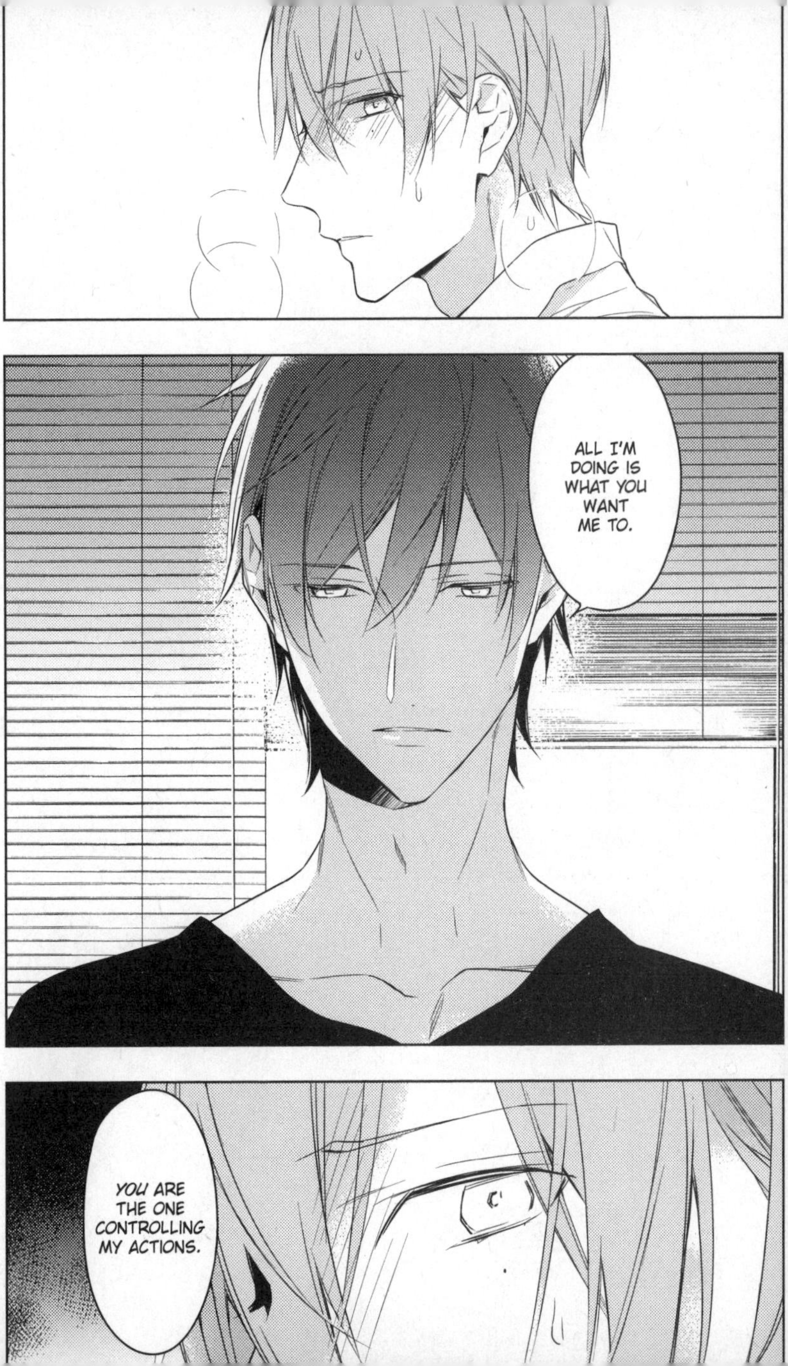
ALL I'M DOING IS WHAT YOU WANT ME TO.
YOU ARE THE ONE CONTROLLING MY ACTIONS.

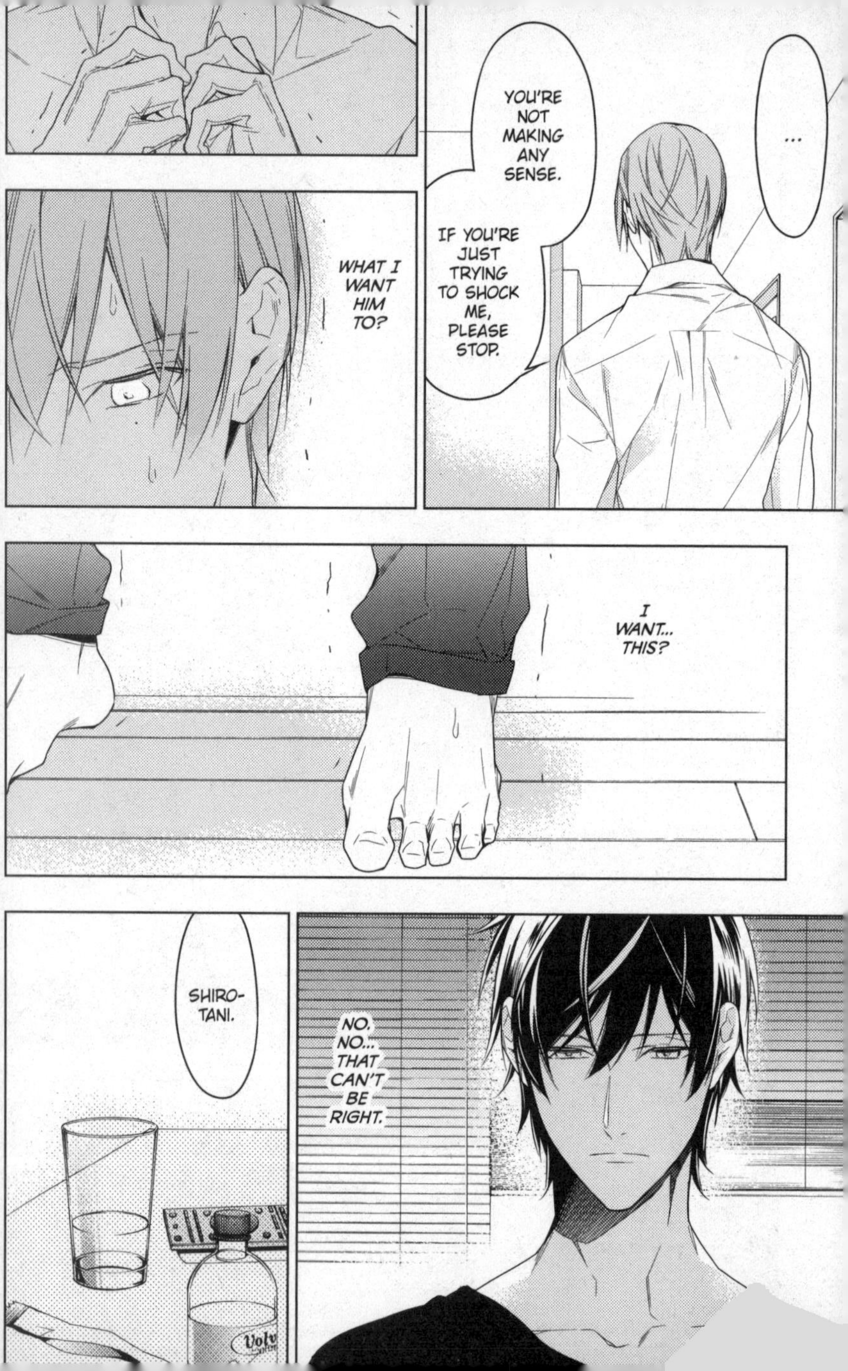
...
YOU'RE NOT MAKING ANY SENSE.
IF YOU'RE JUST TRYING TO SHOCK ME, PLEASE STOP.
WHAT I WANT HIM TO?
I WANT... THIS?
NO. NO... THAT CAN'T BE RIGHT.
SHIRO-TANI.

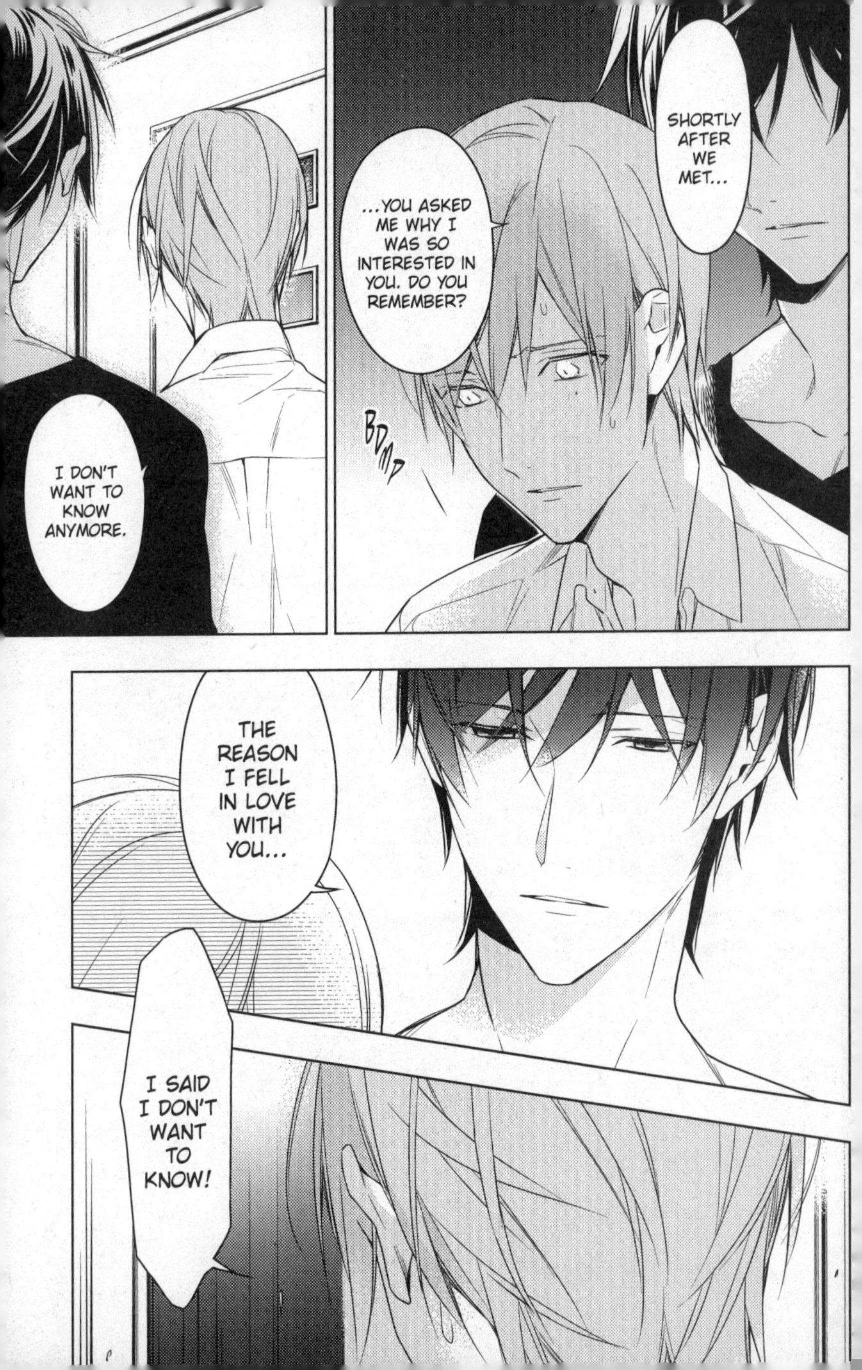
SHORTLY AFTER WE MET...
...YOU ASKED ME WHY I WAS SO INTERESTED IN YOU. DO YOU REMEMBER?
BDMP
I DON'T WANT TO KNOW ANYMORE.
THE REASON I FELL IN LOVE WITH YOU...
I SAID I DON'T WANT TO KNOW!

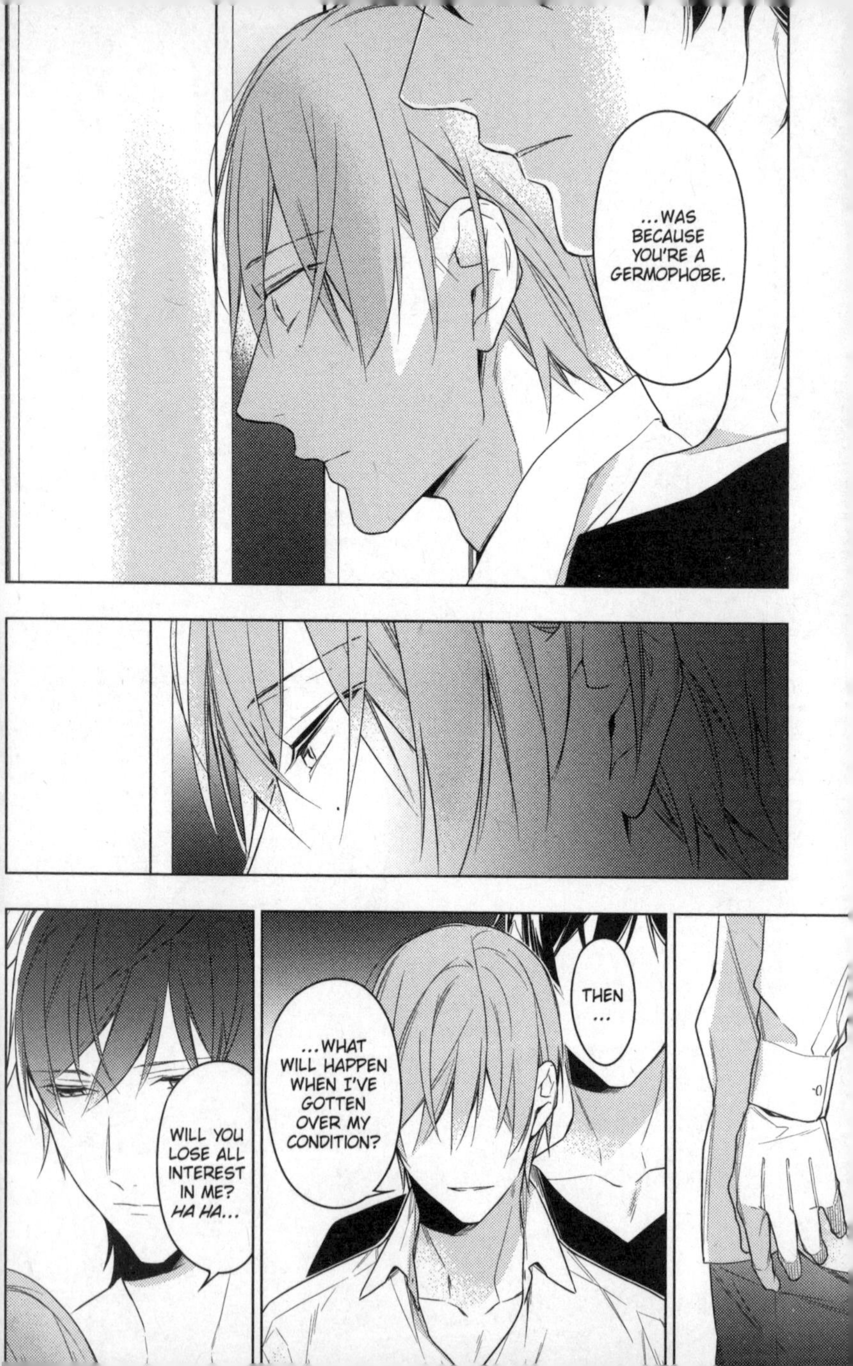
...WAS BECAUSE YOU'RE A GERMOPHOBE.
THEN...
...WHAT WILL HAPPEN WHEN I'VE GOTTEN OVER MY CONDITION?
WILL YOU LOSE ALL INTEREST IN ME? *HA HA...*

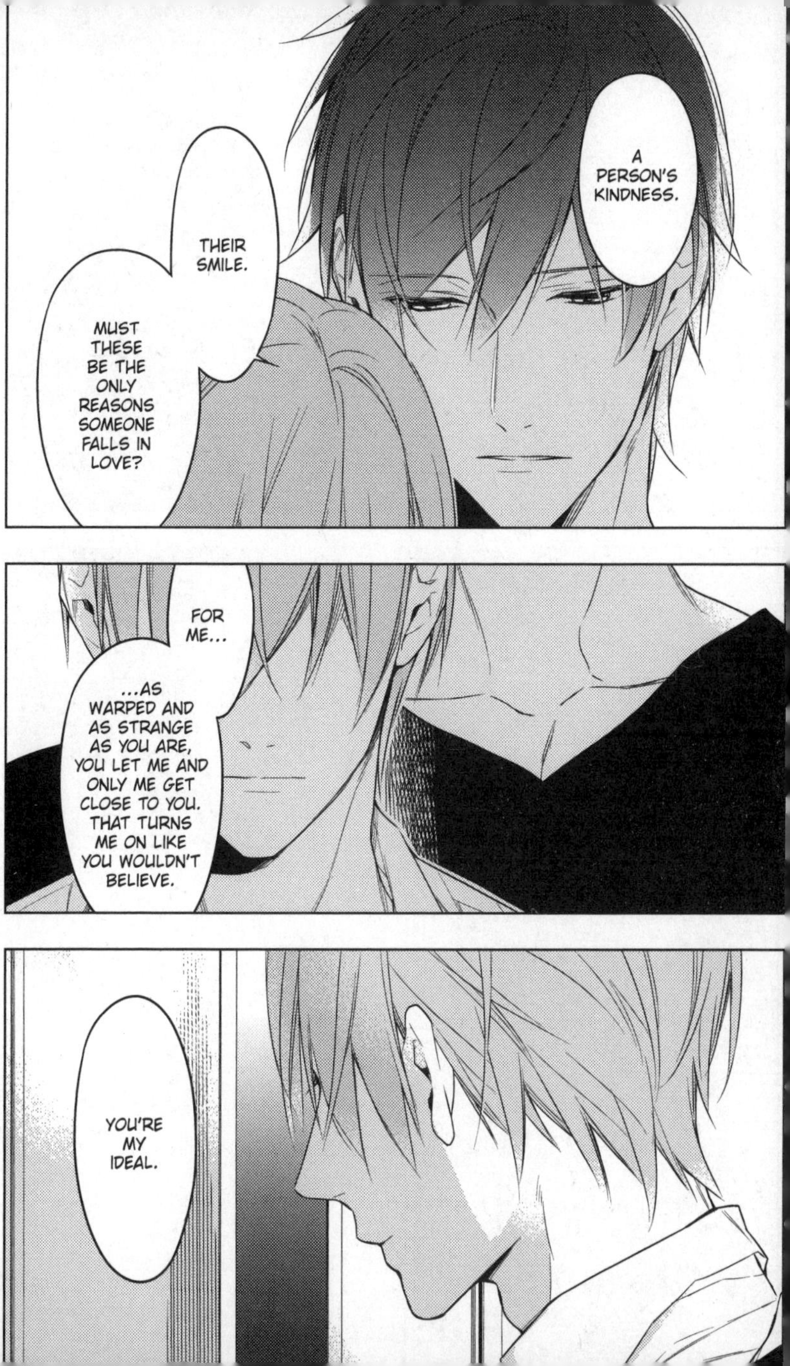
A PERSON'S KINDNESS.
THEIR SMILE.
MUST THESE BE THE ONLY REASONS SOMEONE FALLS IN LOVE?
FOR ME...
...AS WARPED AND AS STRANGE AS YOU ARE, YOU LET ME AND ONLY ME GET CLOSE TO YOU. THAT TURNS ME ON LIKE YOU WOULDN'T BELIEVE.
YOU'RE MY IDEAL.

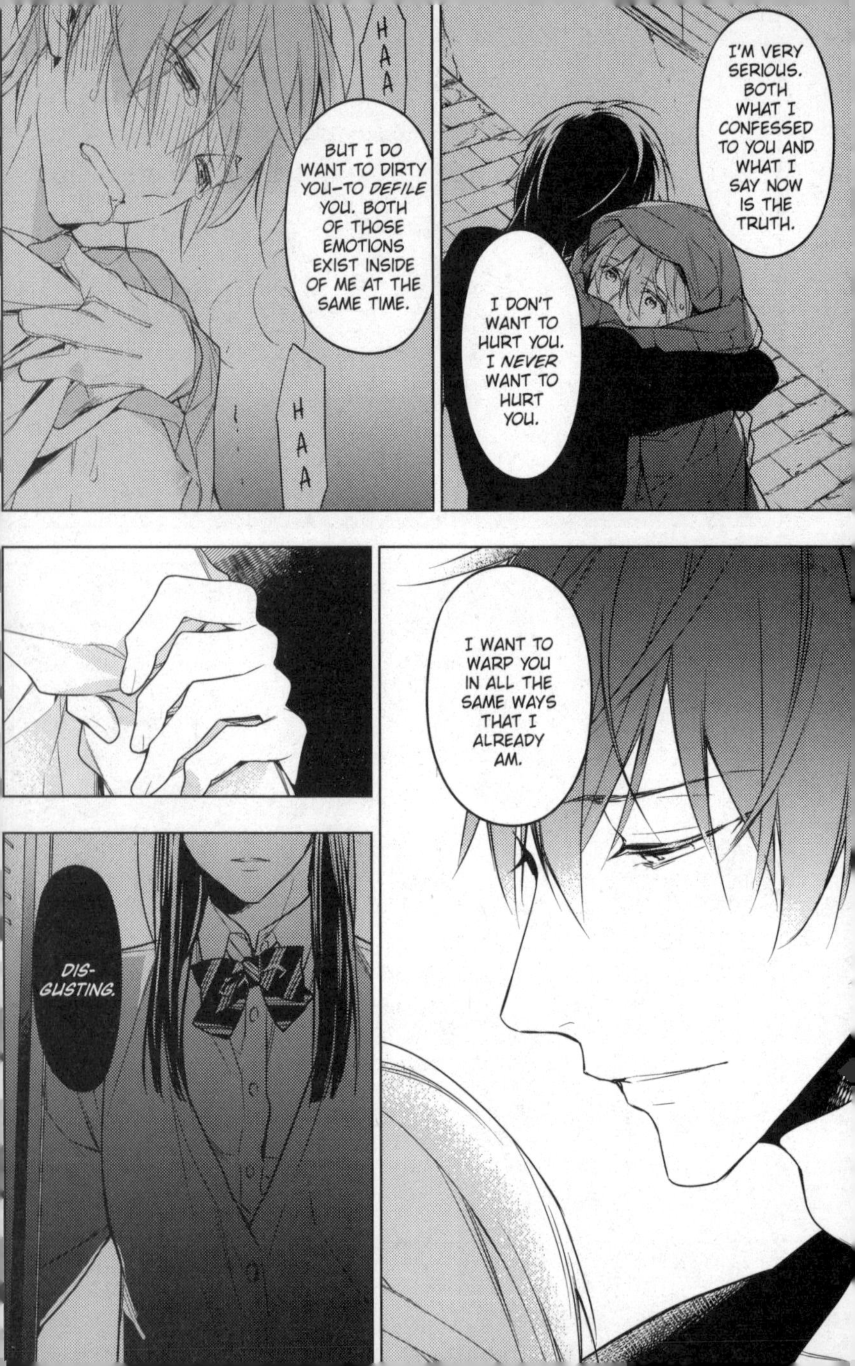
I'M VERY SERIOUS. BOTH WHAT I CONFESSED TO YOU AND WHAT I SAY NOW IS THE TRUTH.
I DON'T WANT TO HURT YOU. I *NEVER* WANT TO HURT YOU.
HAA
BUT I DO WANT TO DIRTY YOU—TO *DEFILE* YOU. BOTH OF THOSE EMOTIONS EXIST INSIDE OF ME AT THE SAME TIME.
HAA
I WANT TO WARP YOU IN ALL THE SAME WAYS THAT I ALREADY AM.
DIS-GUSTING.

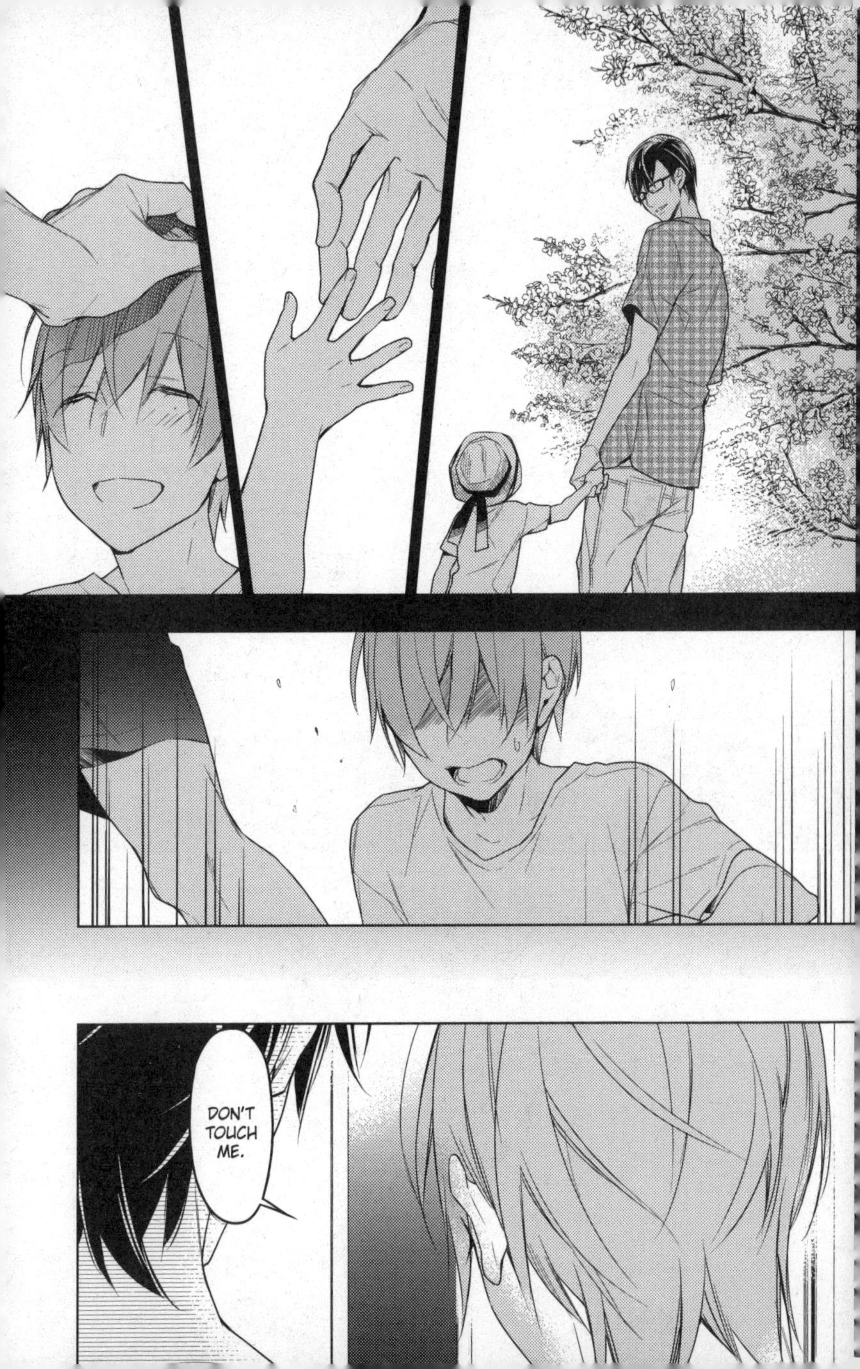
DON'T TOUCH ME.

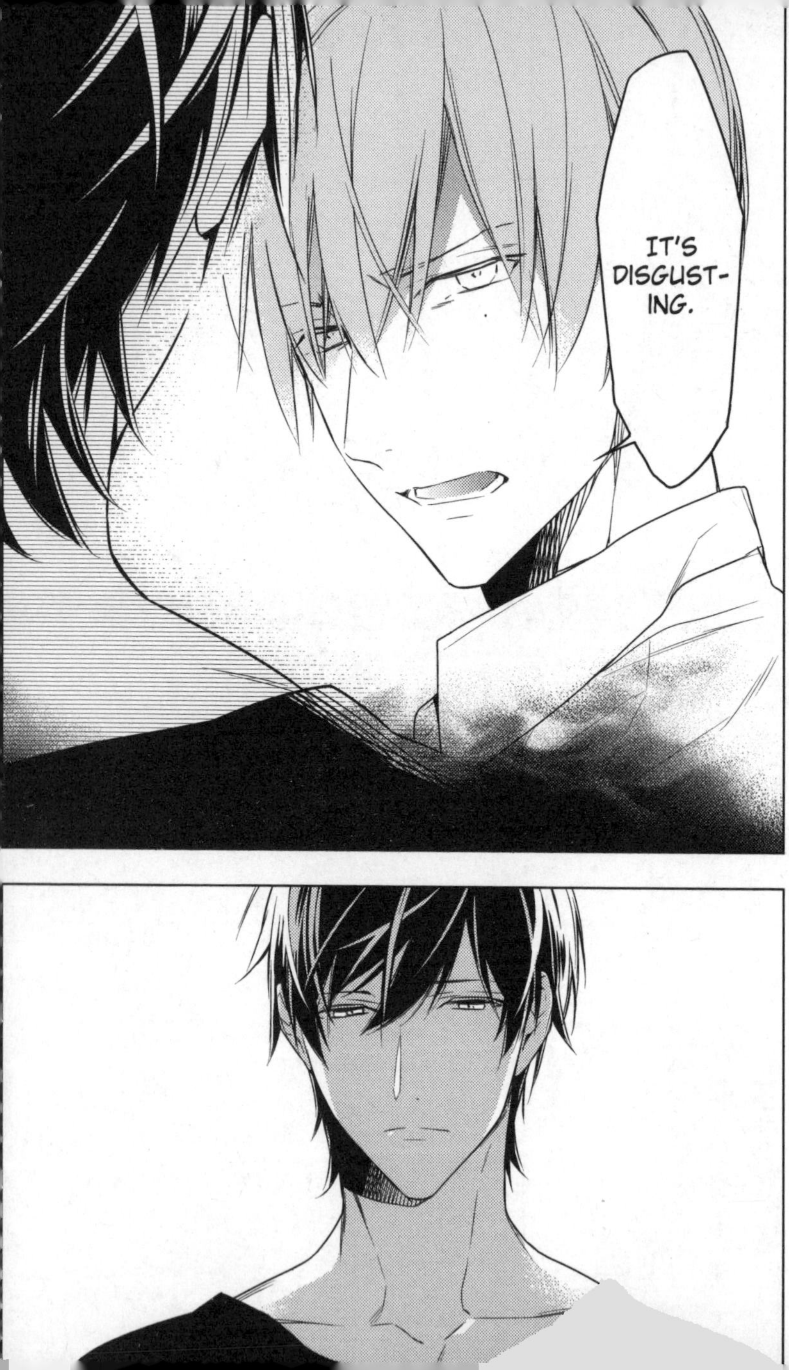
IT'S DISGUST-ING.

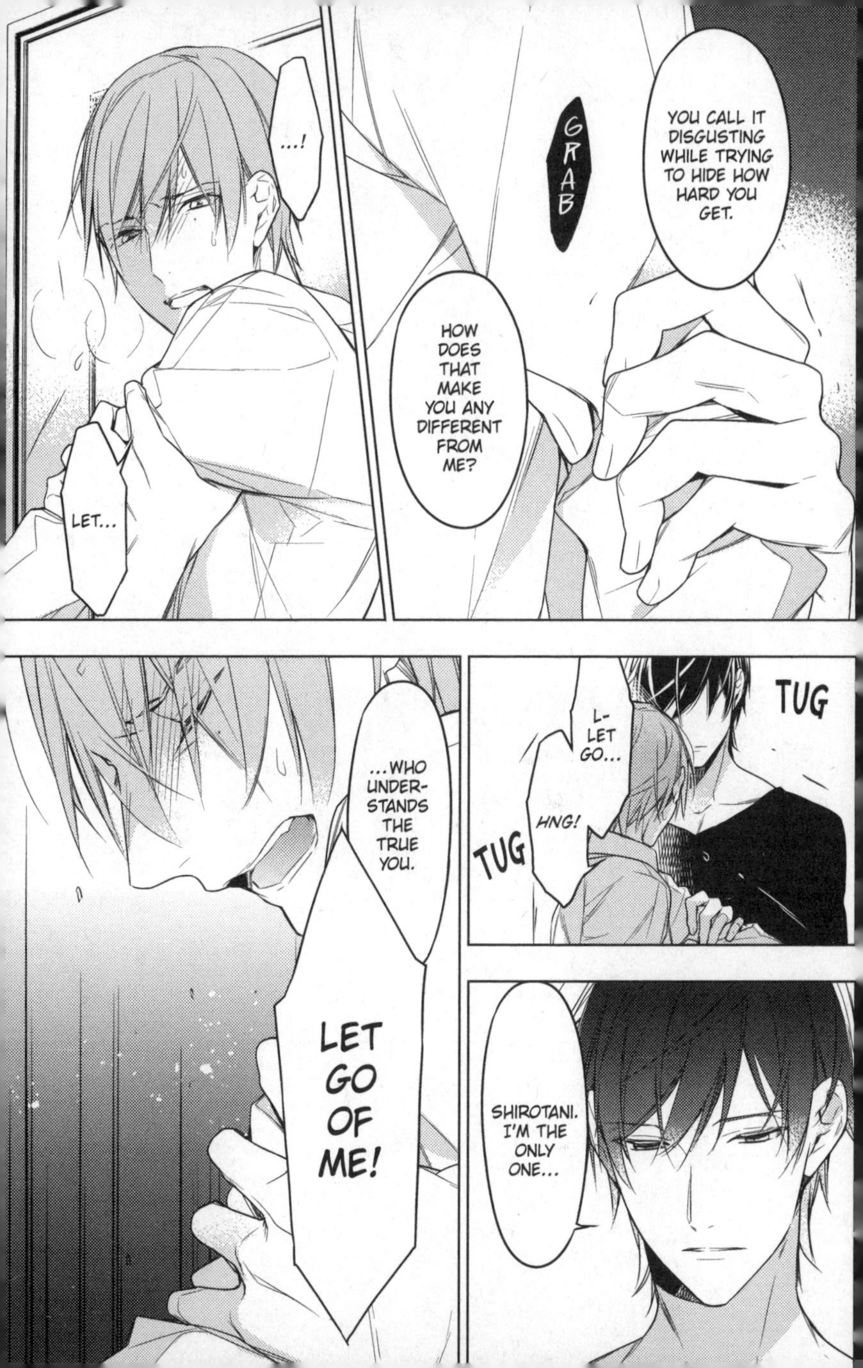
GRAB
YOU CALL IT DISGUSTING WHILE TRYING TO HIDE HOW HARD YOU GET.
HOW DOES THAT MAKE YOU ANY DIFFERENT FROM ME?
...!
LET...
TUG
L- LET GO...
HNG!
TUG
SHIROTANI. I'M THE ONLY ONE...
...WHO UNDERSTANDS THE TRUE YOU.
LET GO OF ME!

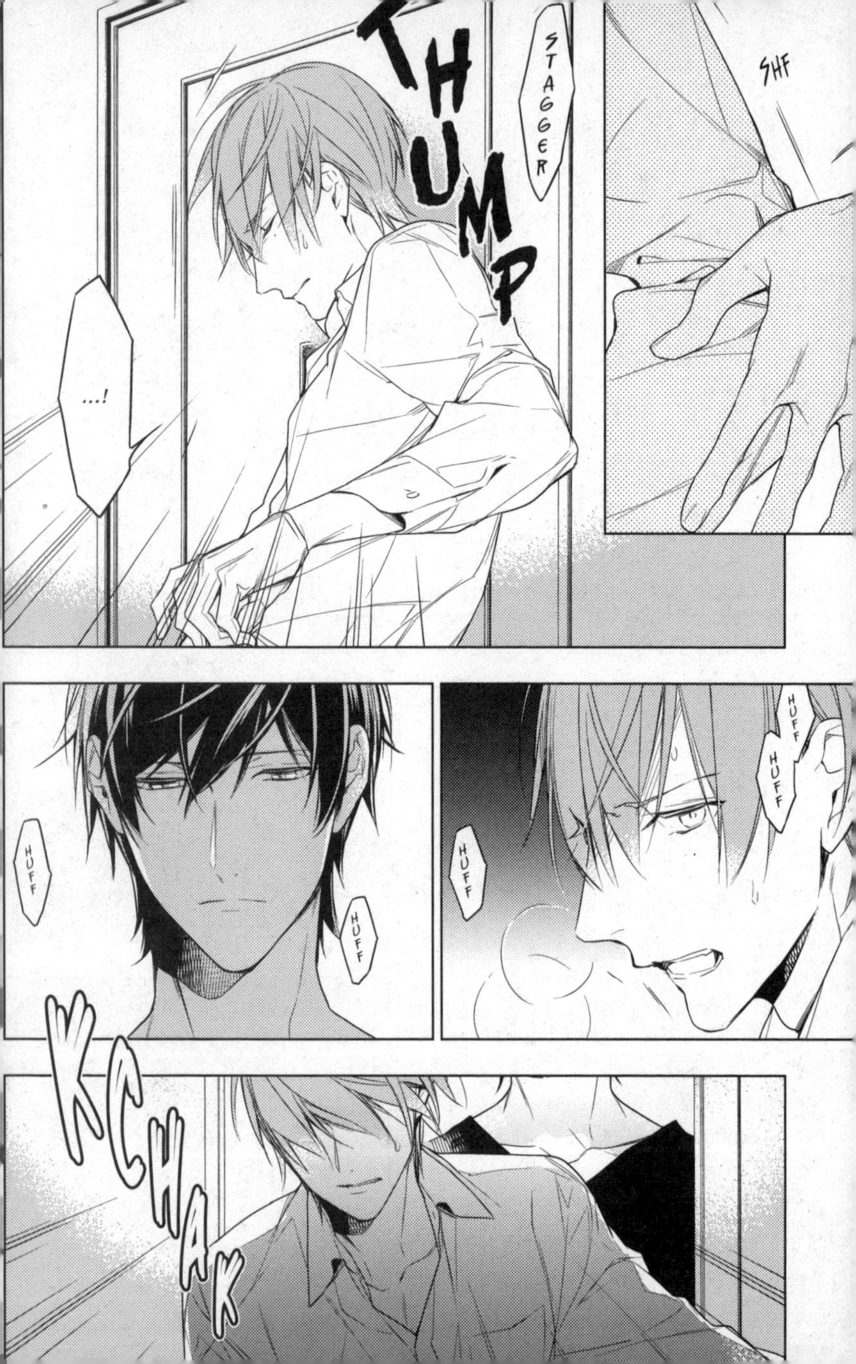
SHF
STAGGER
THUMP
...!
HUFF
HUFF
HUFF
HUFF
HUFF
KCHAK

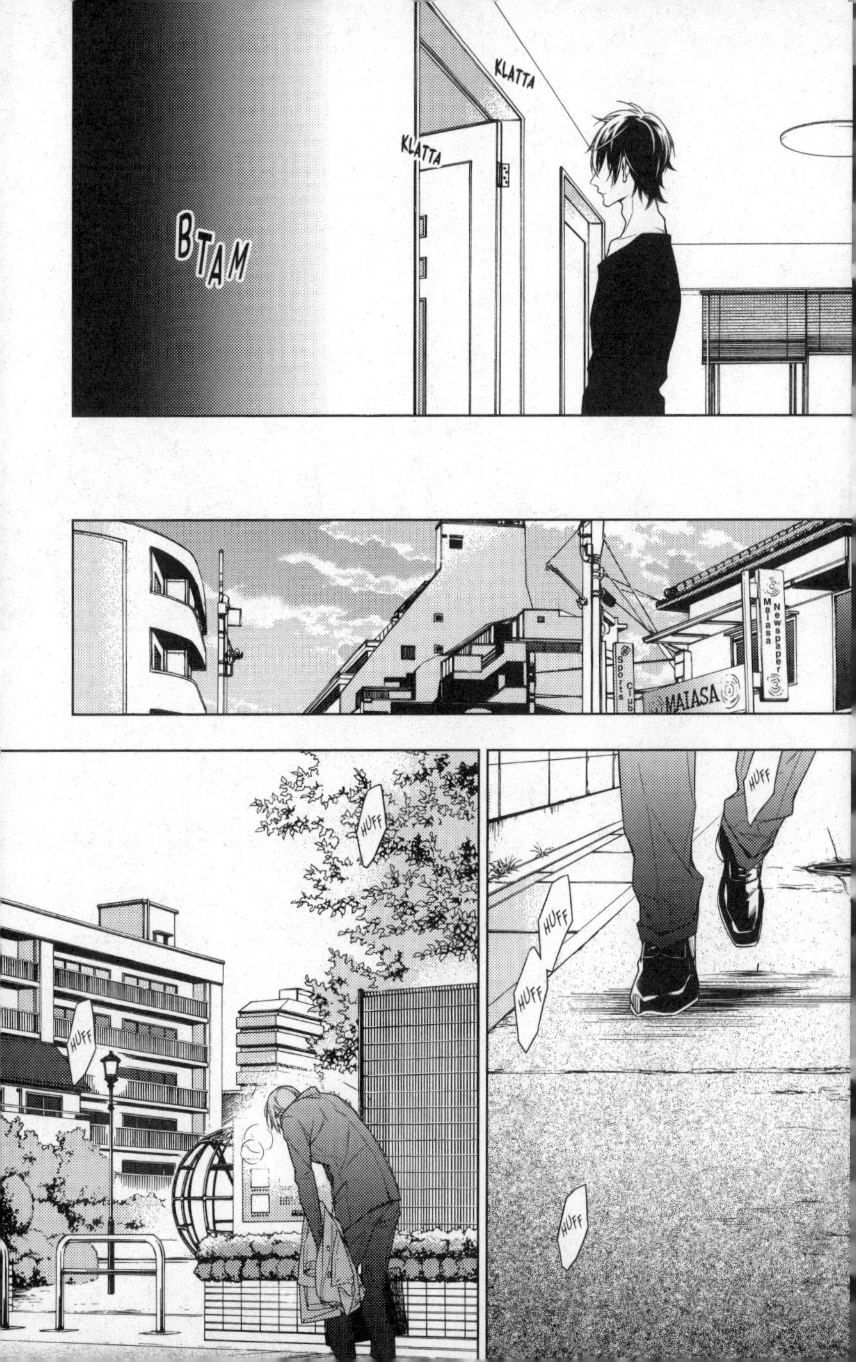

KLATTA
KLATTA
BTAM
Maiasa Newspaper
MAIASA
Sports Club
HUFF
HUFF
HUFF
HUFF
HUFF
HUFF

I DON'T WANT TO HURT YOU. I NEVER WANT TO HURT YOU.

BUT I DO WANT TO DIRTY YOU—TO DEFILE YOU. BOTH OF THOSE EMOTIONS EXIST INSIDE OF ME AT THE SAME TIME.

HUFF

HUFF

HUFF

HUFF

YOU'VE GOT TO BE KIDDING ME!

NO. JUST NO!

HUFF

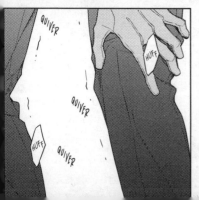

QUIVER

HUFF

QUIVER

HUFF

QUIVER

I KNEW IT.

THIS WHOLE TIME HE'S BEEN LOOKING DOWN ON ME, MAKING ME DO THINGS I DON'T LIKE WHILE LAUGHING AT ME.

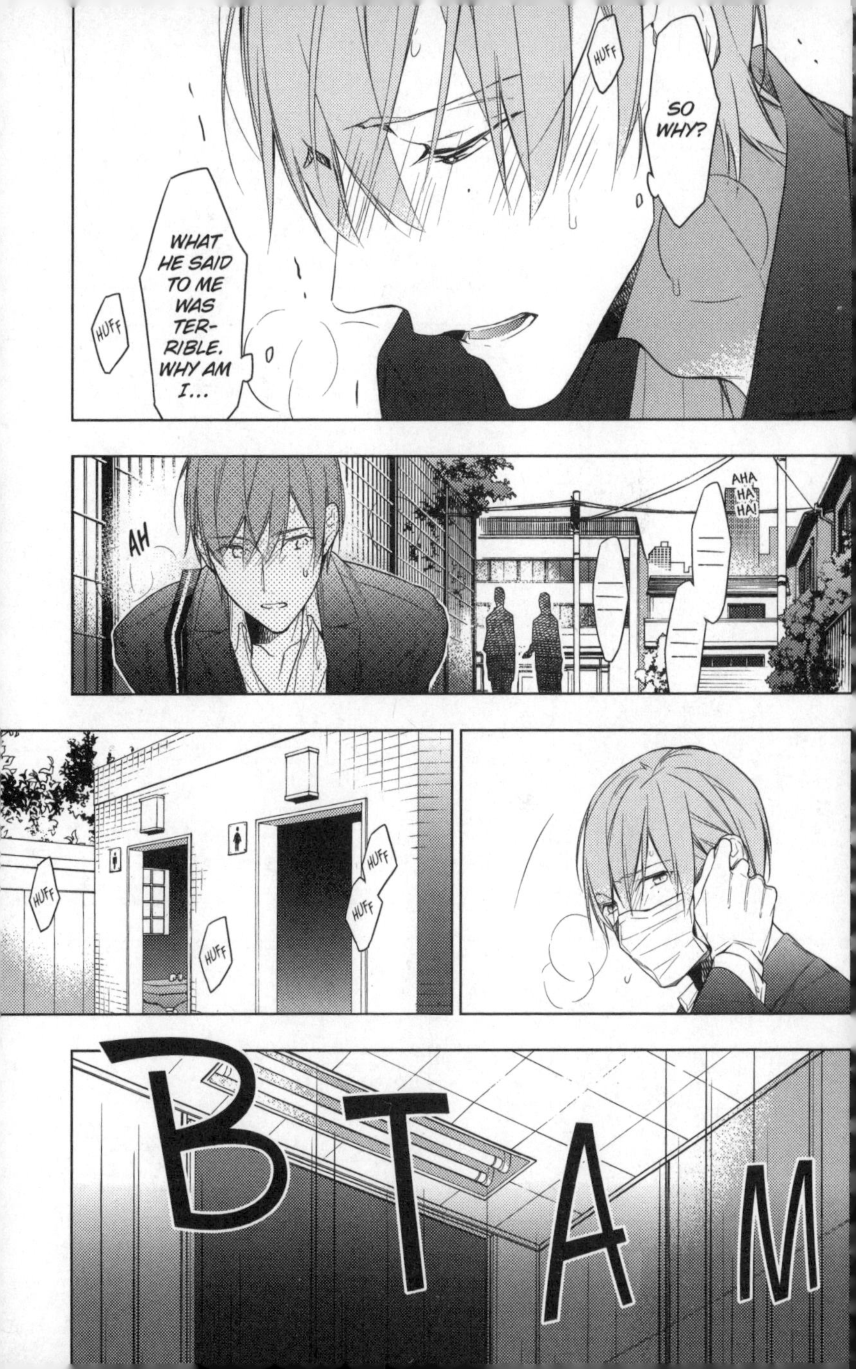
HUFF
SO WHY?
WHAT HE SAID TO ME WAS TER-RIBLE. WHY AM I...
HUFF
AHA HA HA!
AH
HUFF
HUFF
HUFF
HUFF
BTAM

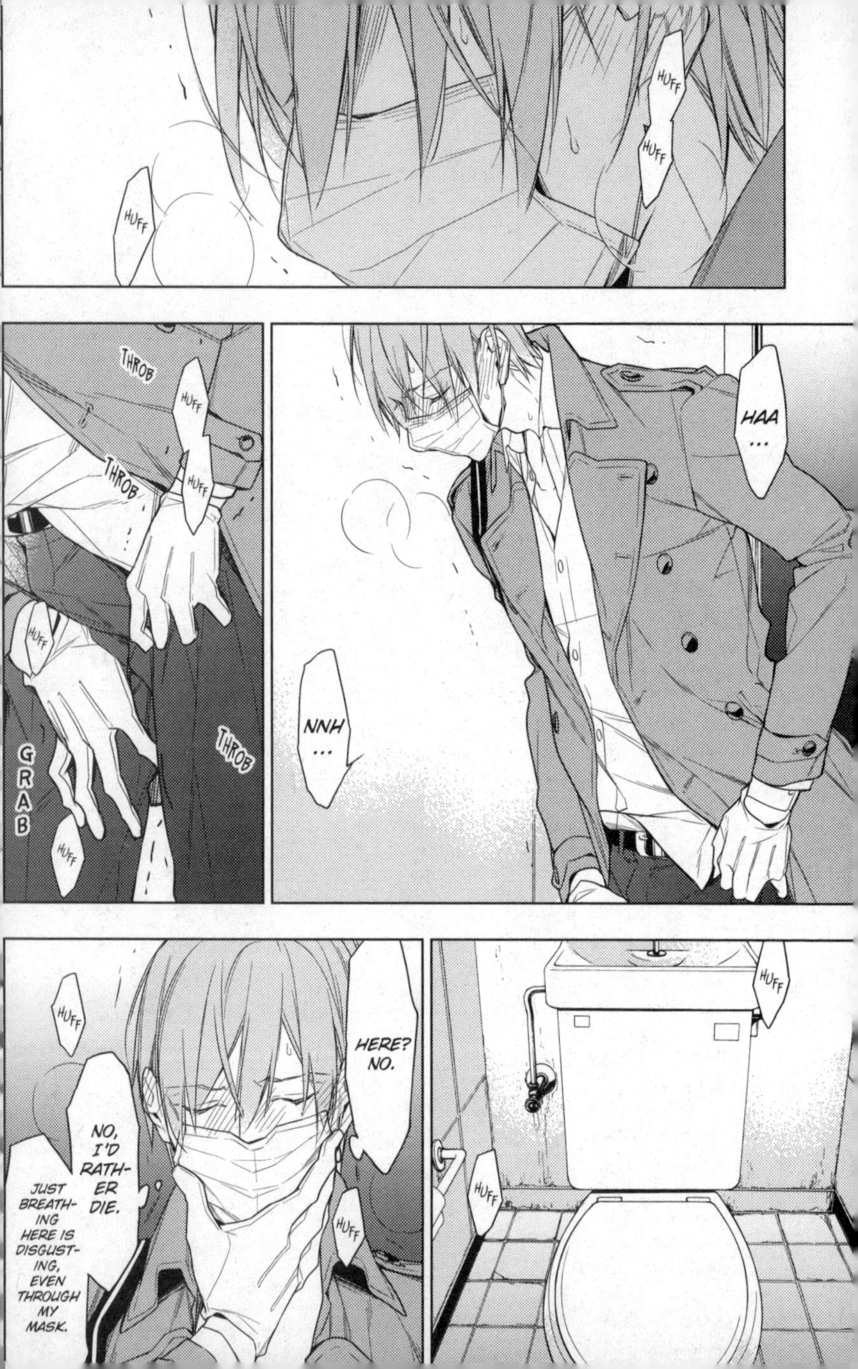
HUFF
HUFF
HUFF
HAA ...
NNH ...
THROB
HUFF
THROB
HUFF
HUFF
THROB
GRAB
HUFF
HUFF
HUFF
HERE? NO.
NO, I'D RATHER DIE.
HUFF
JUST BREATHING HERE IS DISGUSTING, EVEN THROUGH MY MASK.
HUFF

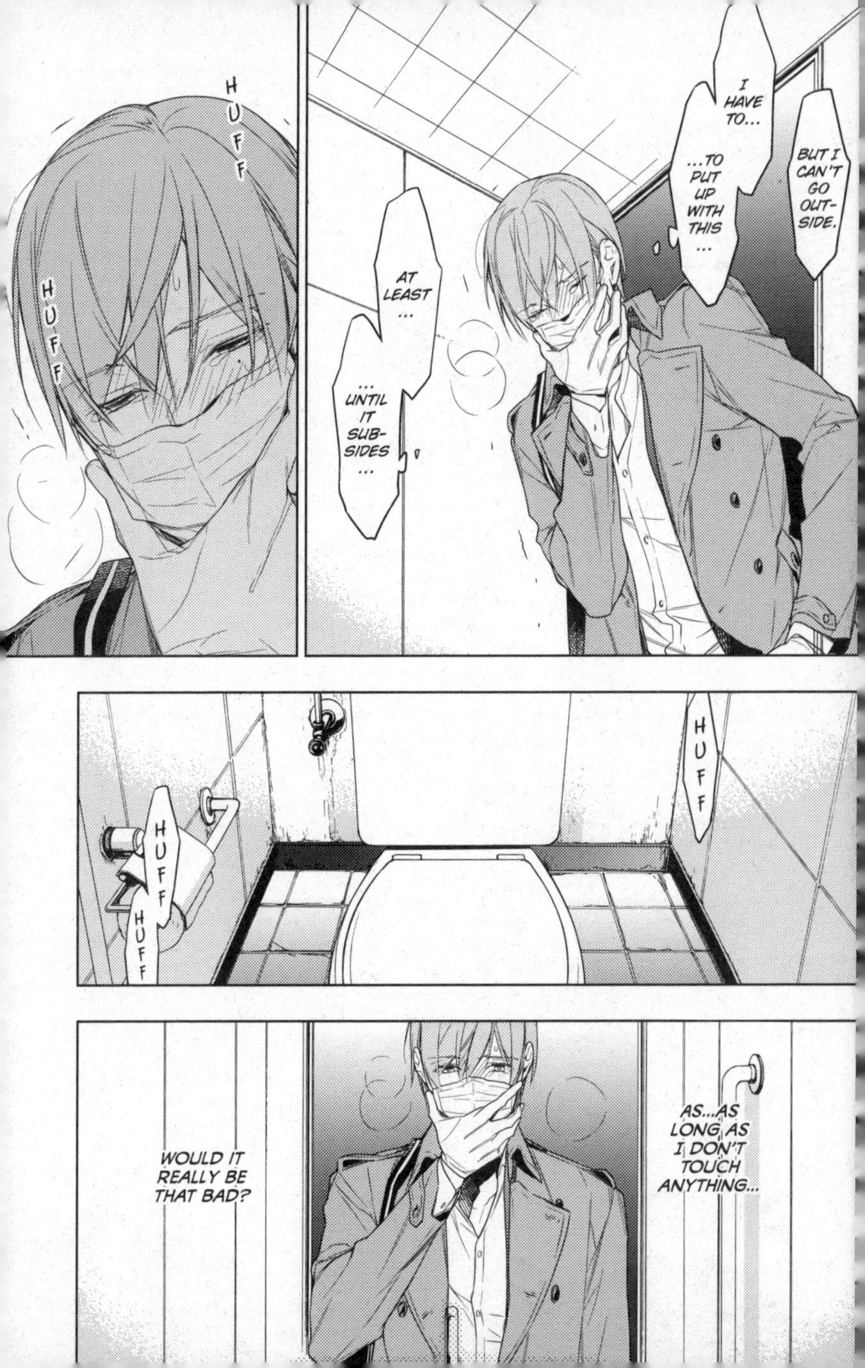
BUT I CAN'T GO OUTSIDE.
I HAVE TO...
...TO PUT UP WITH THIS...
AT LEAST...
...UNTIL IT SUBSIDES...
HUFF
HUFF
HUFF
HUFF
HUFF
AS...AS LONG AS I DON'T TOUCH ANYTHING...
WOULD IT REALLY BE THAT BAD?

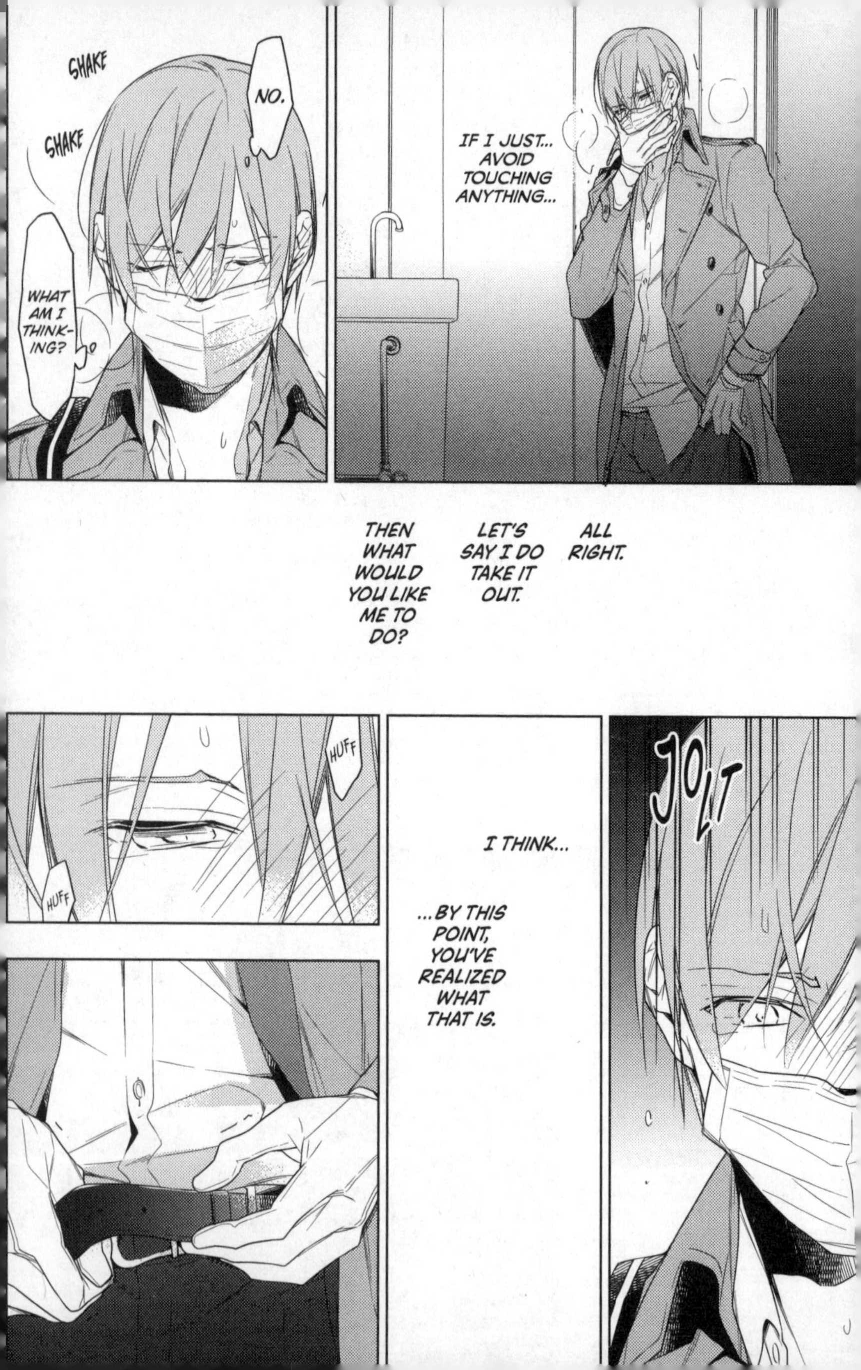
IF I JUST... AVOID TOUCHING ANYTHING...
NO.
SHAKE
SHAKE
WHAT AM I THINKING?
ALL RIGHT.
LET'S SAY I DO TAKE IT OUT.
THEN WHAT WOULD YOU LIKE ME TO DO?
JOLT
I THINK...
...BY THIS POINT, YOU'VE REALIZED WHAT THAT IS.
HUFF
HUFF

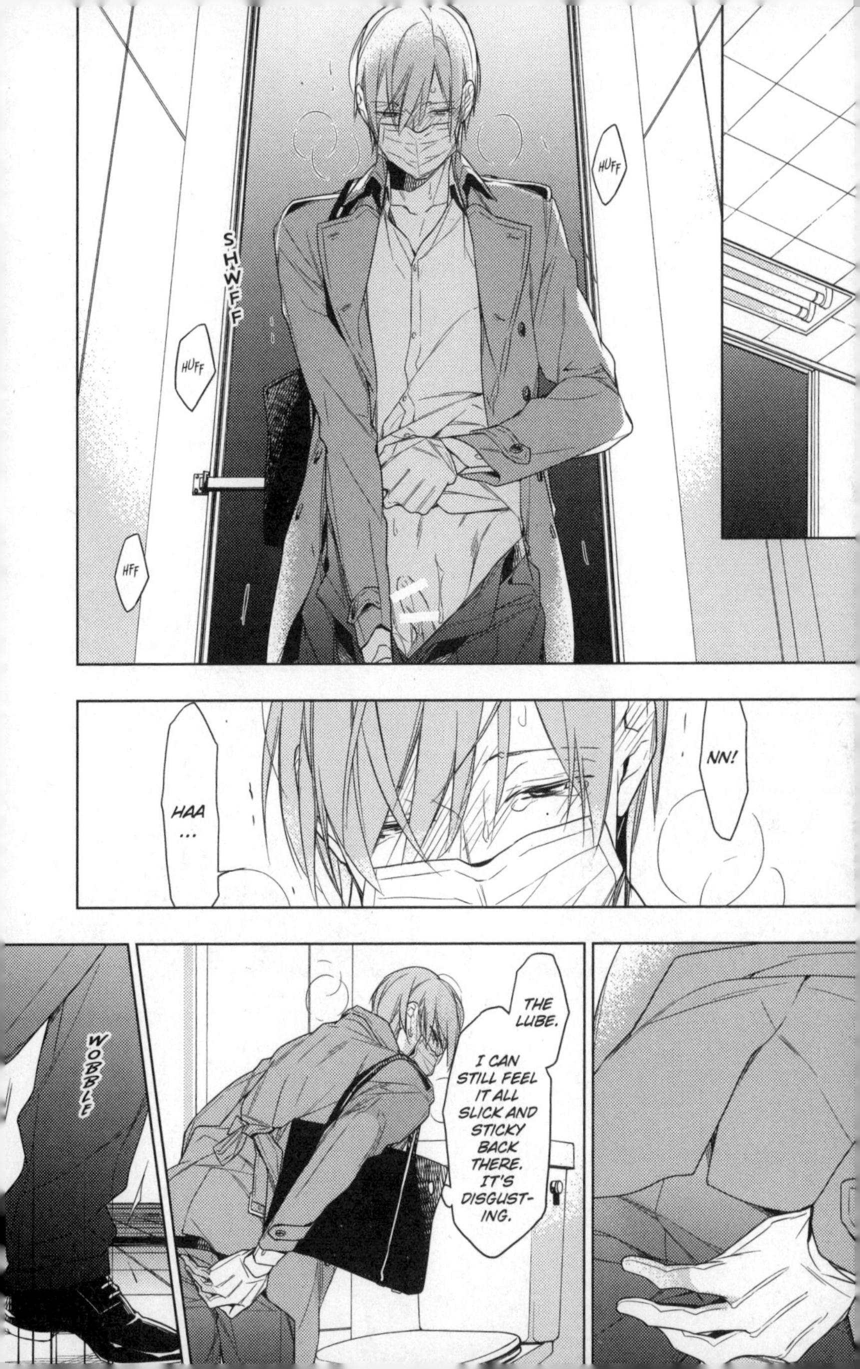
HUFF
SHWFF
HUFF
HFF
NN!
HAA ...
THE LUBE.
I CAN STILL FEEL IT ALL SLICK AND STICKY BACK THERE. IT'S DISGUSTING.
WOBBLE

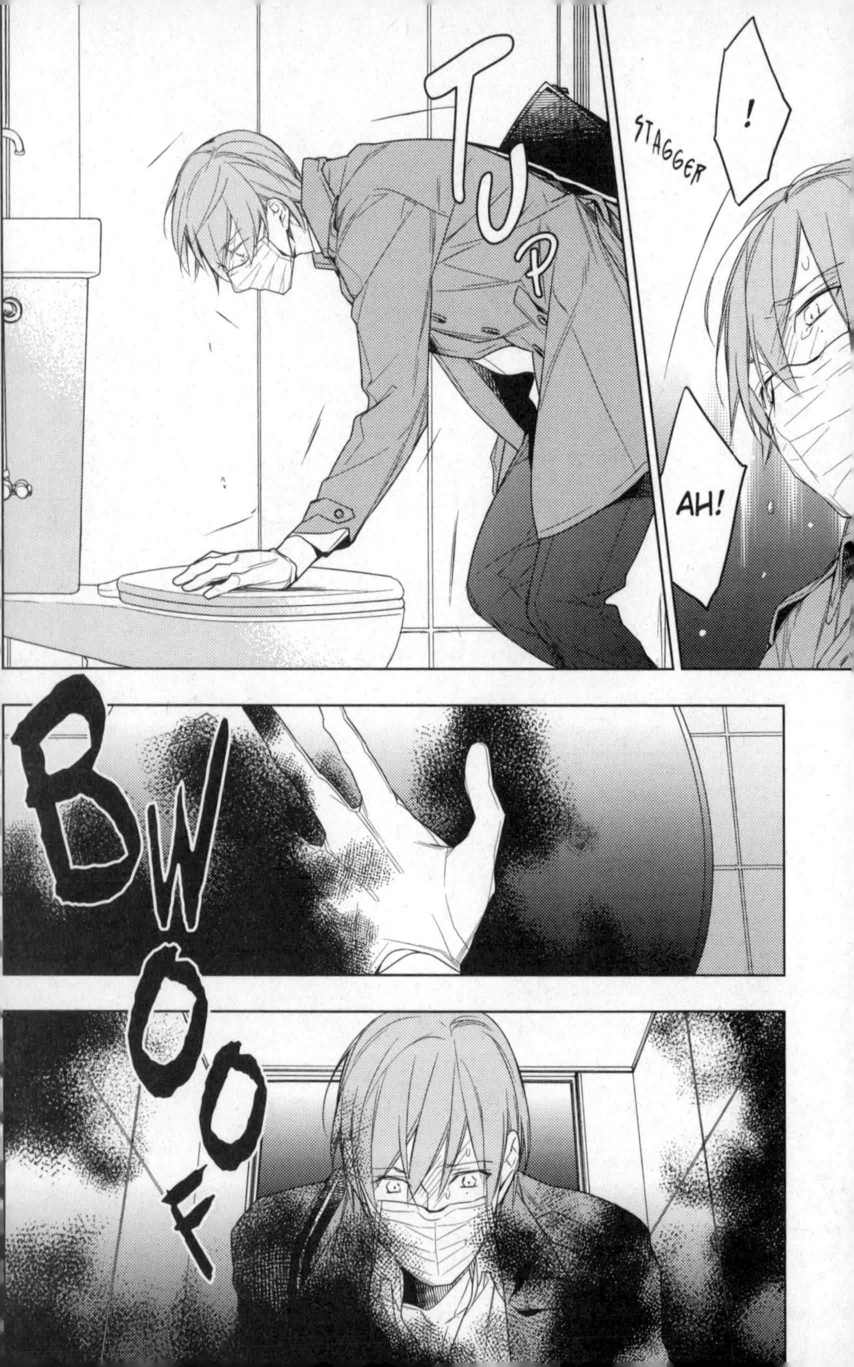
!
AH!
STAGGER
TUP
BWOOF

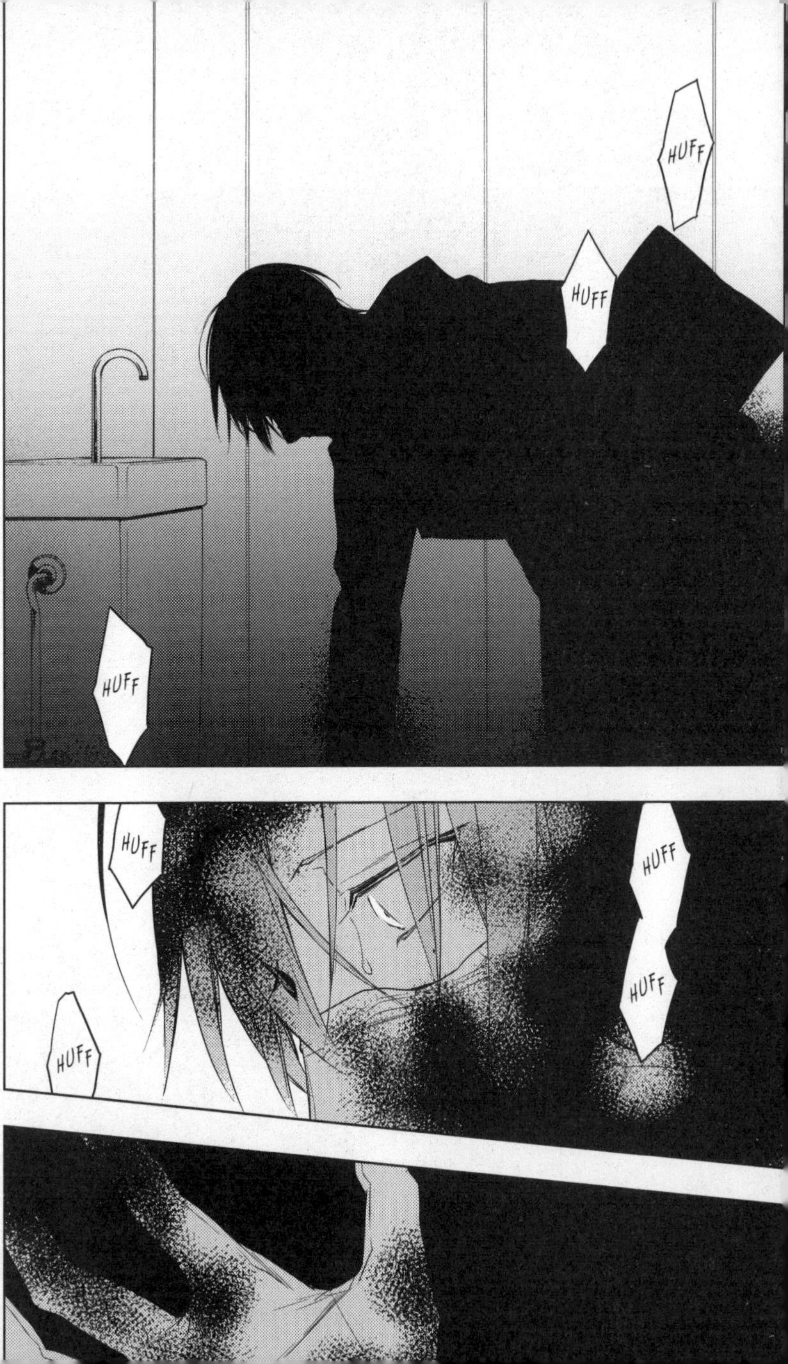
HUFF
HUFF
HUFF
HUFF
HUFF
HUFF
HUFF

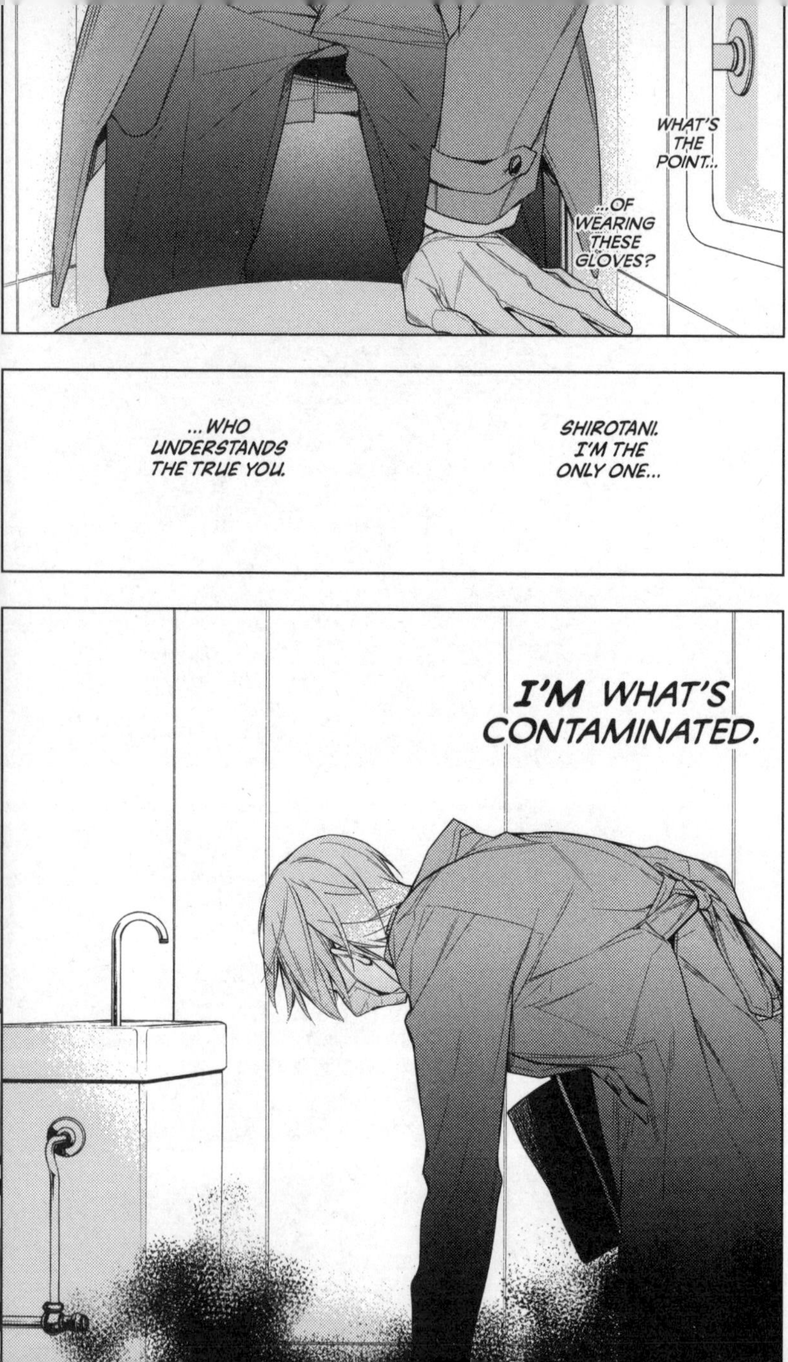
WHAT'S THE POINT...
...OF WEARING THESE GLOVES?
SHIROTANI. I'M THE ONLY ONE...
...WHO UNDERSTANDS THE TRUE YOU.
I'M WHAT'S CONTAMINATED.

ten count by rihito takarai

ten count by rihito takarai

TEN COUNT 21

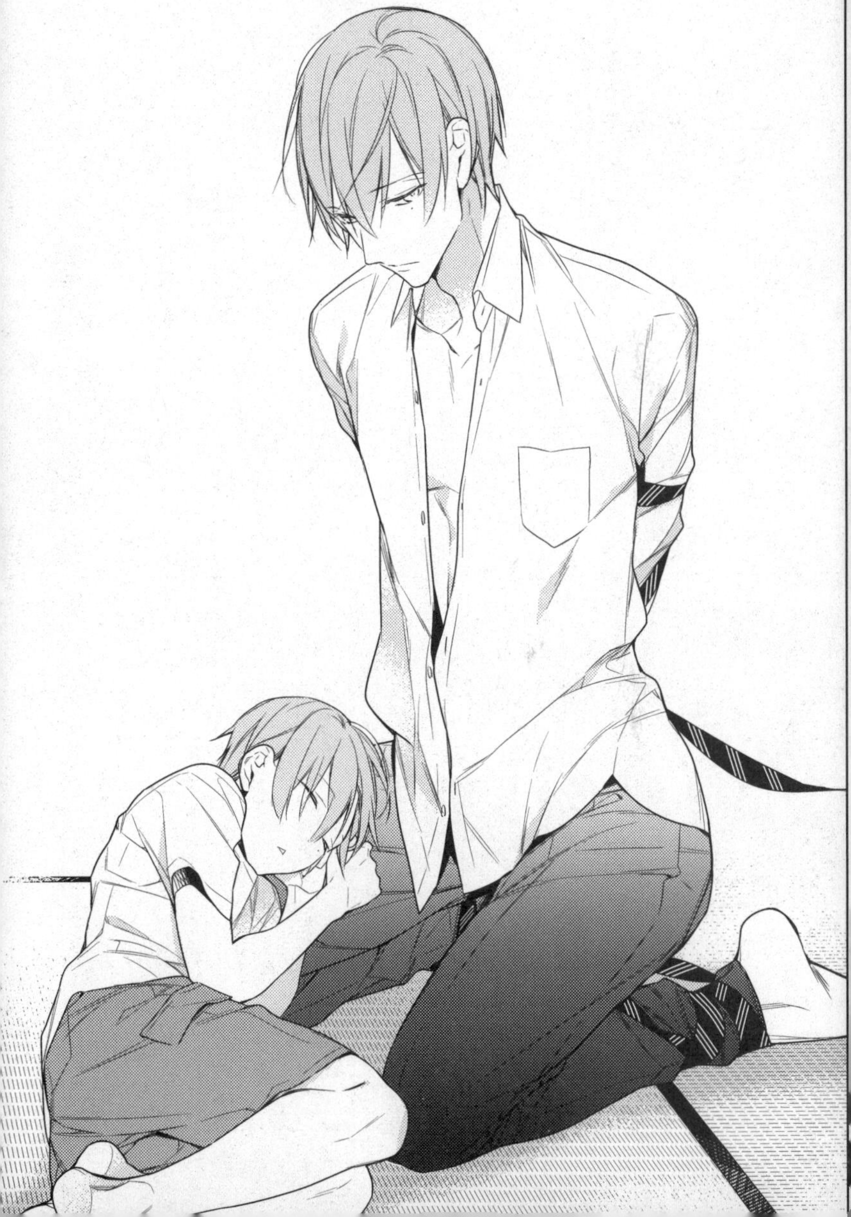

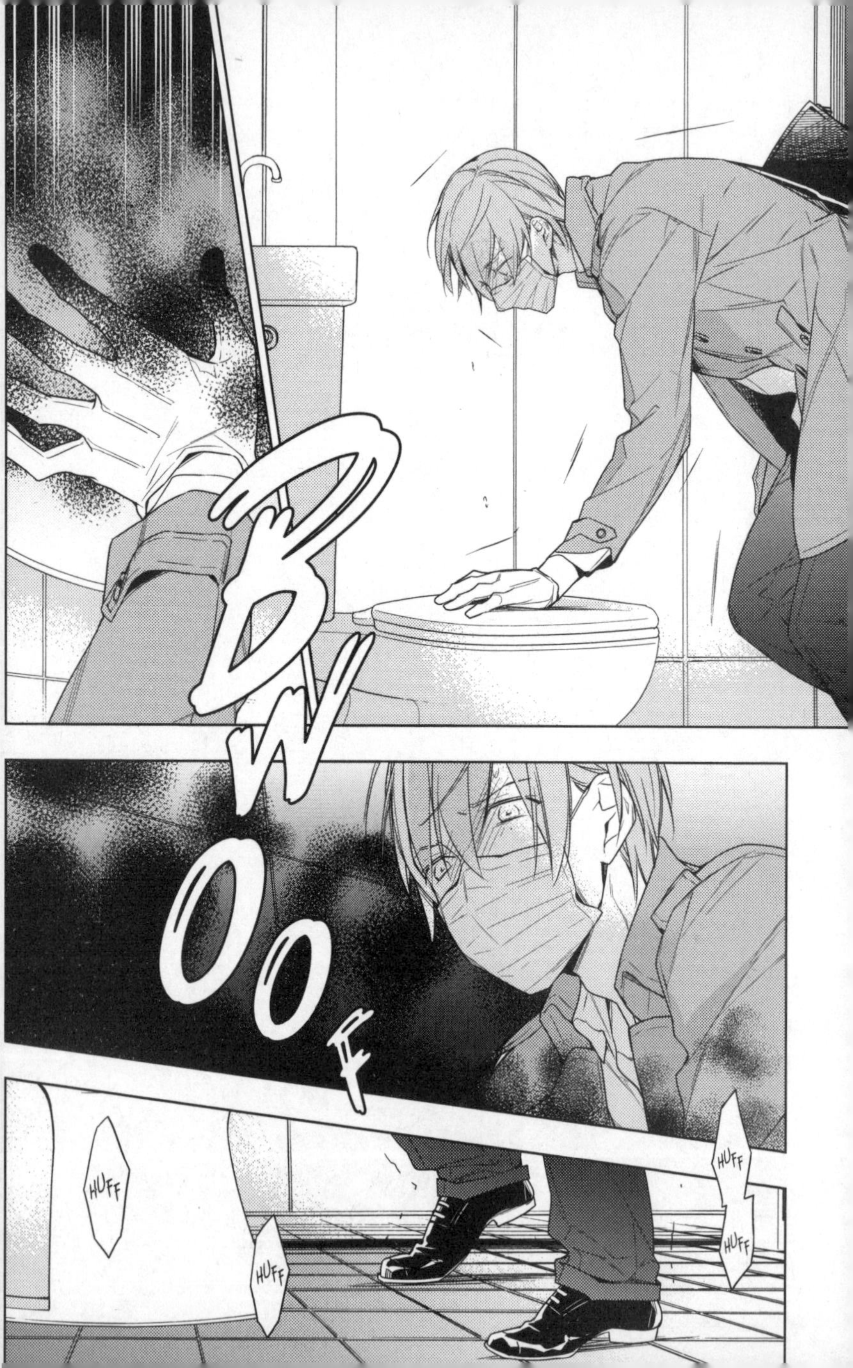
HUFF
HUFF
HUFF
HUFF

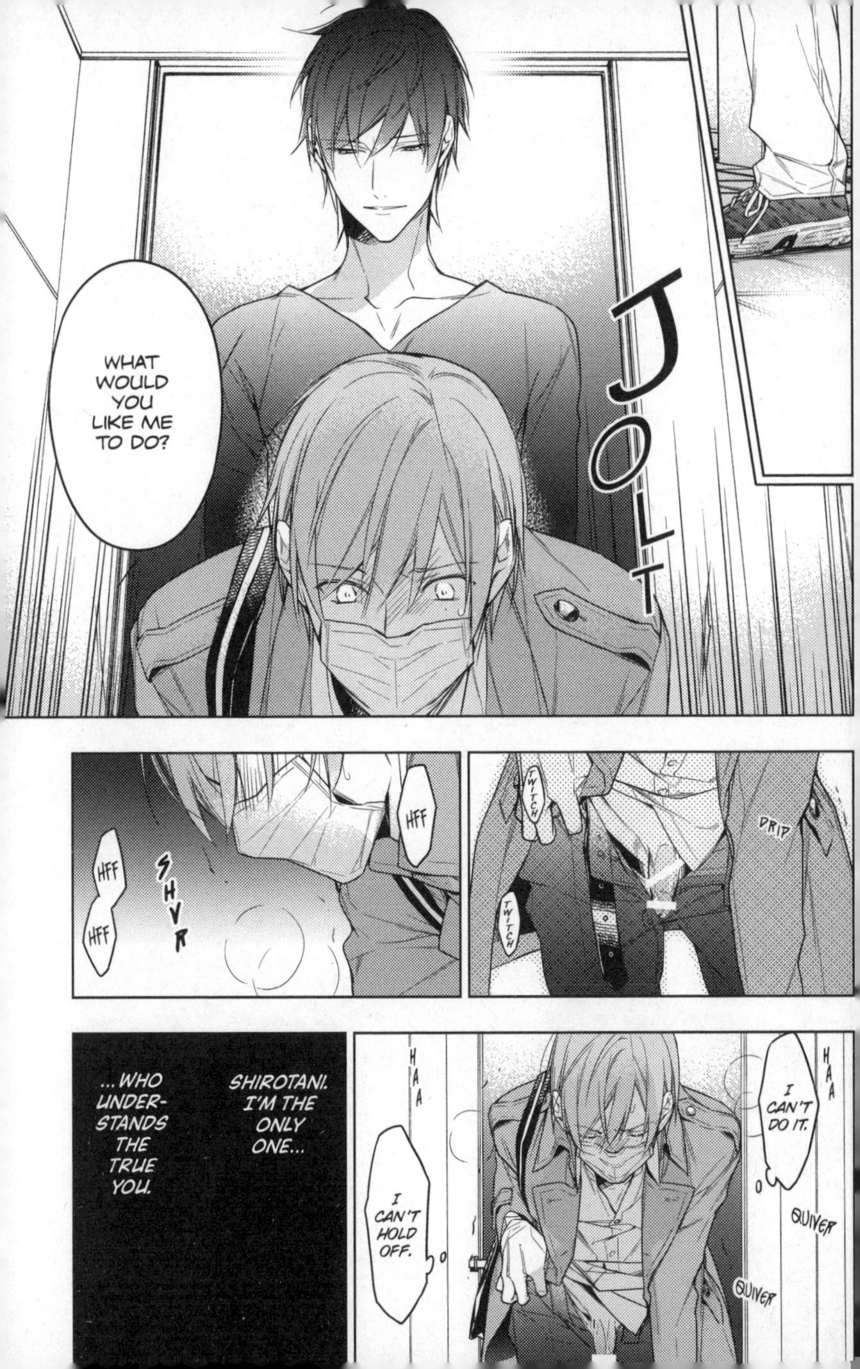
JOLT
WHAT WOULD YOU LIKE ME TO DO?
TWITCH
DRIP
TWITCH
HFF
SHVR
HFF
HFF
HAA
I CAN'T DO IT.
HAA
I CAN'T HOLD OFF.
QUIVER
QUIVER
SHIROTANI. I'M THE ONLY ONE...
...WHO UNDER-STANDS THE TRUE YOU.

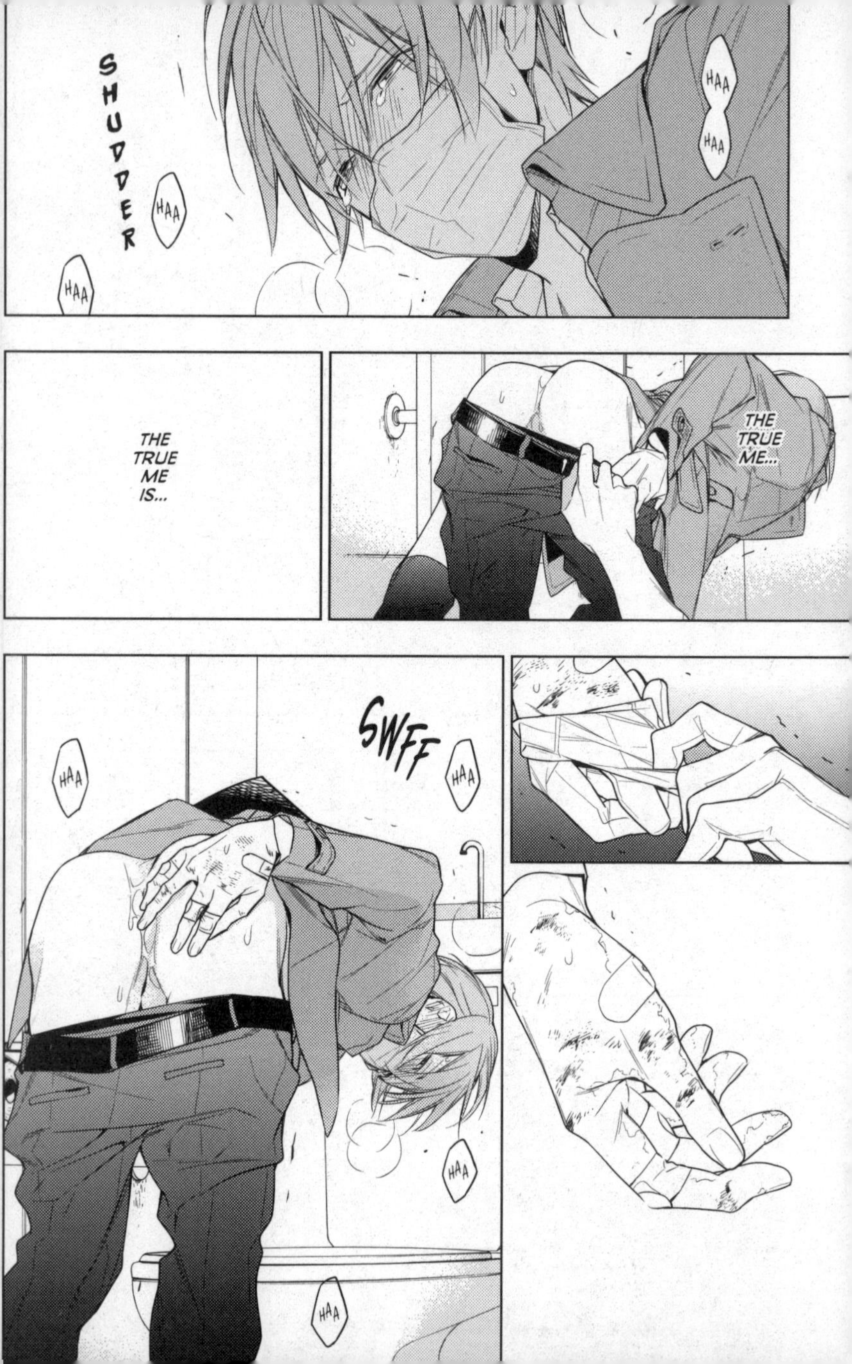
HAA
HAA
SHUDDER
HAA
HAA
THE TRUE ME...
THE TRUE ME IS...
SWFF
HAA
HAA
HAA
HAA

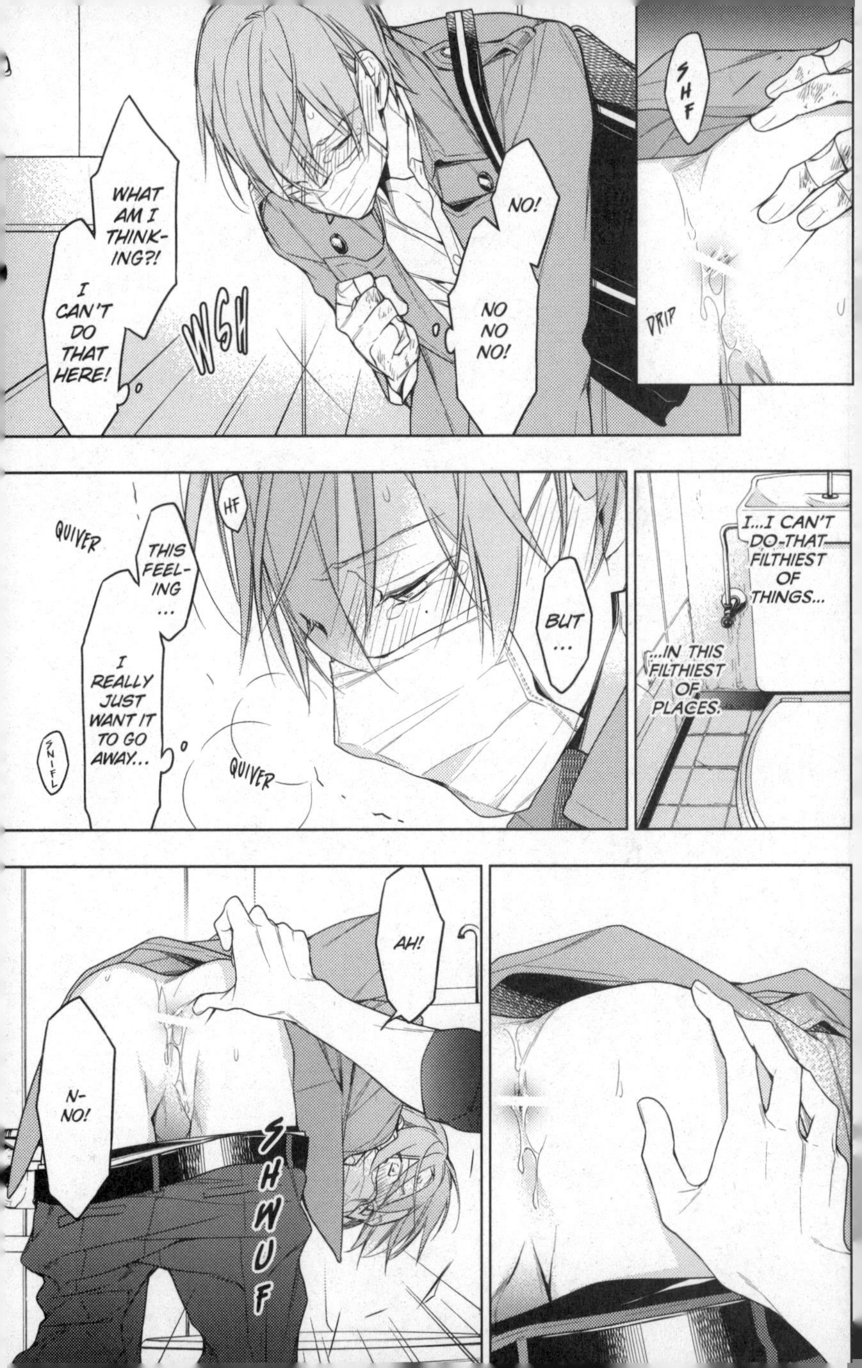
SHF
DRIP
NO!
NO NO NO!
WSH
WHAT AM I THINKING?!
I CAN'T DO THAT HERE!
I...I CAN'T DO THAT FILTHIEST OF THINGS...
...IN THIS FILTHIEST OF PLACES.
HF
BUT...
QUIVER
THIS FEELING...
I REALLY JUST WANT IT TO GO AWAY...
QUIVER
SNIFL
AH!
SHWUF
N-NO!

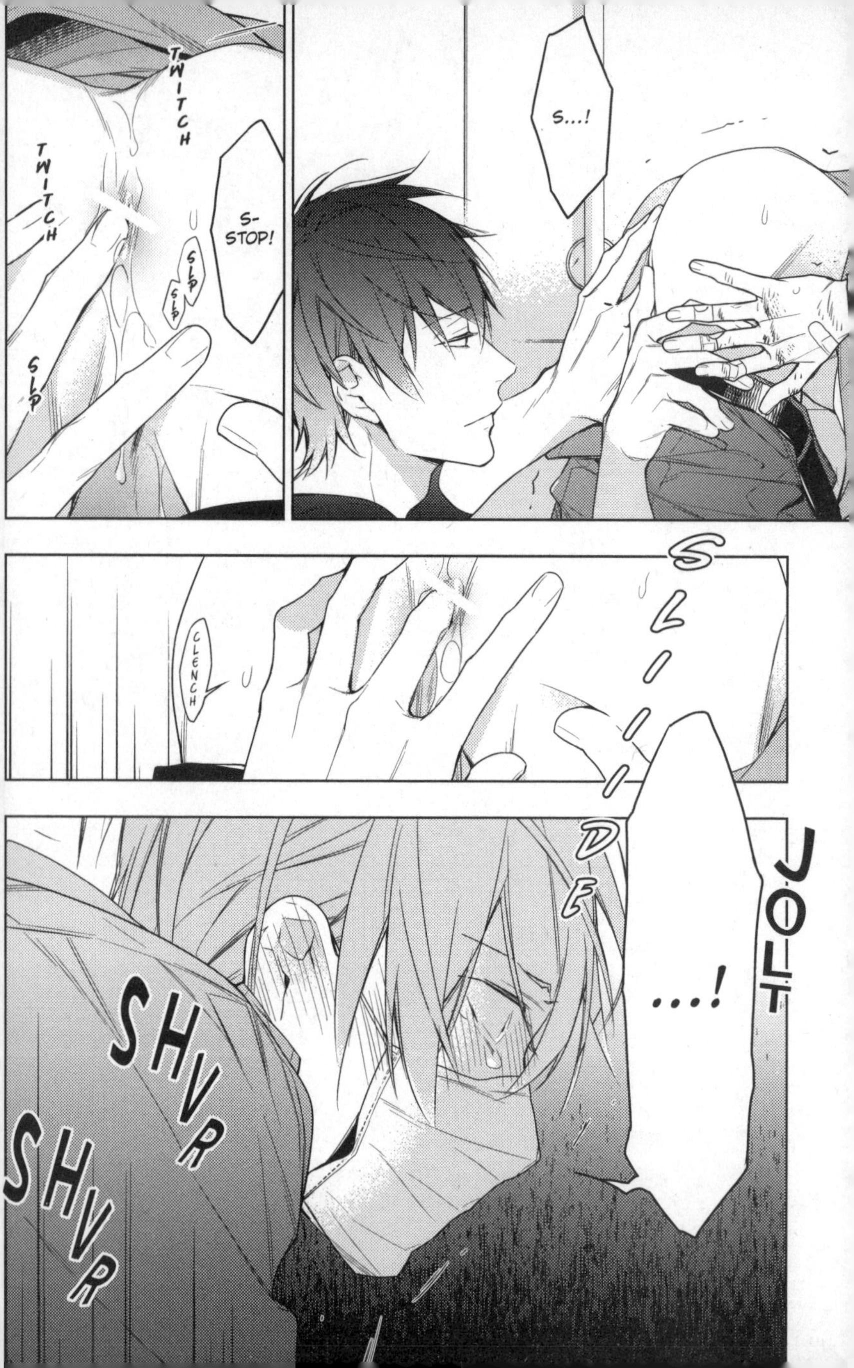
S...!
S-
STOP!
TWITCH
TWITCH
SLP
SLP
SLP
SLIIIDE
CLENCH
JOLT
...!
SHVR
SHVR

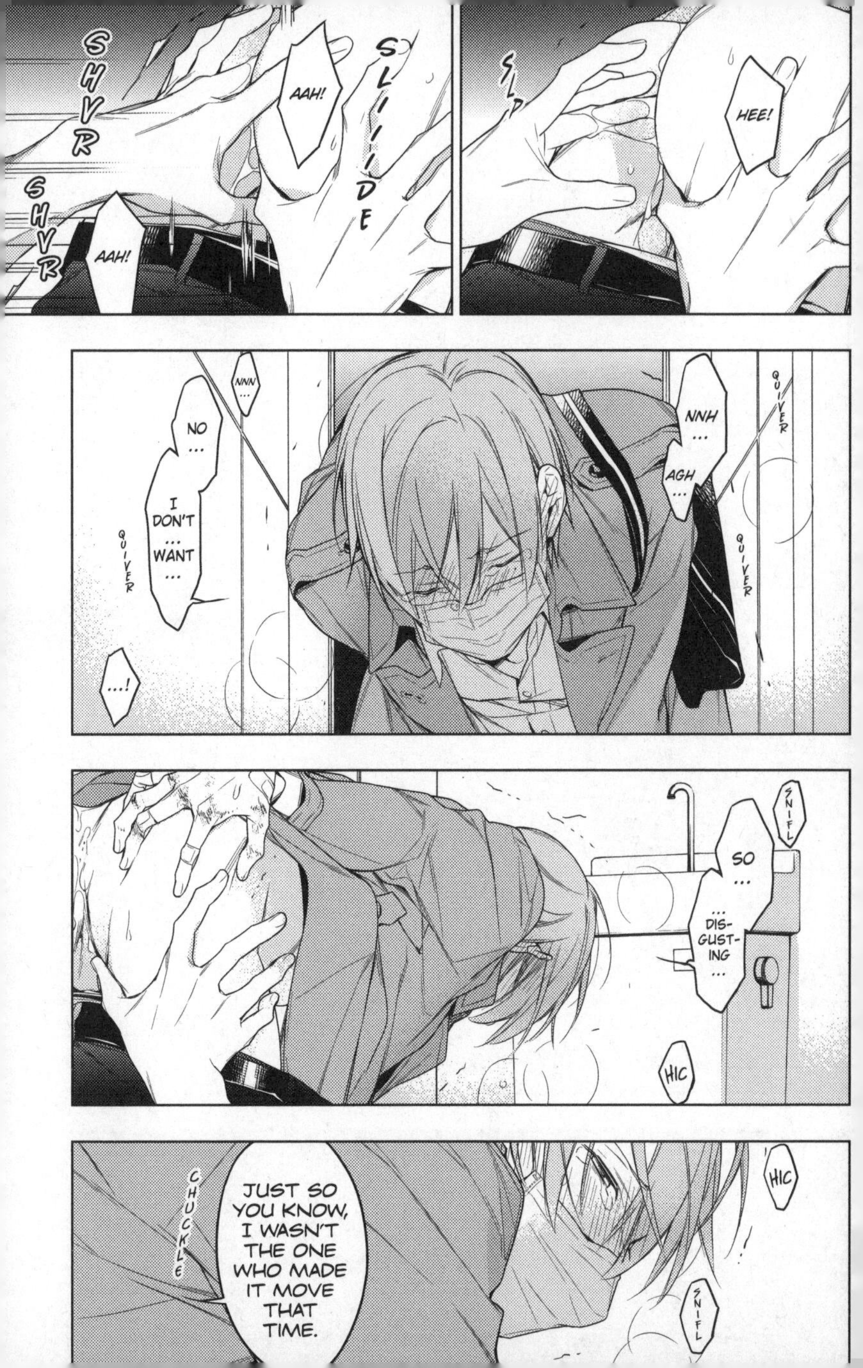
SLP
HEE!
AAH!
SLIIIIDE
SHVR
SHVR
AAH!
QUIVER
NNH... AGH...
QUIVER
NNN...
NO... I DON'T... WANT...
QUIVER
...!
SNIFL
SO... ...DISGUSTING...
HIC
HIC
SNIFL
JUST SO YOU KNOW, I WASN'T THE ONE WHO MADE IT MOVE THAT TIME.
CHUCKLE

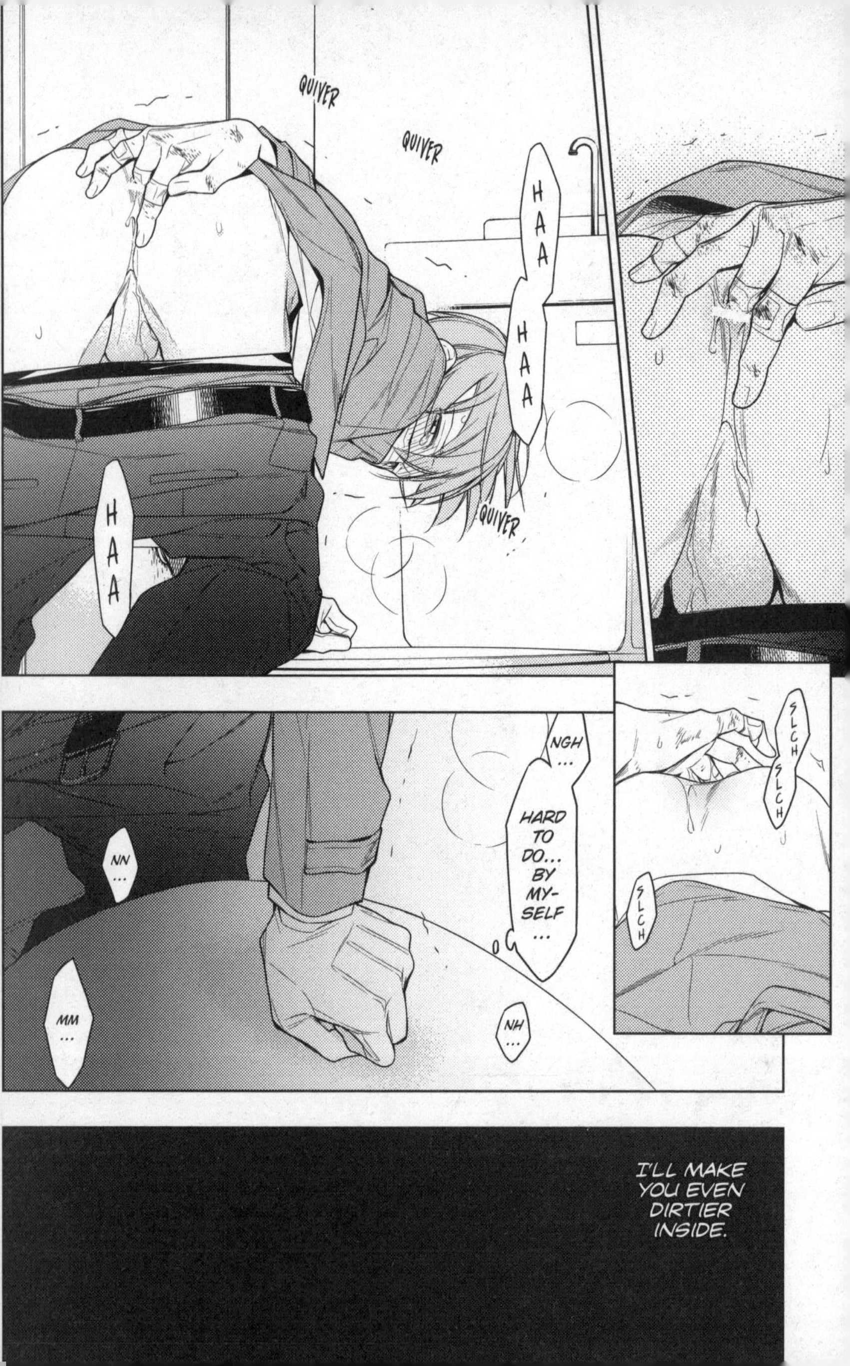

QUIVER
QUIVER
HAA HAA
QUIVER
HAA
SLCH SLCH
SLCH
NGH...
HARD TO DO... BY MY-SELF...
NH...
NN...
MM...
I'LL MAKE YOU EVEN DIRTIER INSIDE.

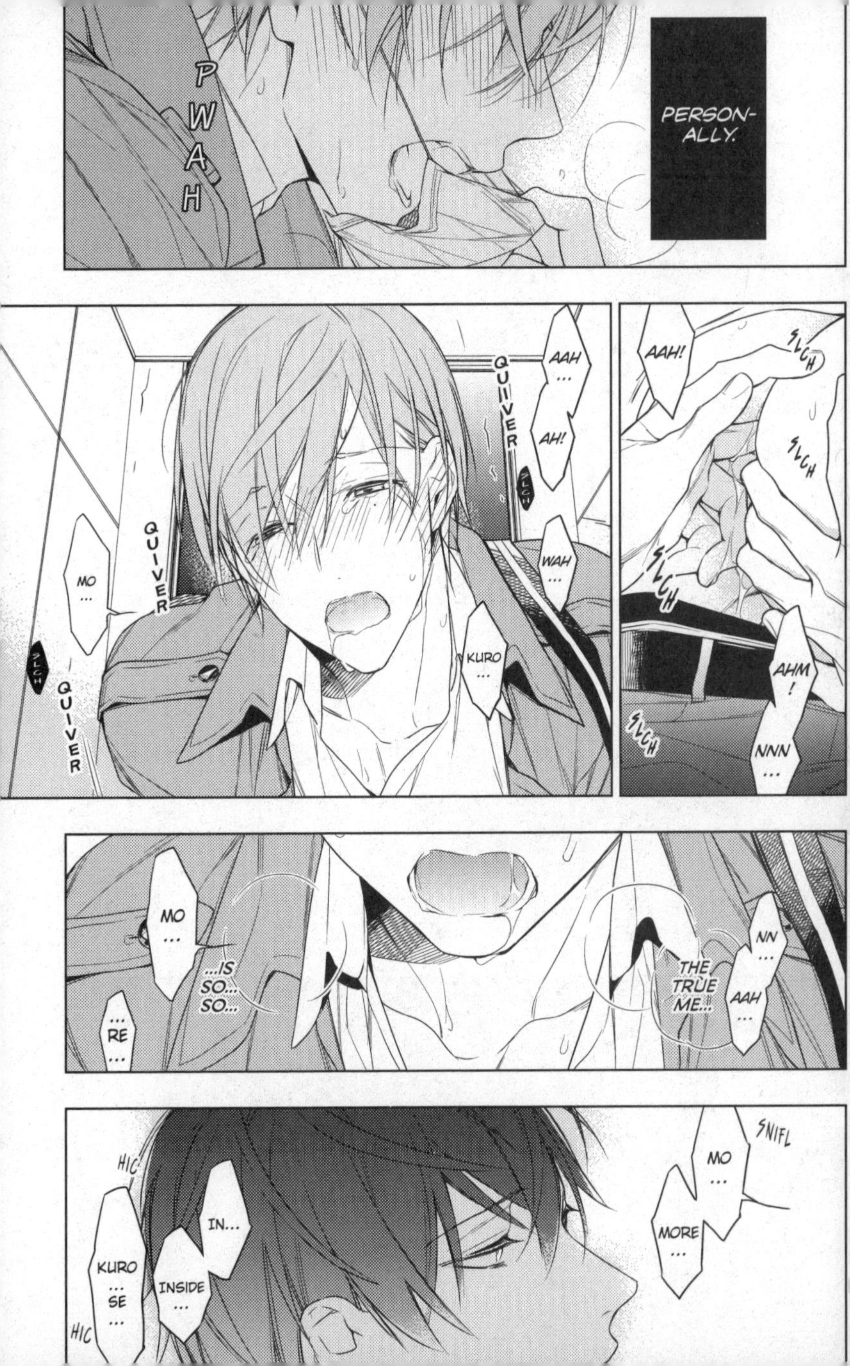
PERSON-ALLY.
PWAH
AAH!
SLCH
SLCH
SLCH
AHM!
SLCH
NNN...
AAH... AH!
QUIVER
SLCH
WAH...
KURO...
QUIVER
MO...
SLCH
QUIVER
NN... AAH...
THE TRUE ME...
...IS SO... SO...
MO...
...RE...
SNIFL
MO...
MORE...
IN...
INSIDE...
HIC
KURO... SE...
HIC

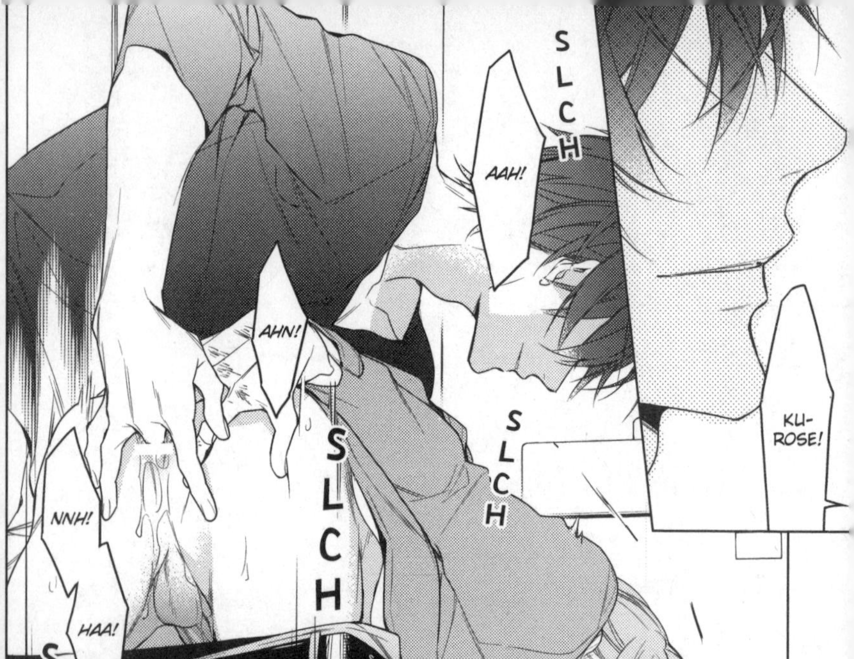
SLCH
AAH!
KU-ROSE!
SLCH
AHN!
SLCH
NNH!
HAA!
SLCH
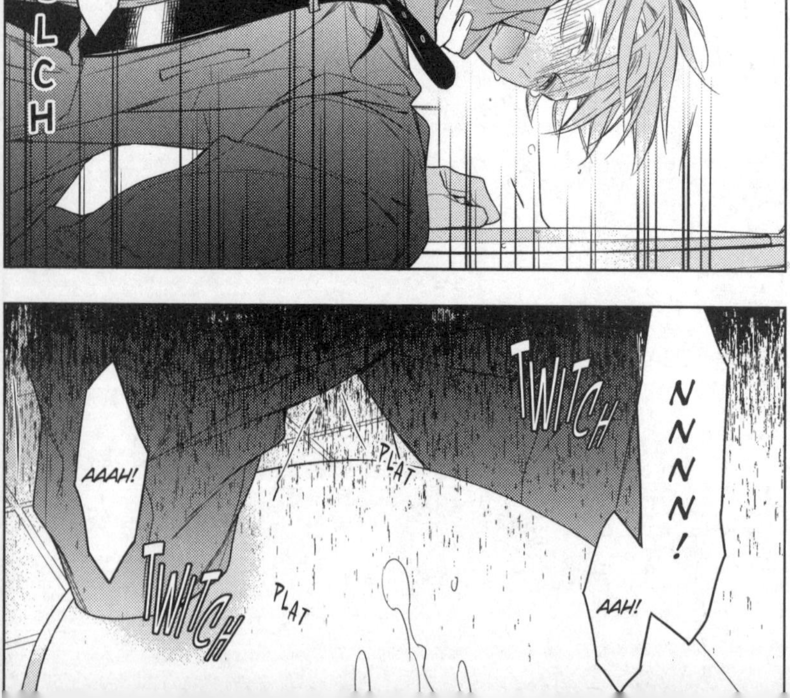
NNNNN!
AAH!
TWITCH
PLAT
AAAH!
TWITCH
PLAT

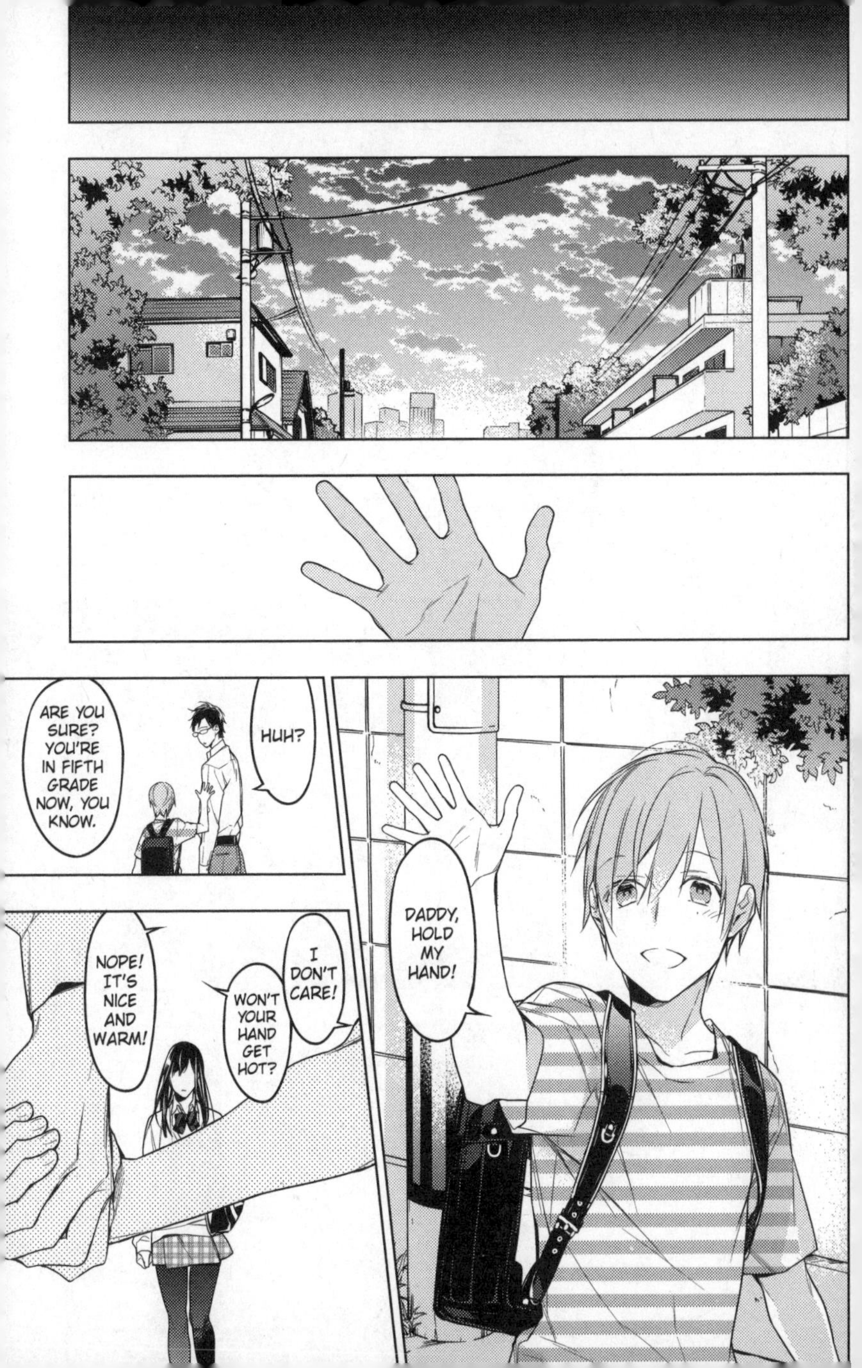
DADDY, HOLD MY HAND!
HUH?
ARE YOU SURE? YOU'RE IN FIFTH GRADE NOW, YOU KNOW.
I DON'T CARE!
WON'T YOUR HAND GET HOT?
NOPE! IT'S NICE AND WARM!

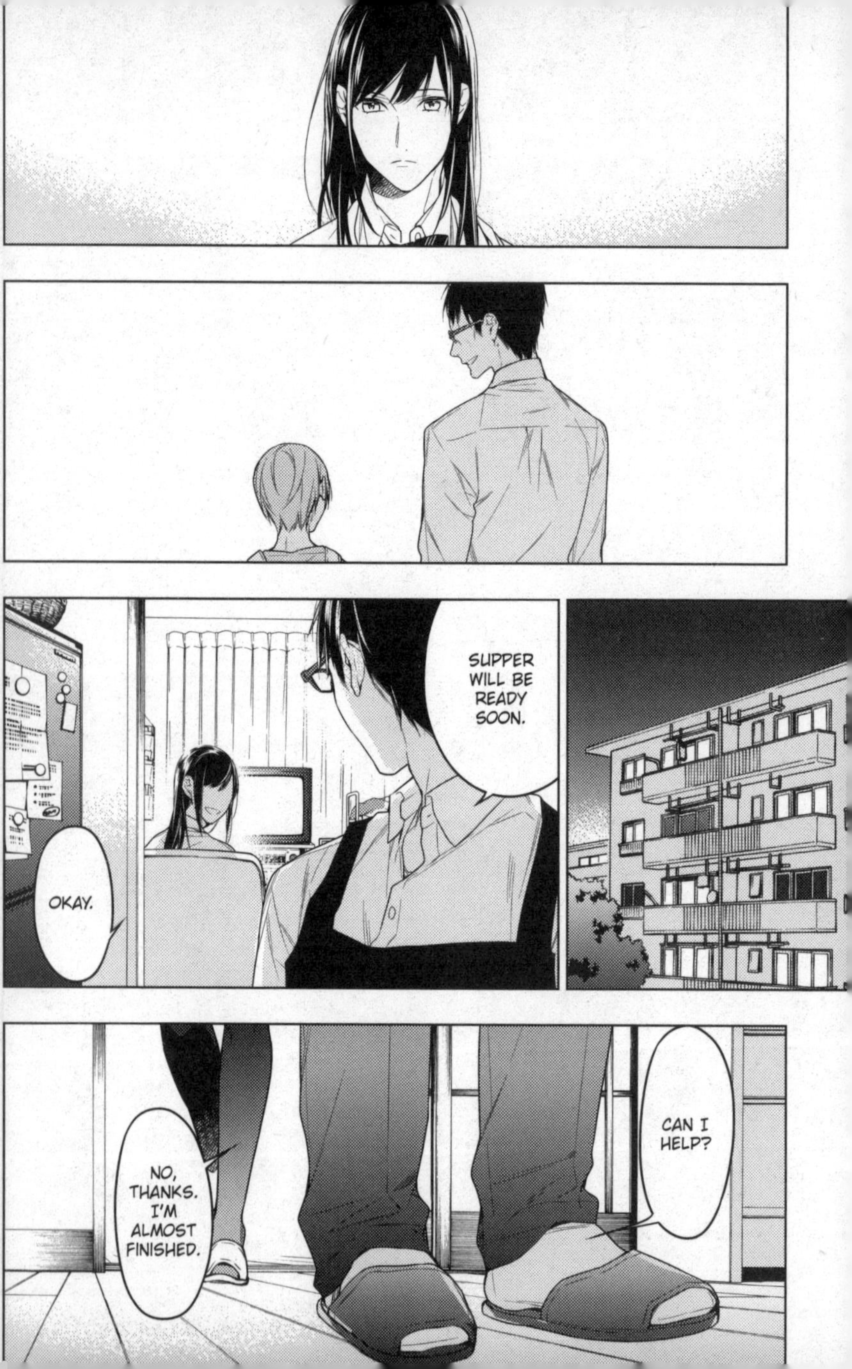
SUPPER WILL BE READY SOON.
OKAY.
CAN I HELP?
NO, THANKS. I'M ALMOST FINISHED.

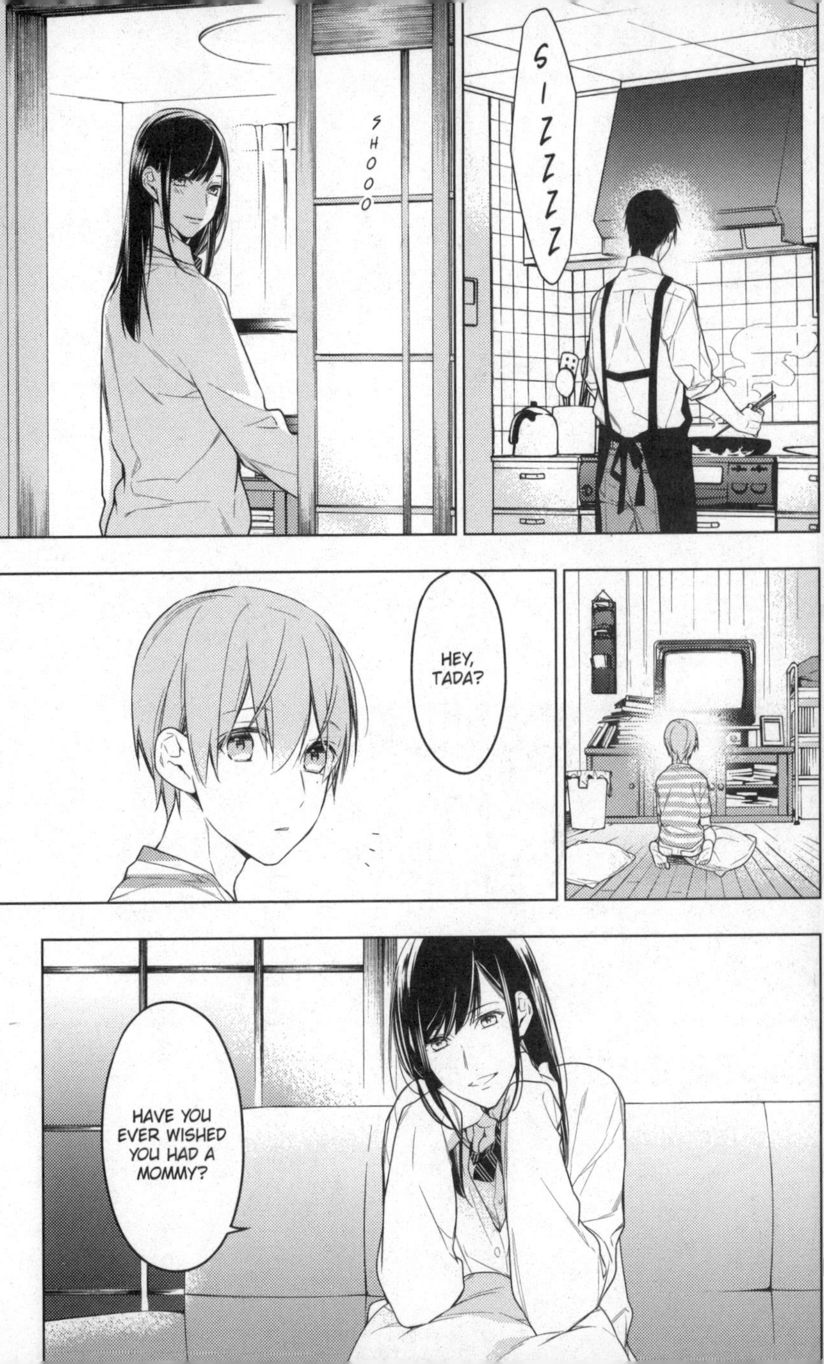
SIZZZZ
SHOOO
HEY, TADA?
HAVE YOU EVER WISHED YOU HAD A MOMMY?

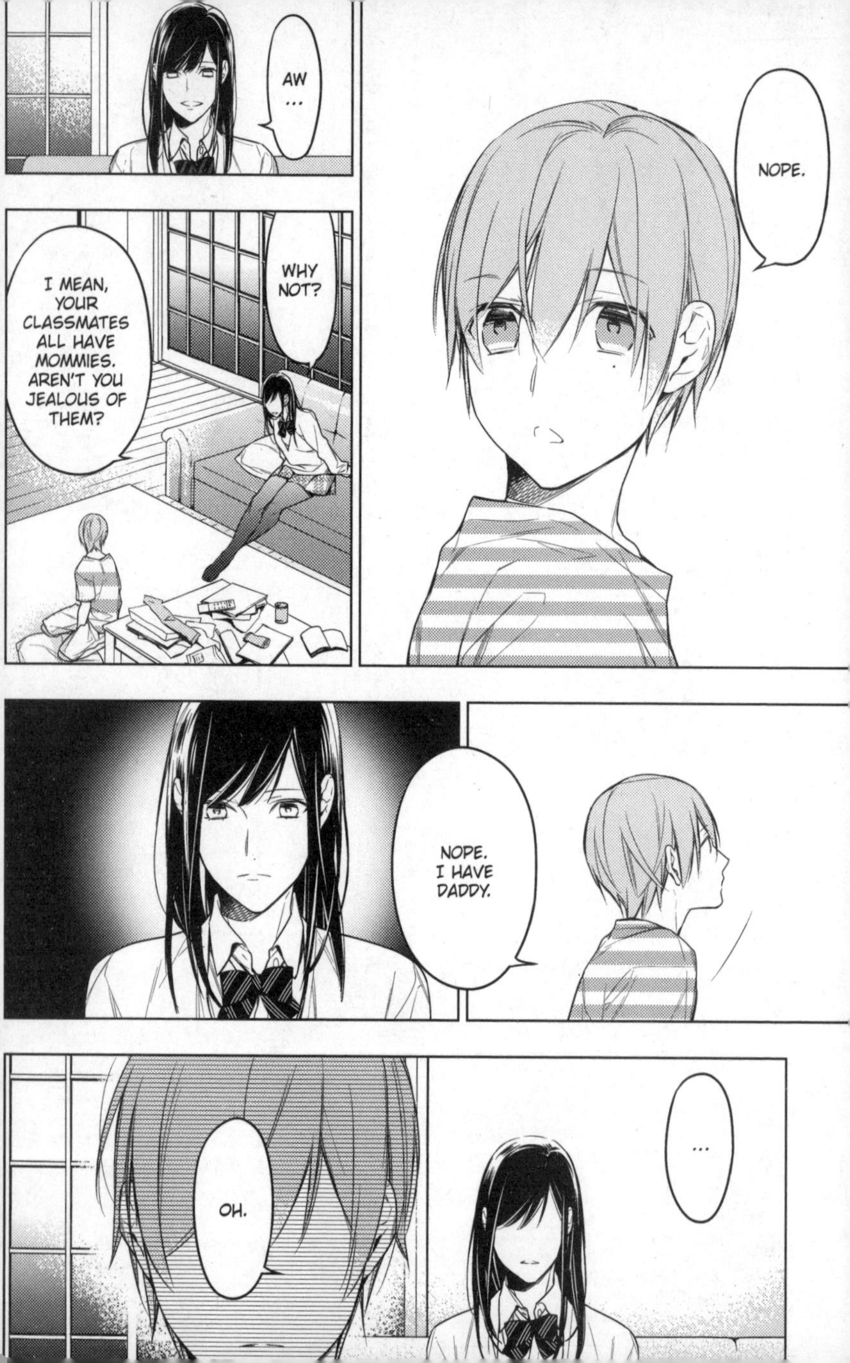
NOPE.
AW ...
WHY NOT?
I MEAN, YOUR CLASSMATES ALL HAVE MOMMIES. AREN'T YOU JEALOUS OF THEM?
NOPE. I HAVE DADDY.
...
OH.

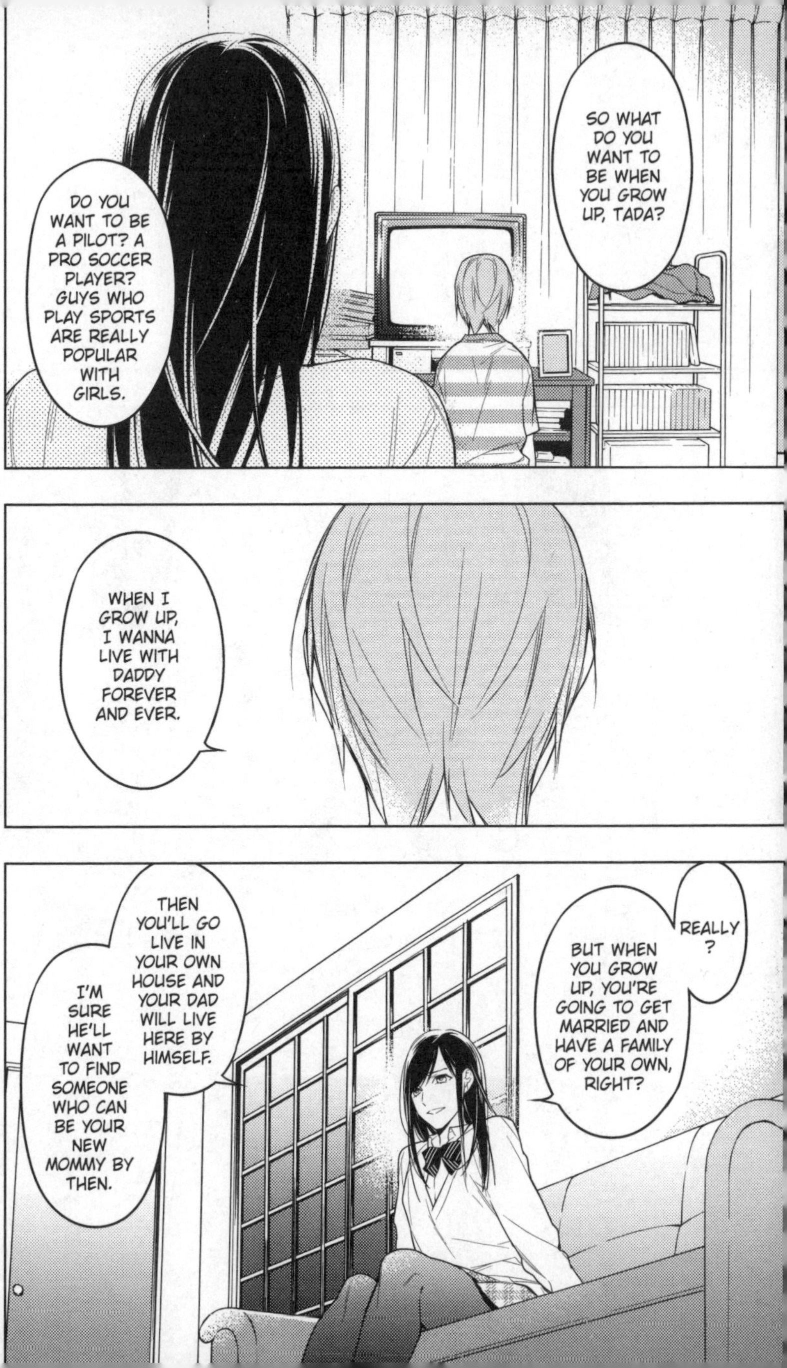
SO WHAT DO YOU WANT TO BE WHEN YOU GROW UP, TADA?
DO YOU WANT TO BE A PILOT? A PRO SOCCER PLAYER? GUYS WHO PLAY SPORTS ARE REALLY POPULAR WITH GIRLS.
WHEN I GROW UP, I WANNA LIVE WITH DADDY FOREVER AND EVER.
REALLY?
BUT WHEN YOU GROW UP, YOU'RE GOING TO GET MARRIED AND HAVE A FAMILY OF YOUR OWN, RIGHT?
THEN YOU'LL GO LIVE IN YOUR OWN HOUSE AND YOUR DAD WILL LIVE HERE BY HIMSELF.
I'M SURE HE'LL WANT TO FIND SOMEONE WHO CAN BE YOUR NEW MOMMY BY THEN.

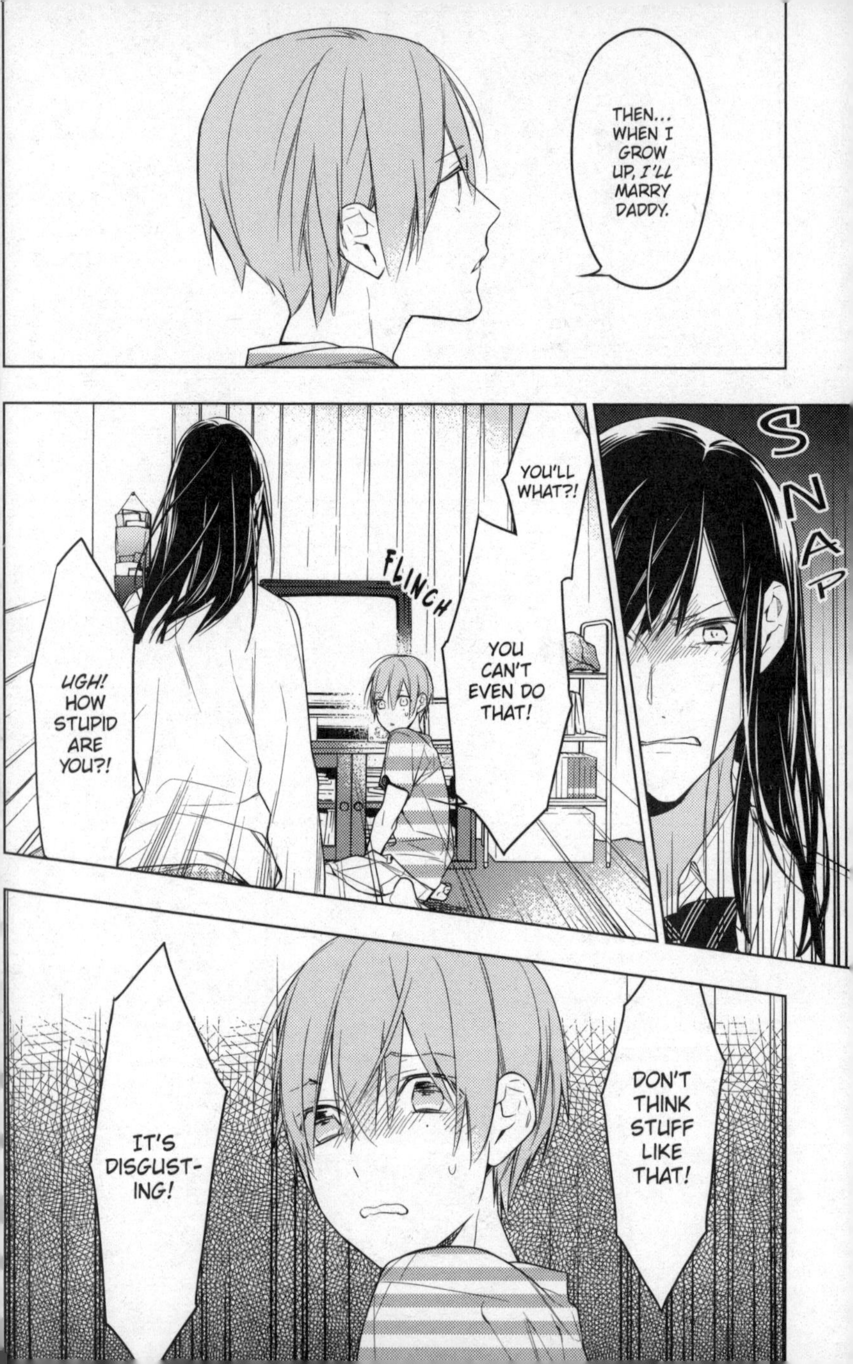
THEN... WHEN I GROW UP, I'LL MARRY DADDY.
SNAP
YOU'LL WHAT?!
FLINCH
YOU CAN'T EVEN DO THAT!
UGH! HOW STUPID ARE YOU?!
DON'T THINK STUFF LIKE THAT!
IT'S DISGUST-ING!

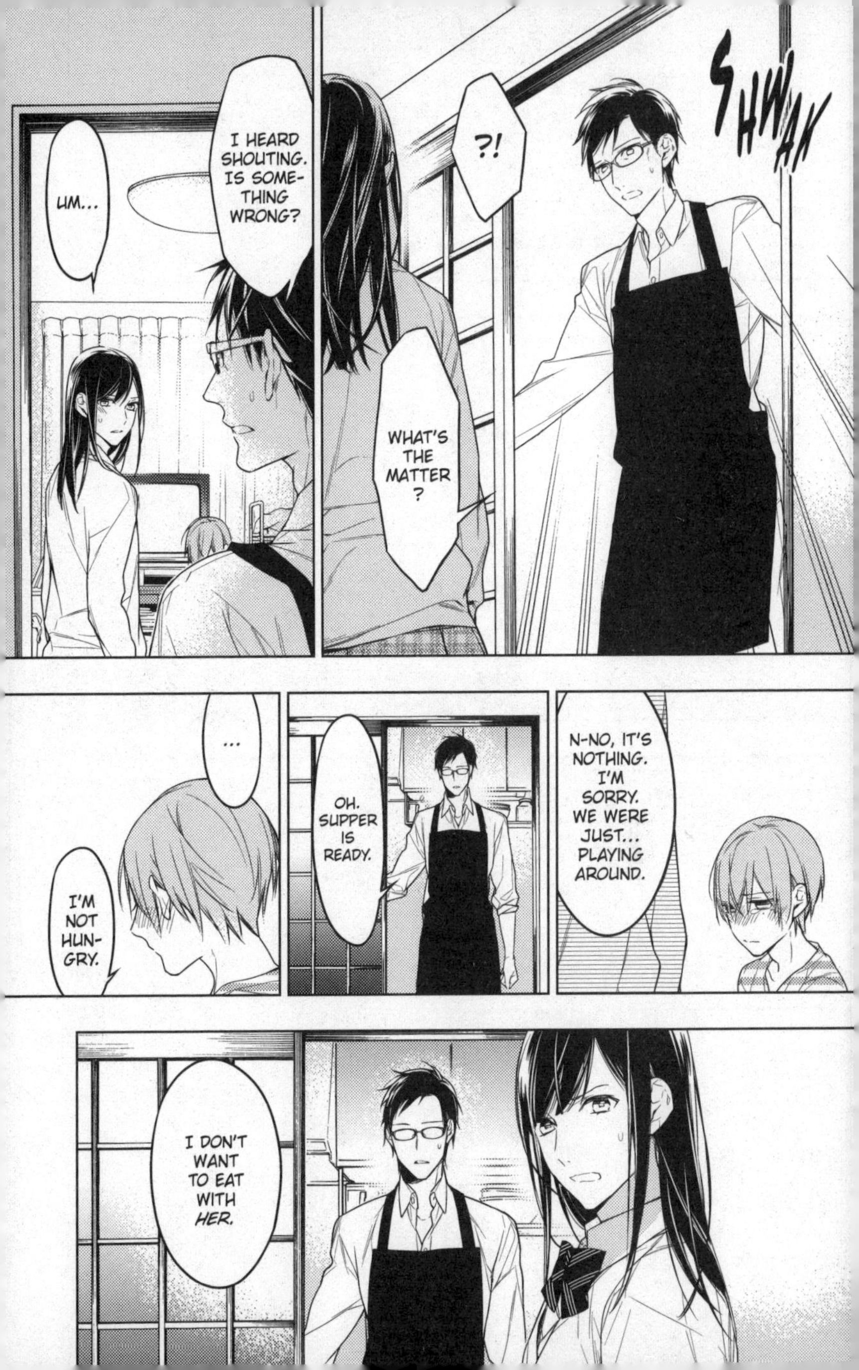
SHWAK
?!
WHAT'S THE MATTER?
I HEARD SHOUTING. IS SOMETHING WRONG?
UM...
N-NO, IT'S NOTHING. I'M SORRY. WE WERE JUST... PLAYING AROUND.
OH. SUPPER IS READY.
...
I'M NOT HUNGRY.
I DON'T WANT TO EAT WITH *HER*.

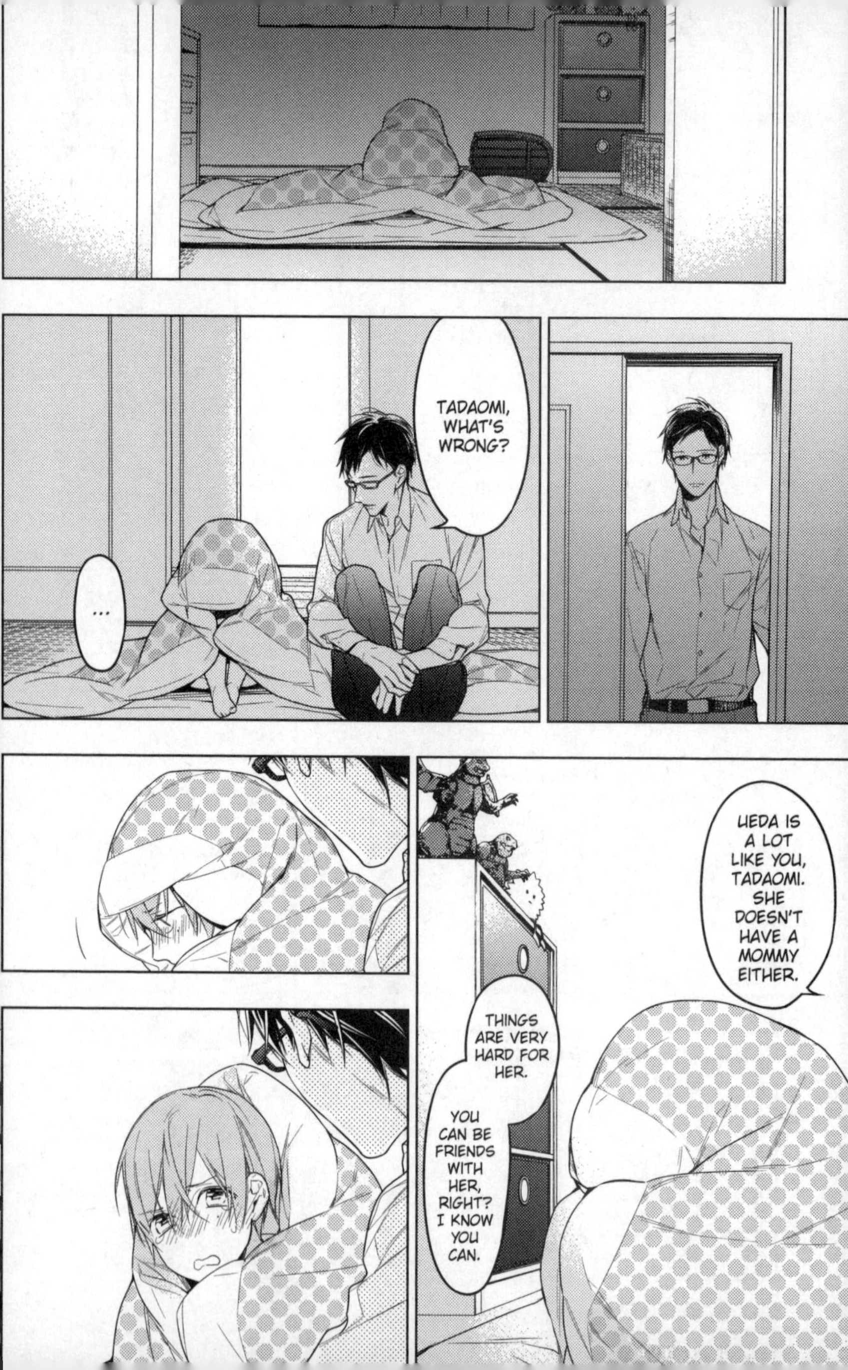
TADAOMI, WHAT'S WRONG?
...
UEDA IS A LOT LIKE YOU, TADAOMI. SHE DOESN'T HAVE A MOMMY EITHER.
THINGS ARE VERY HARD FOR HER.
YOU CAN BE FRIENDS WITH HER, RIGHT? I KNOW YOU CAN.

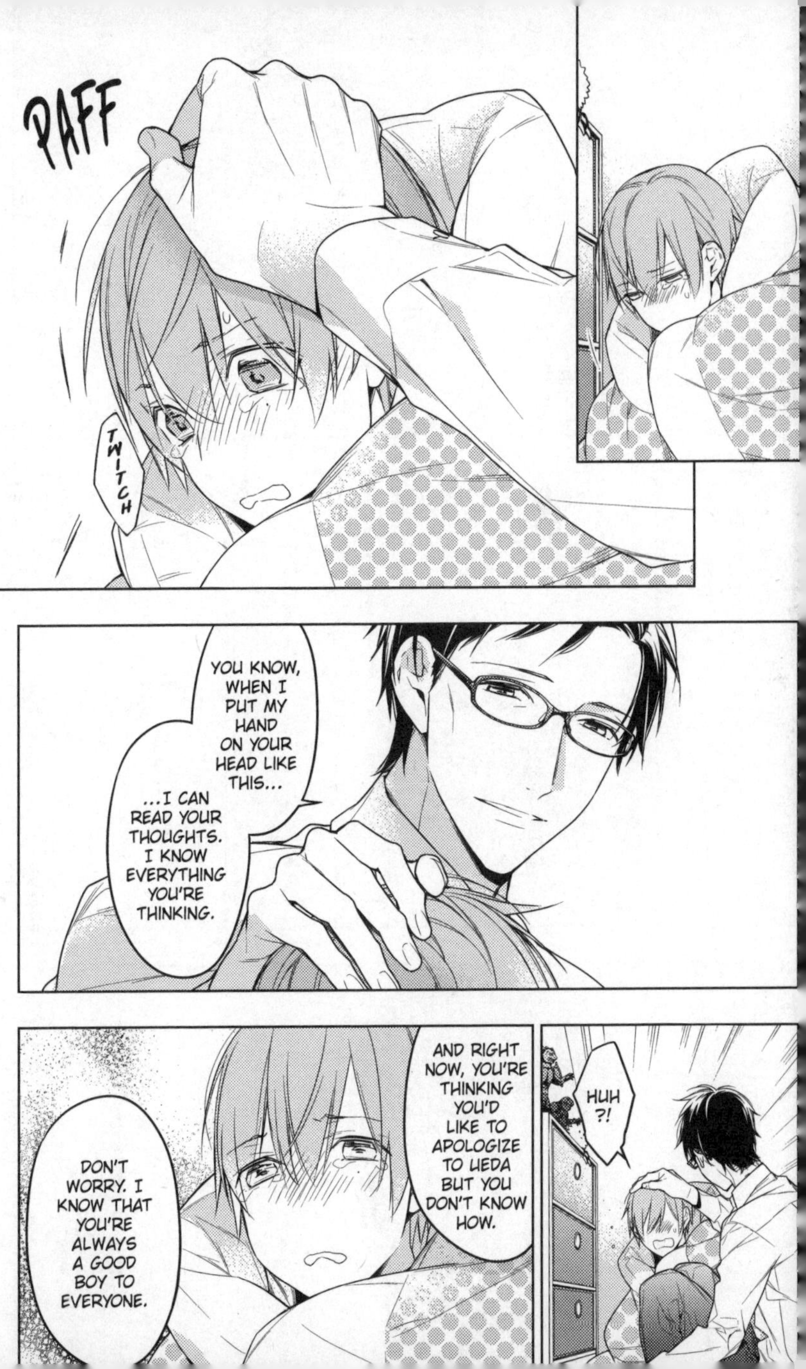
PAFF
TWITCH
YOU KNOW, WHEN I PUT MY HAND ON YOUR HEAD LIKE THIS...
...I CAN READ YOUR THOUGHTS. I KNOW EVERYTHING YOU'RE THINKING.
HUH?!
AND RIGHT NOW, YOU'RE THINKING YOU'D LIKE TO APOLOGIZE TO UEDA BUT YOU DON'T KNOW HOW.
DON'T WORRY. I KNOW THAT YOU'RE ALWAYS A GOOD BOY TO EVERYONE.

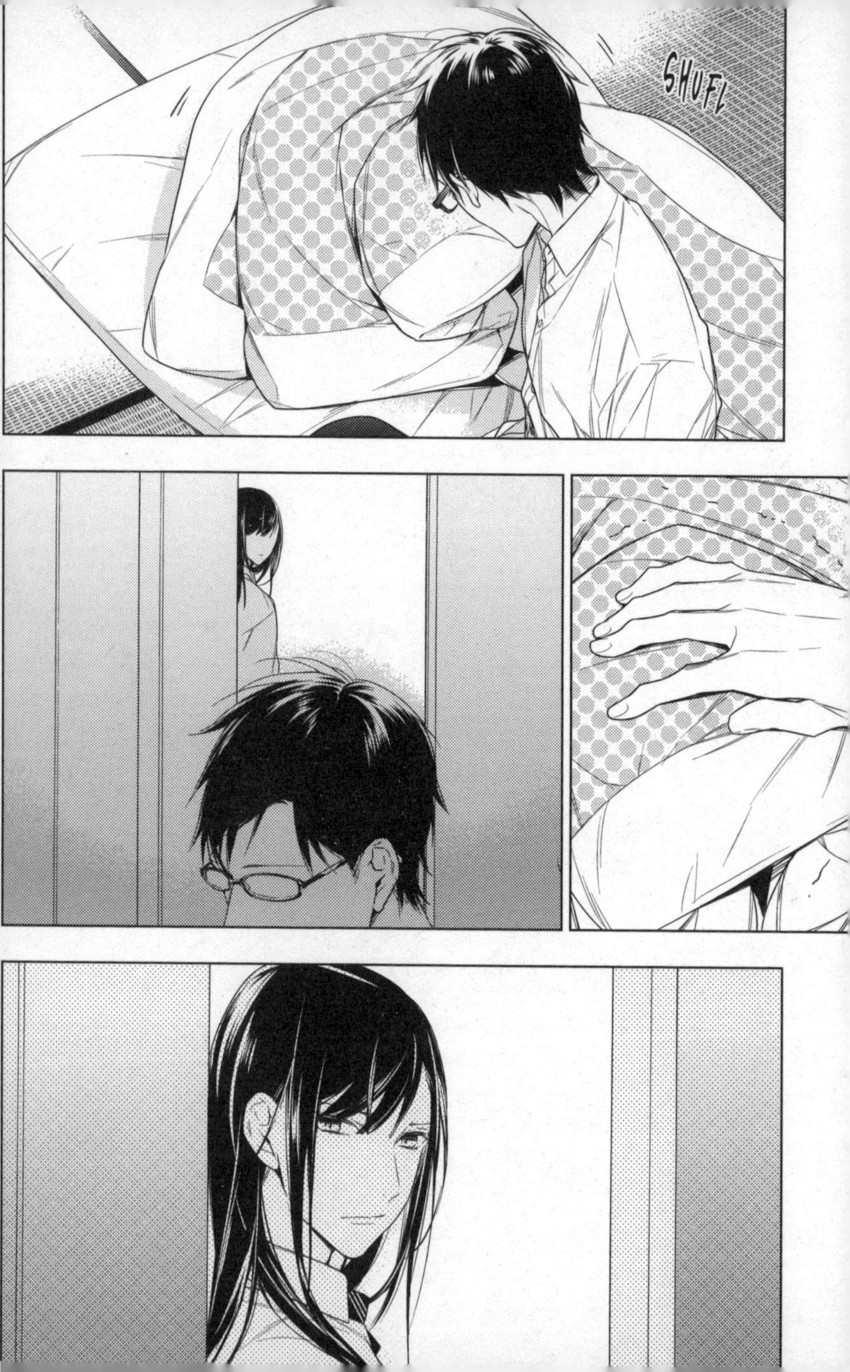
SHUFL

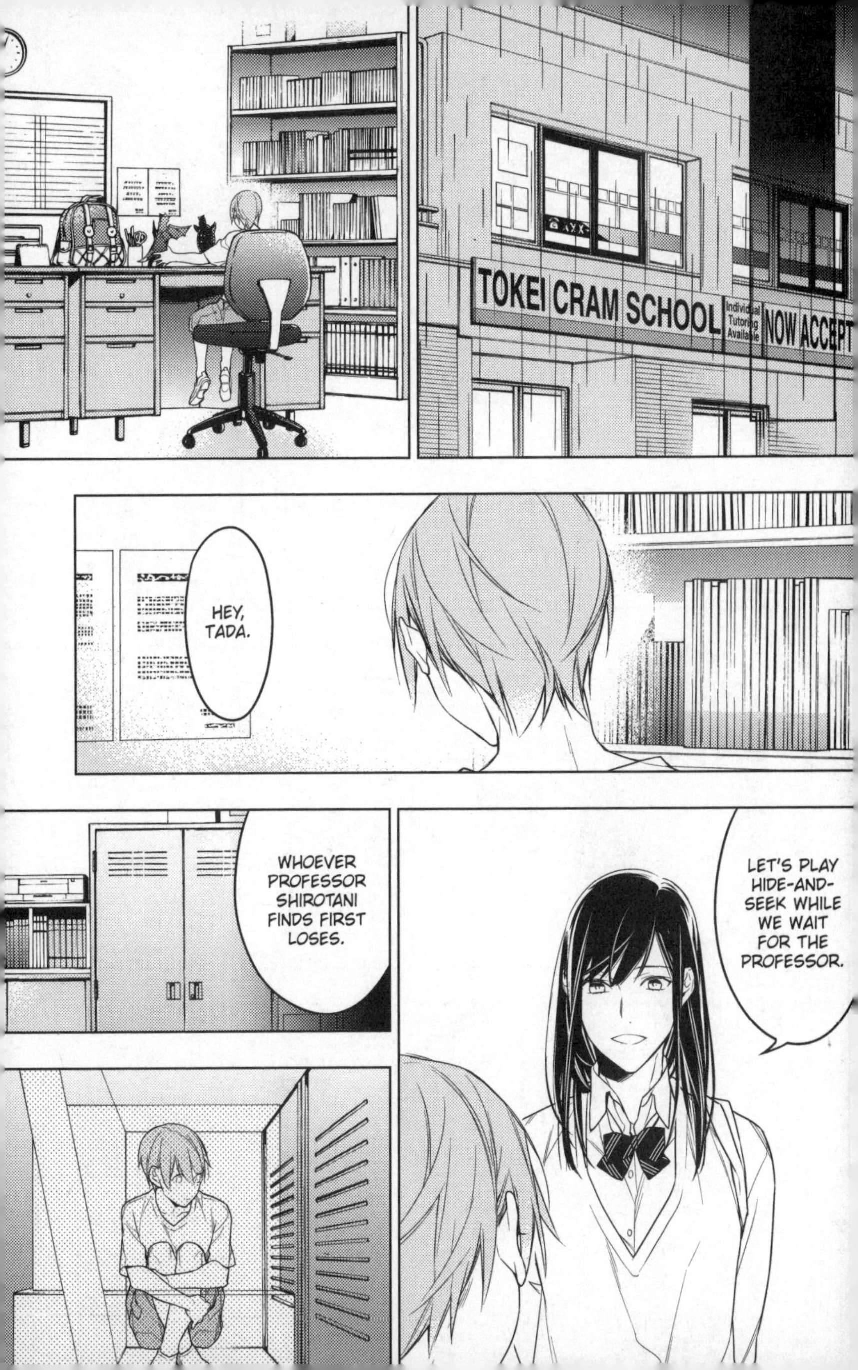
TOKEI CRAM SCHOOL
Individual Tutoring Available
NOW ACCEPT
HEY, TADA.
LET'S PLAY HIDE-AND-SEEK WHILE WE WAIT FOR THE PROFESSOR.
WHOEVER PROFESSOR SHIROTANI FINDS FIRST LOSES.

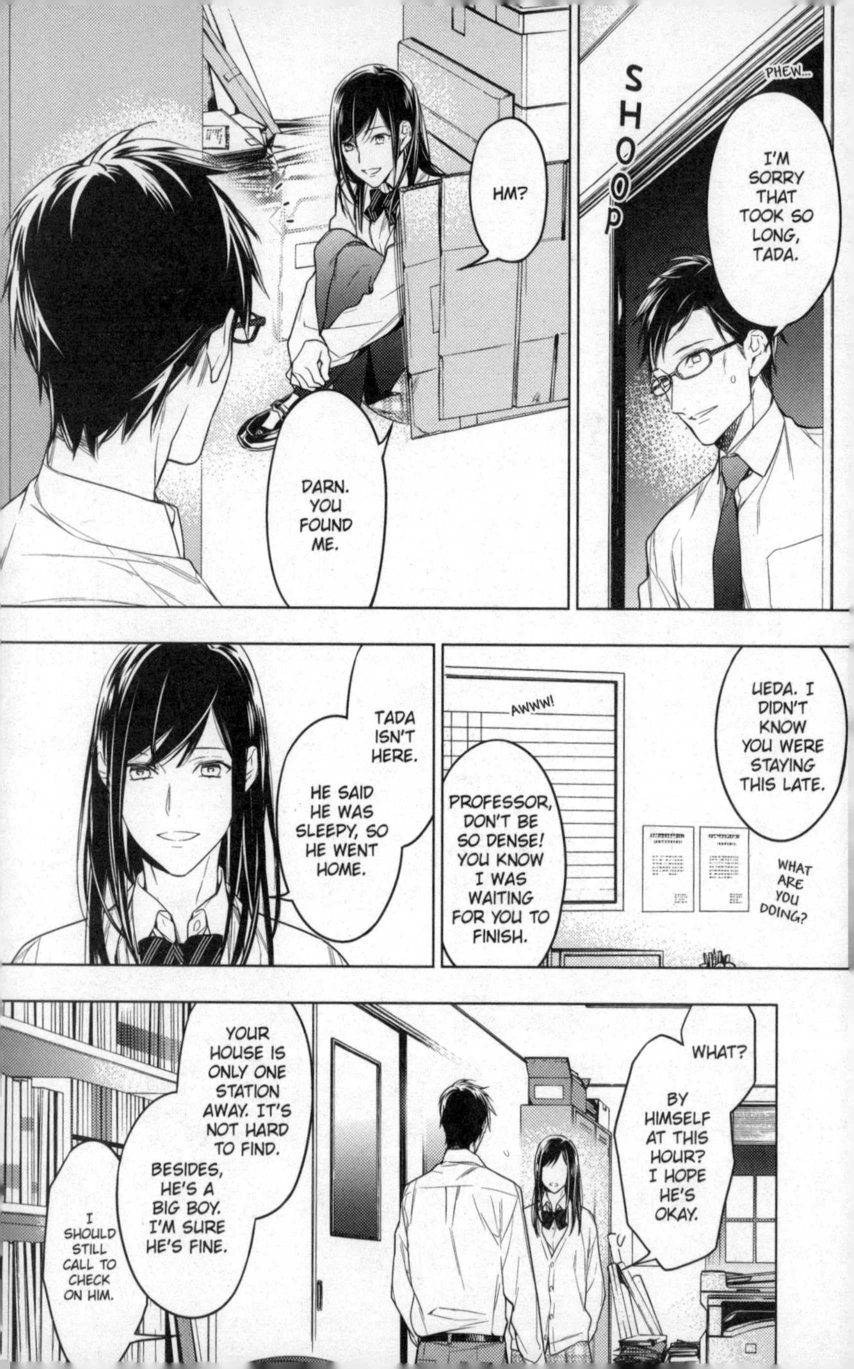
SHOOP
PHEW...
I'M SORRY THAT TOOK SO LONG, TADA.
HM?
DARN. YOU FOUND ME.
UEDA. I DIDN'T KNOW YOU WERE STAYING THIS LATE.
WHAT ARE YOU DOING?
AWWW!
PROFESSOR, DON'T BE SO DENSE! YOU KNOW I WAS WAITING FOR YOU TO FINISH.
TADA ISN'T HERE.
HE SAID HE WAS SLEEPY, SO HE WENT HOME.
WHAT?
BY HIMSELF AT THIS HOUR? I HOPE HE'S OKAY.
YOUR HOUSE IS ONLY ONE STATION AWAY. IT'S NOT HARD TO FIND.
BESIDES, HE'S A BIG BOY. I'M SURE HE'S FINE.
I SHOULD STILL CALL TO CHECK ON HIM.

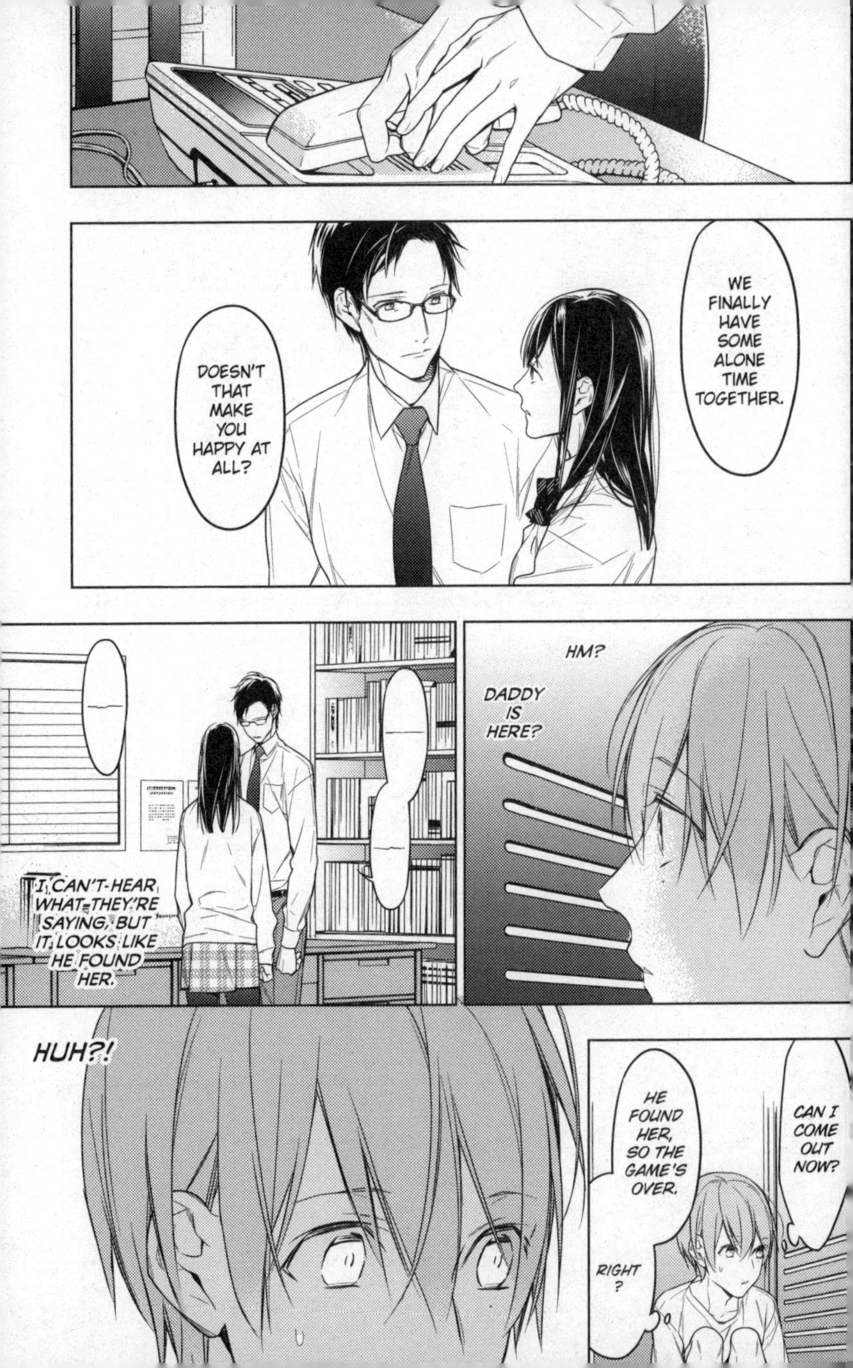
WE FINALLY HAVE SOME ALONE TIME TOGETHER.
DOESN'T THAT MAKE YOU HAPPY AT ALL?
HM?
DADDY IS HERE?
I CAN'T HEAR WHAT THEY'RE SAYING, BUT IT LOOKS LIKE HE FOUND HER.
CAN I COME OUT NOW?
HE FOUND HER, SO THE GAME'S OVER.
RIGHT?
HUH?!

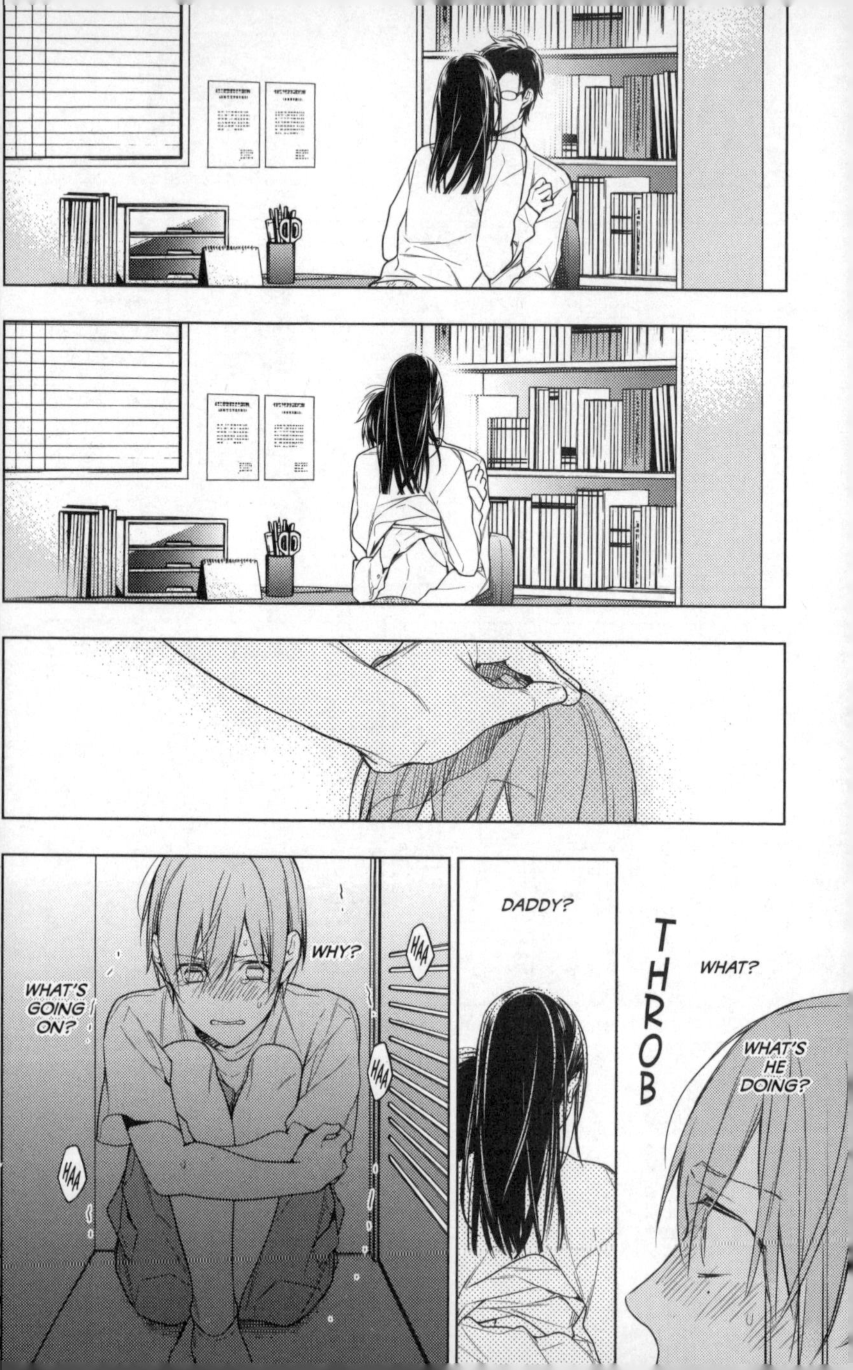
DADDY?
THROB
WHAT?
WHAT'S HE DOING?
HAA
WHY?
HAA
WHAT'S GOING ON?
HAA

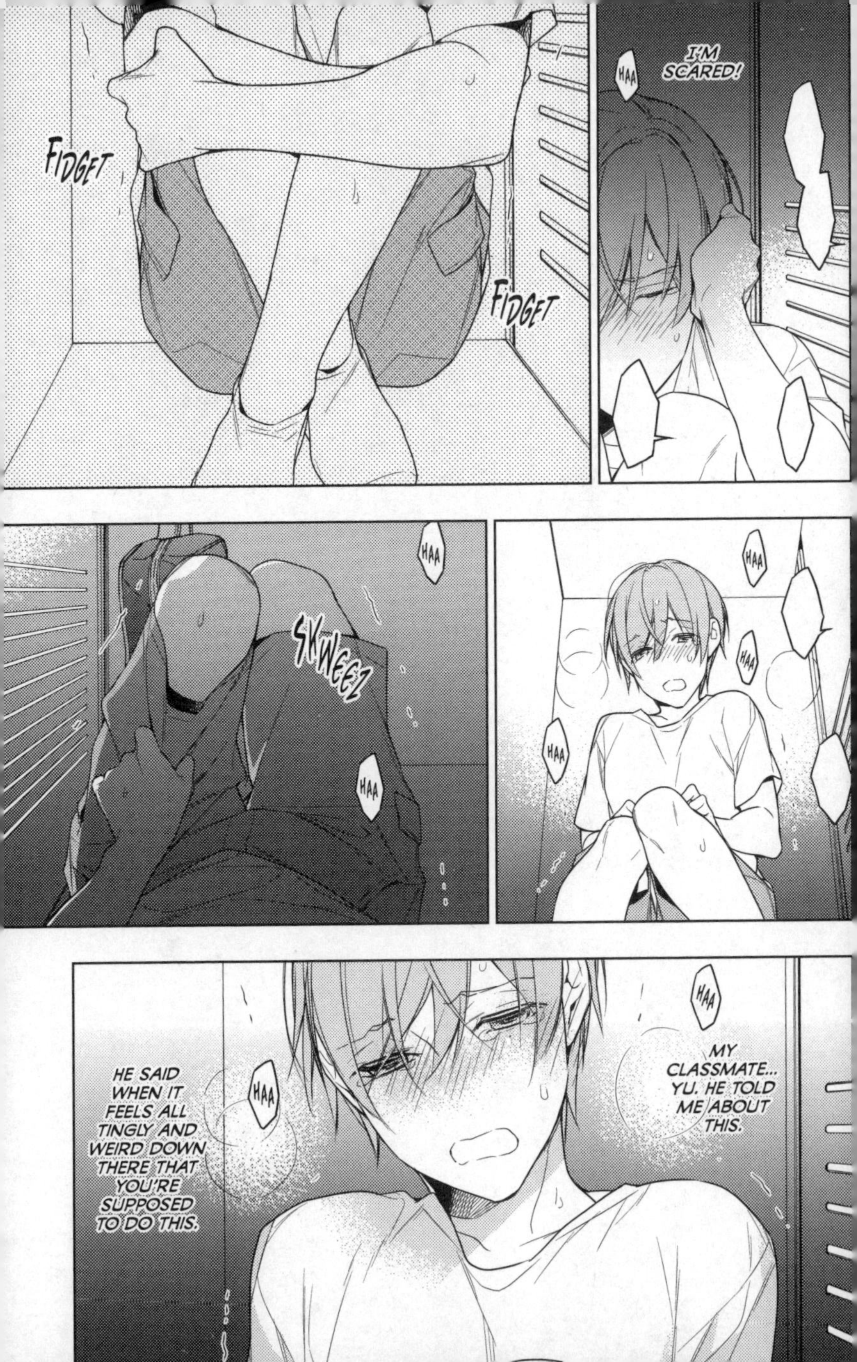
HAA
I'M SCARED!
FIDGET
FIDGET
HAA
HAA
HAA
HAA
SKWEEZ
HAA
HAA
MY CLASSMATE... YU. HE TOLD ME ABOUT THIS.
HAA
HE SAID WHEN IT FEELS ALL TINGLY AND WEIRD DOWN THERE THAT YOU'RE SUPPOSED TO DO THIS.

ten count by rihito takarai

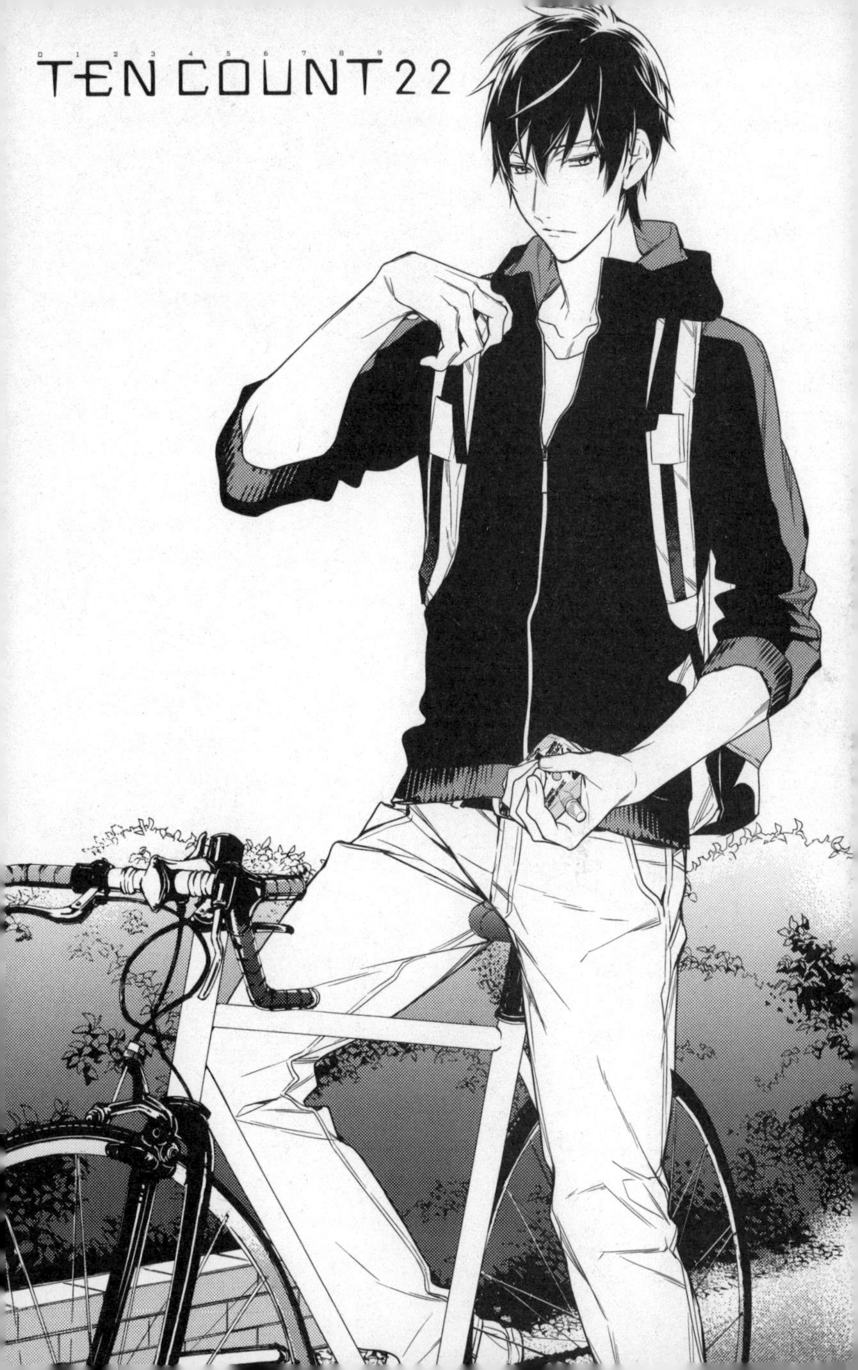
TEN COUNT 22

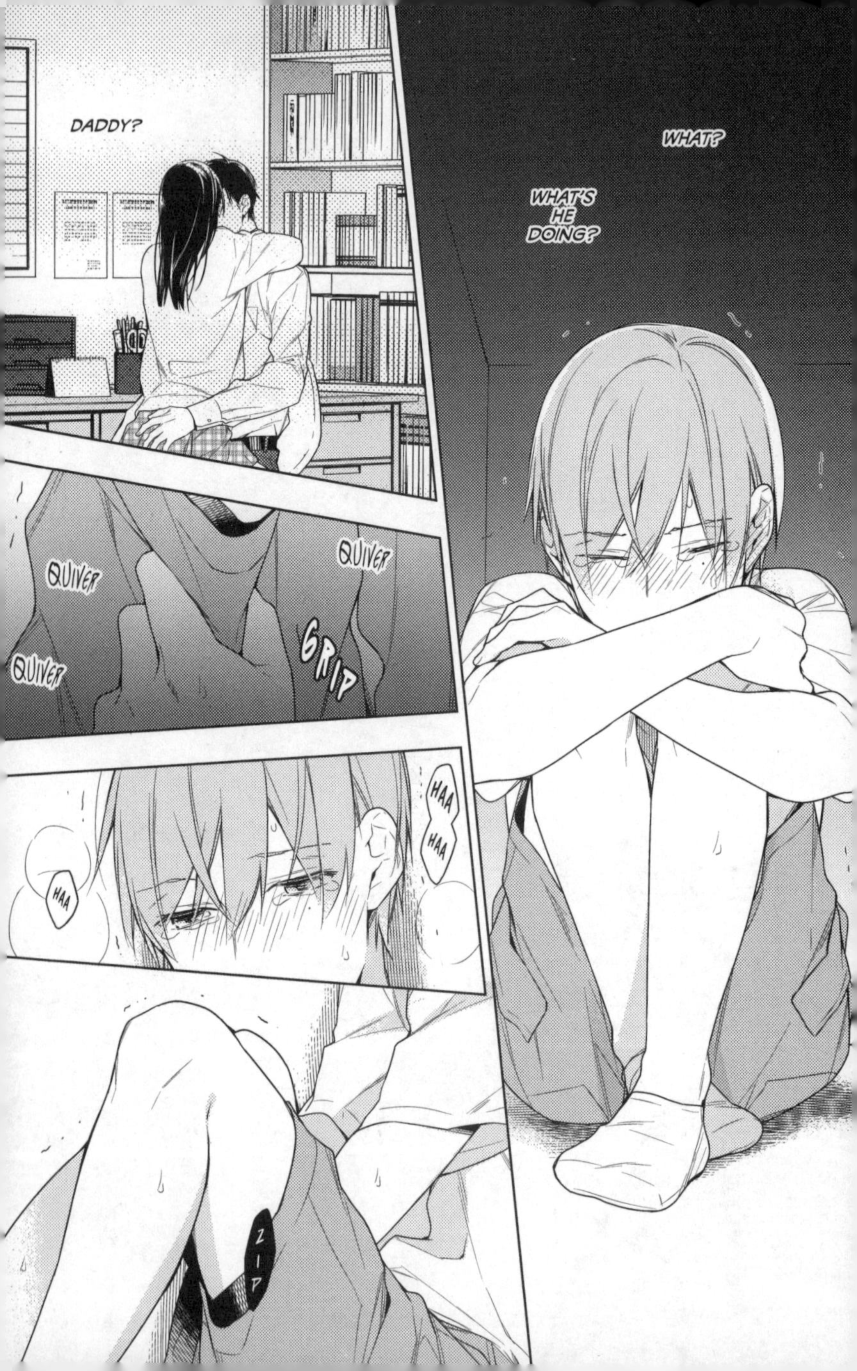
WHAT?
WHAT'S HE DOING?
DADDY?
QUIVER
QUIVER
GRIP
QUIVER
HAA
HAA
HAA
ZIP

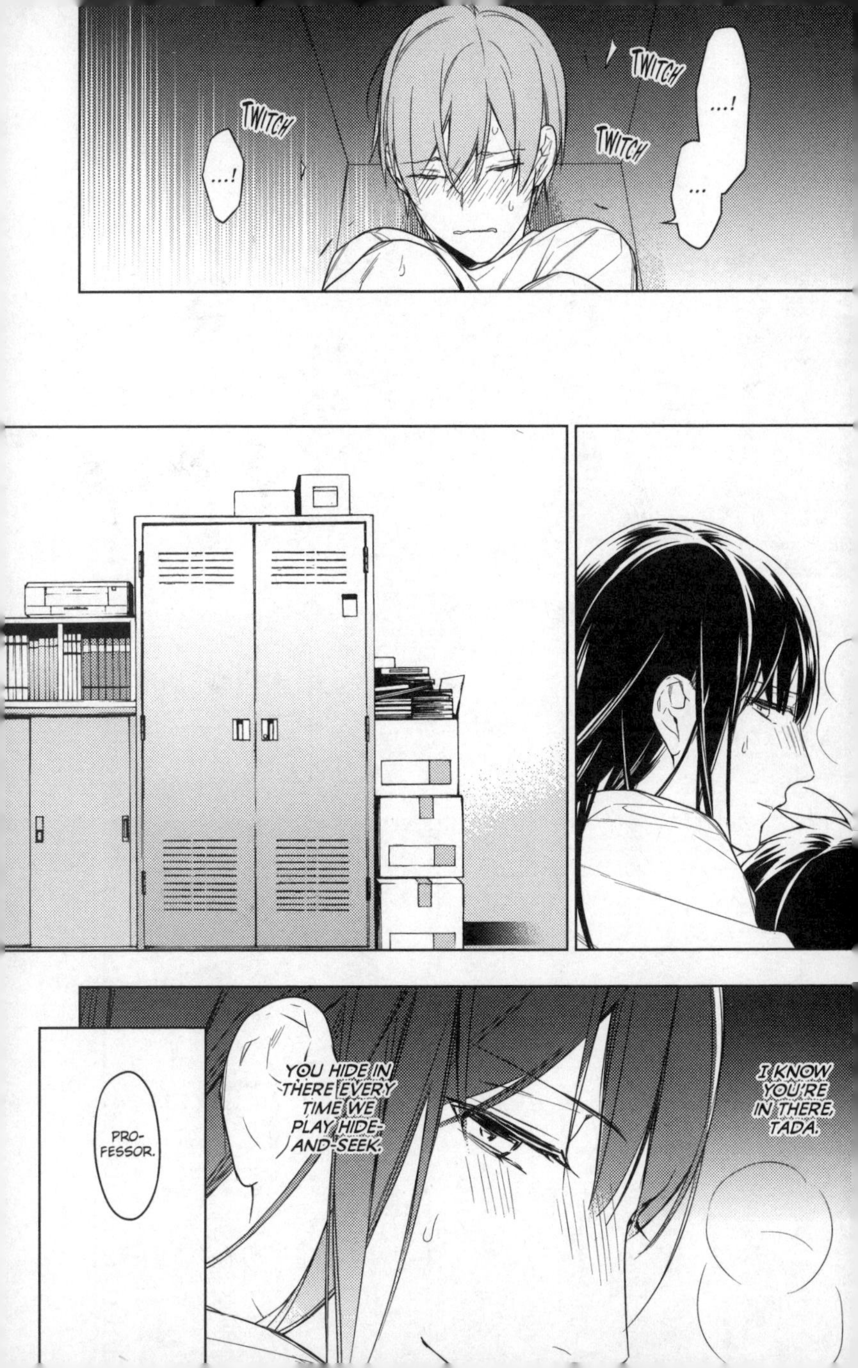
TWITCH
...!
...
TWITCH
TWITCH
...!
I KNOW YOU'RE IN THERE, TADA.
YOU HIDE IN THERE EVERY TIME WE PLAY HIDE-AND-SEEK.
PRO-FESSOR.

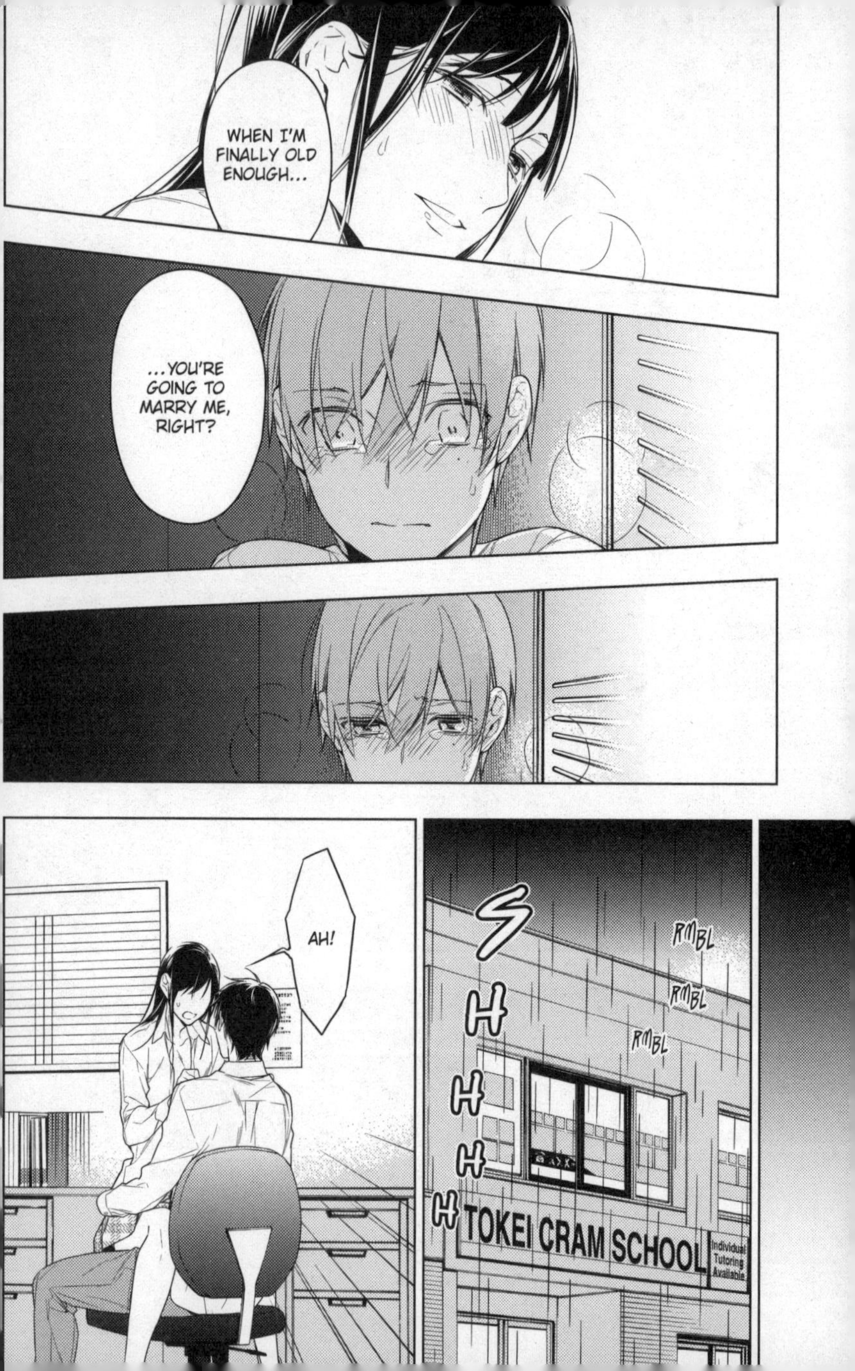
WHEN I'M FINALLY OLD ENOUGH...
...YOU'RE GOING TO MARRY ME, RIGHT?
SHHHHH
RMBL
RMBL
RMBL
TOKEI CRAM SCHOOL
Individual Tutoring Available
AH!

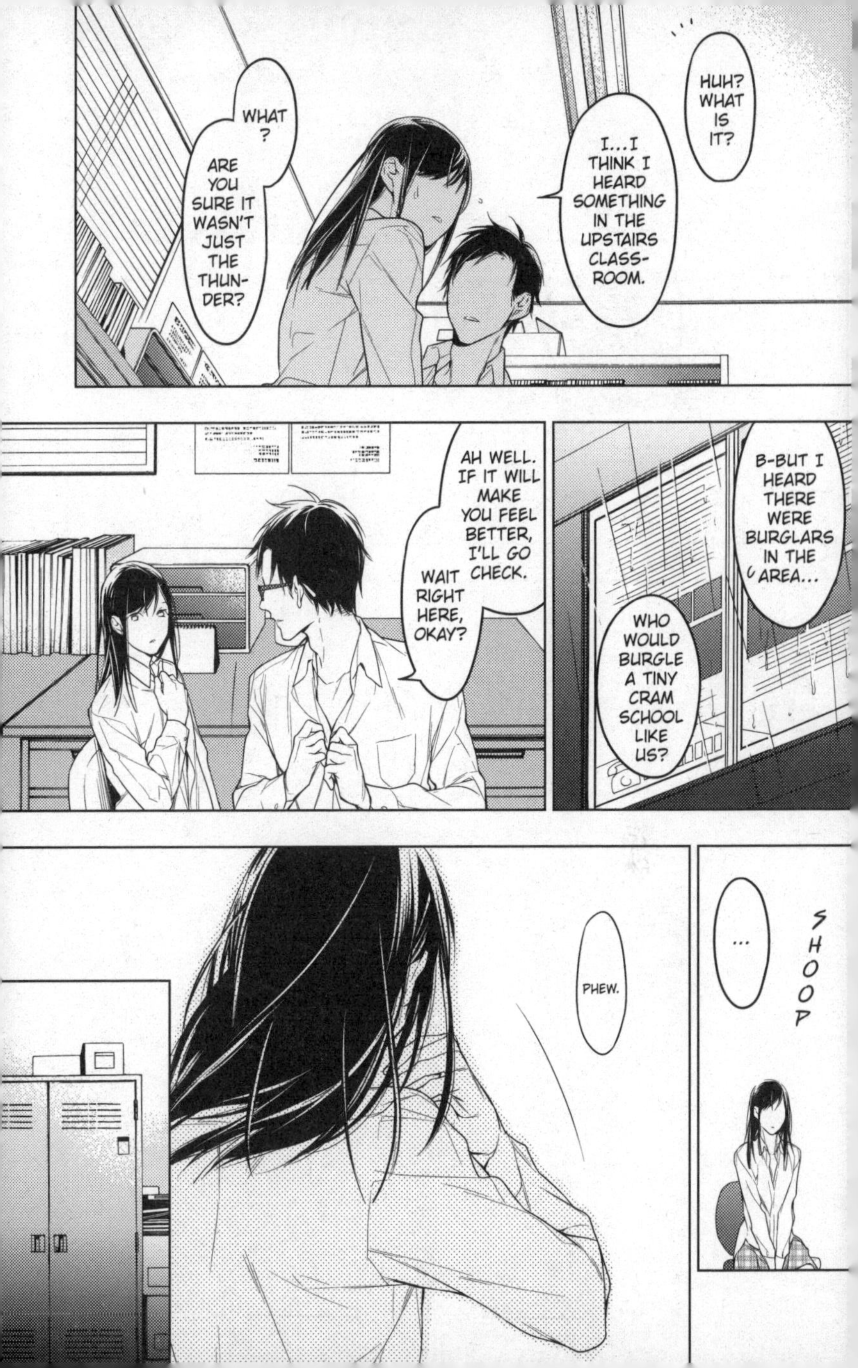
HUH? WHAT IS IT?
I...I THINK I HEARD SOMETHING IN THE UPSTAIRS CLASSROOM.
WHAT? ARE YOU SURE IT WASN'T JUST THE THUNDER?
B-BUT I HEARD THERE WERE BURGLARS IN THE AREA...
WHO WOULD BURGLE A TINY CRAM SCHOOL LIKE US?
AH WELL. IF IT WILL MAKE YOU FEEL BETTER, I'LL GO CHECK.
WAIT RIGHT HERE, OKAY?
...
SHOOP
PHEW.

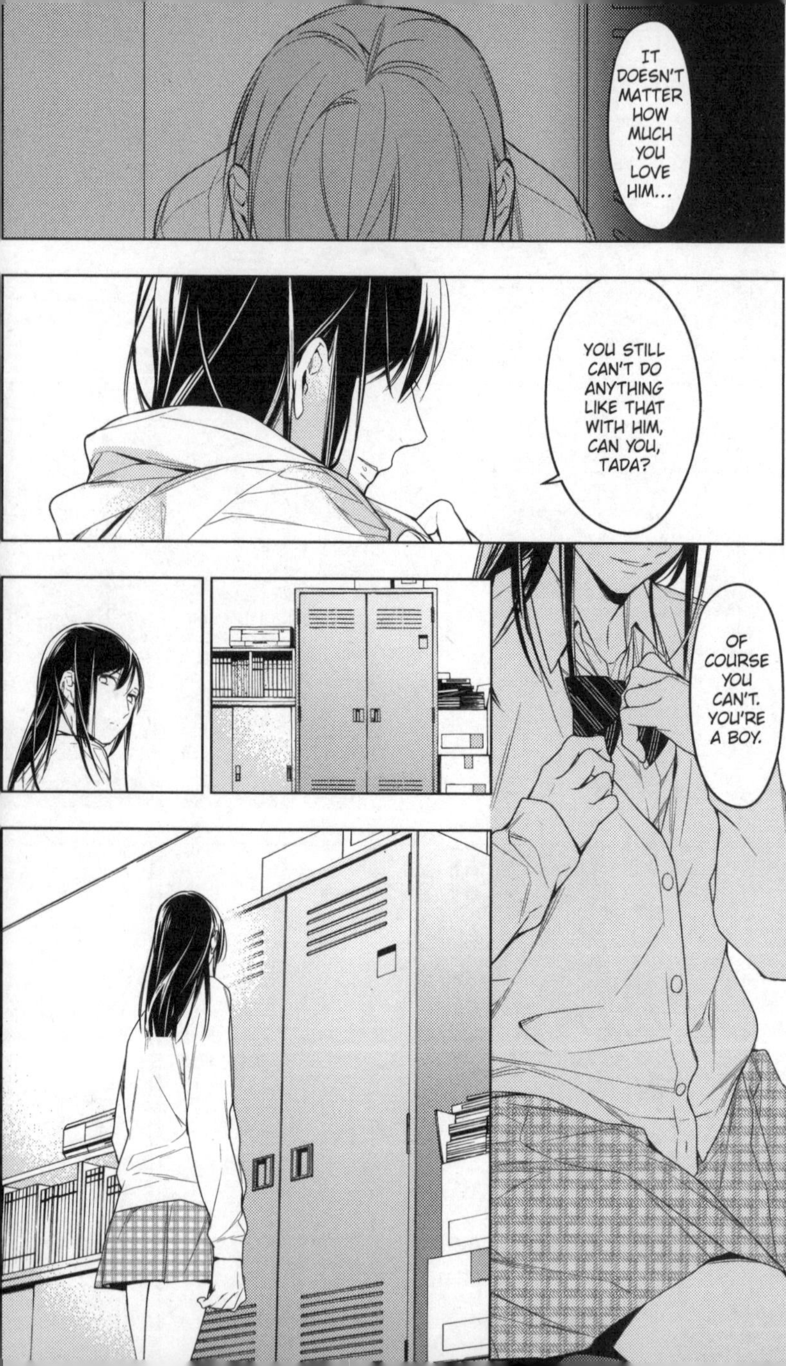
IT DOESN'T MATTER HOW MUCH YOU LOVE HIM...
YOU STILL CAN'T DO ANYTHING LIKE THAT WITH HIM, CAN YOU, TADA?
OF COURSE YOU CAN'T. YOU'RE A BOY.

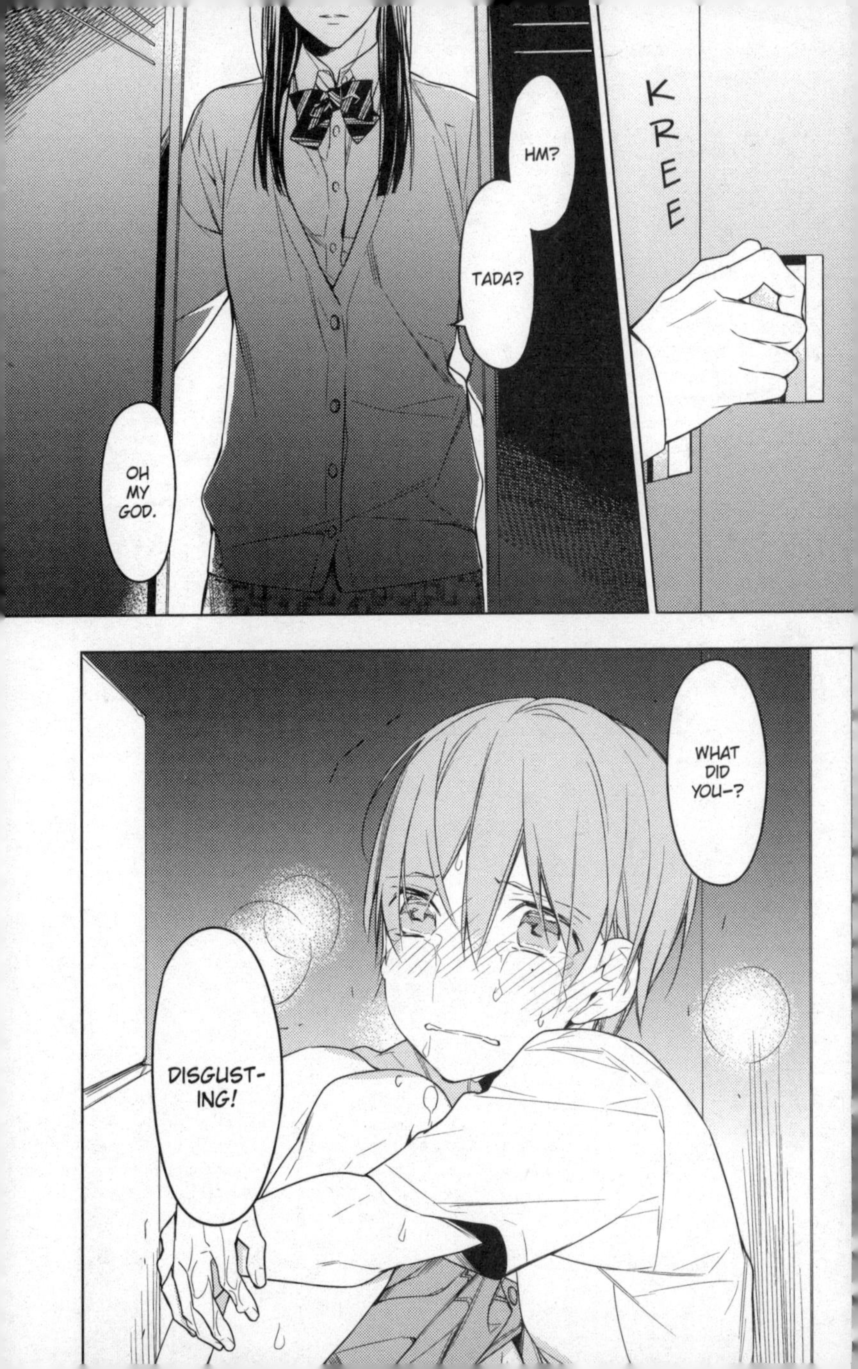
KREE
HM?
TADA?
OH MY GOD.
WHAT DID YOU-?
DISGUST-ING!

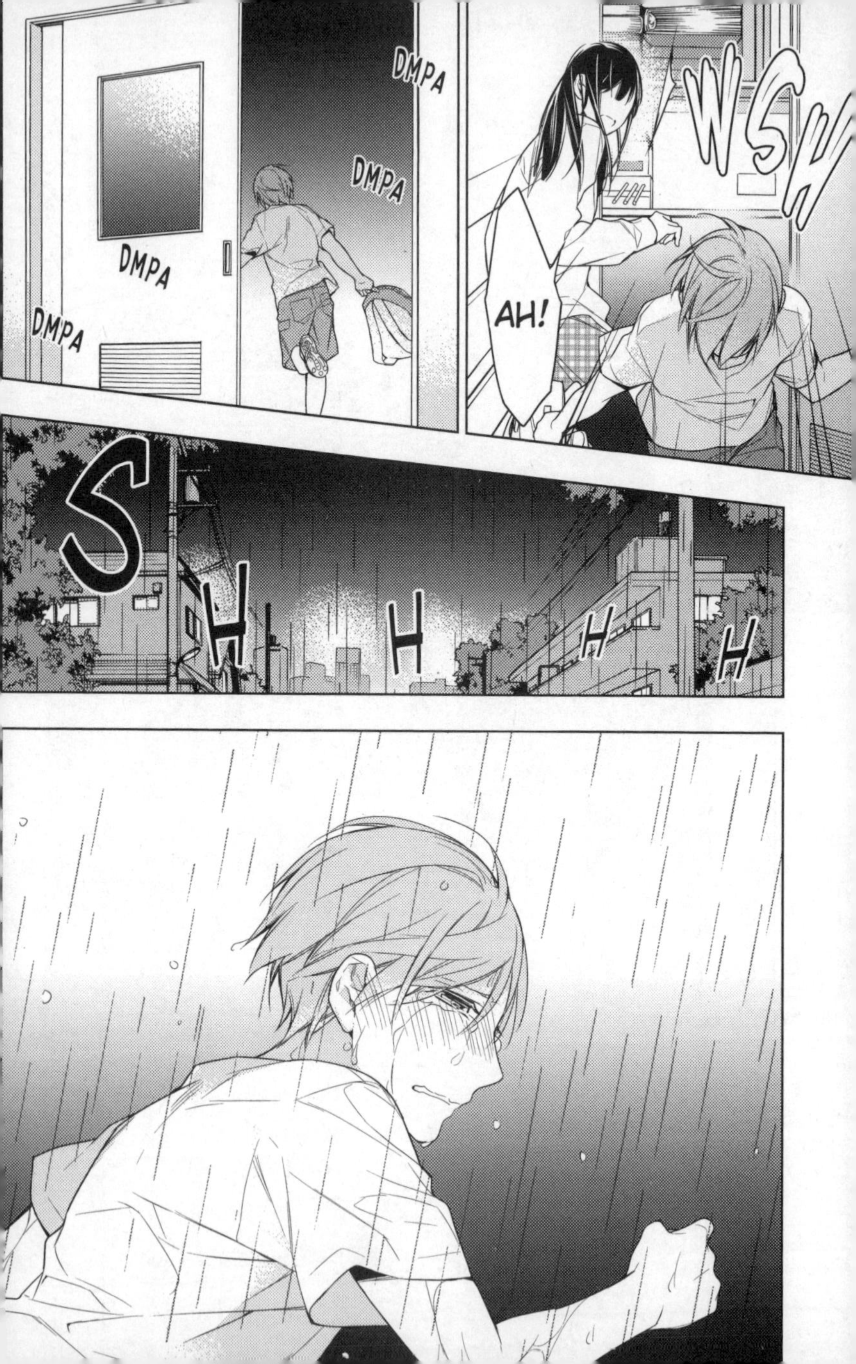
WSH
AH!
DMPA
DMPA
DMPA
DMPA
SHHHH

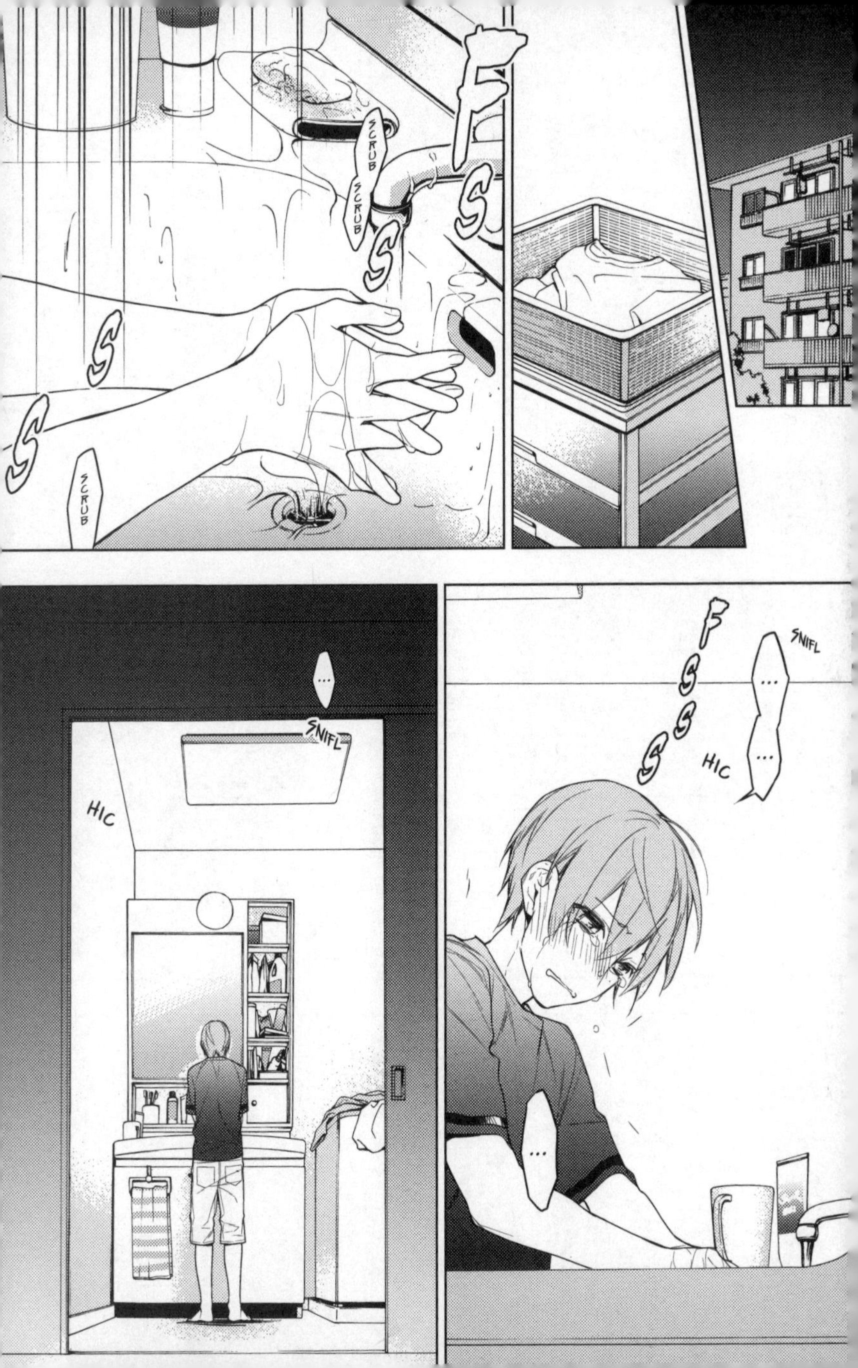
FSS
SCRUB
SCRUB
SS
SCRUB
FSSS
SNIFL
...
...
HIC
...
...
SNIFL
HIC

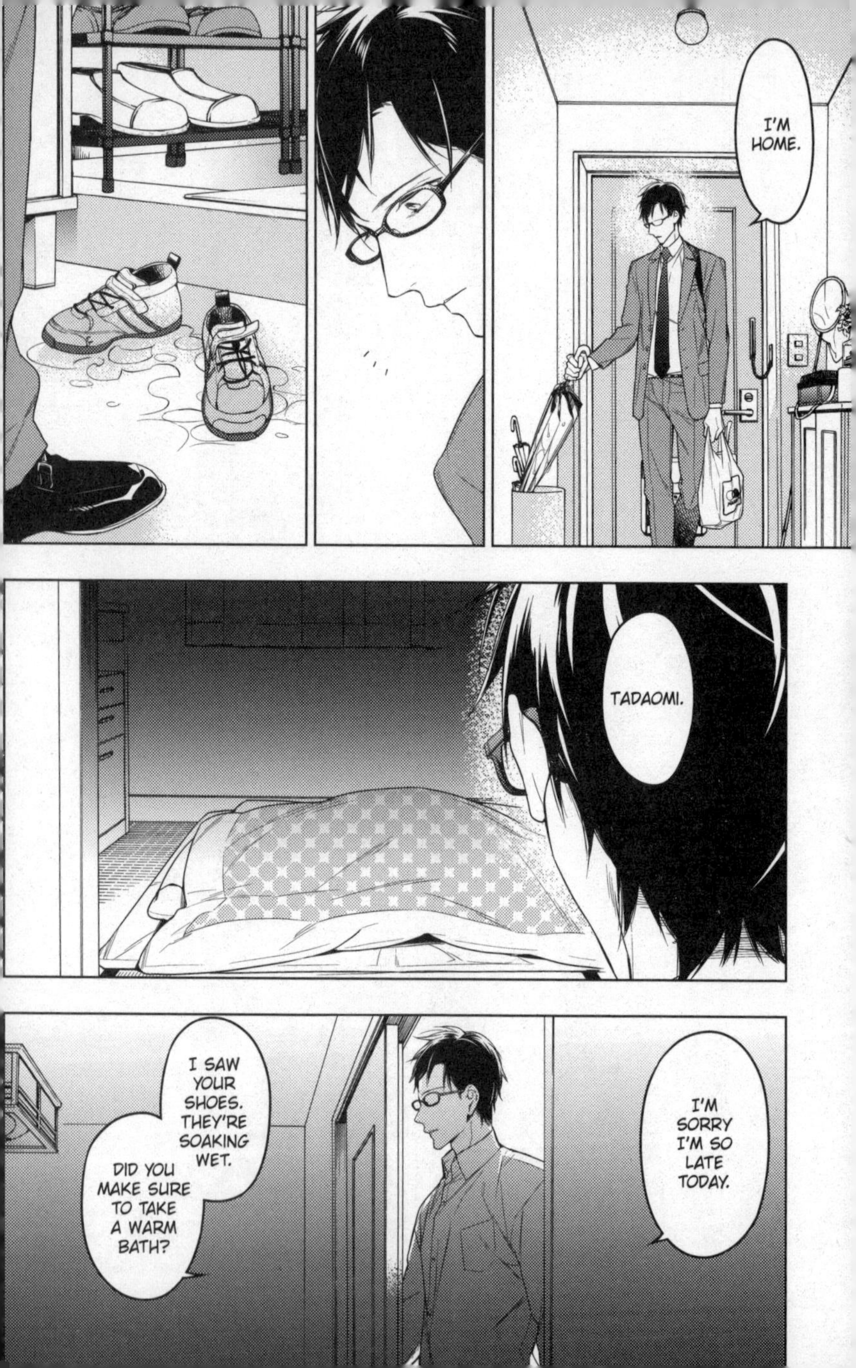
I'M HOME.
TADAOMI.
I'M SORRY I'M SO LATE TODAY.
I SAW YOUR SHOES. THEY'RE SOAKING WET.
DID YOU MAKE SURE TO TAKE A WARM BATH?

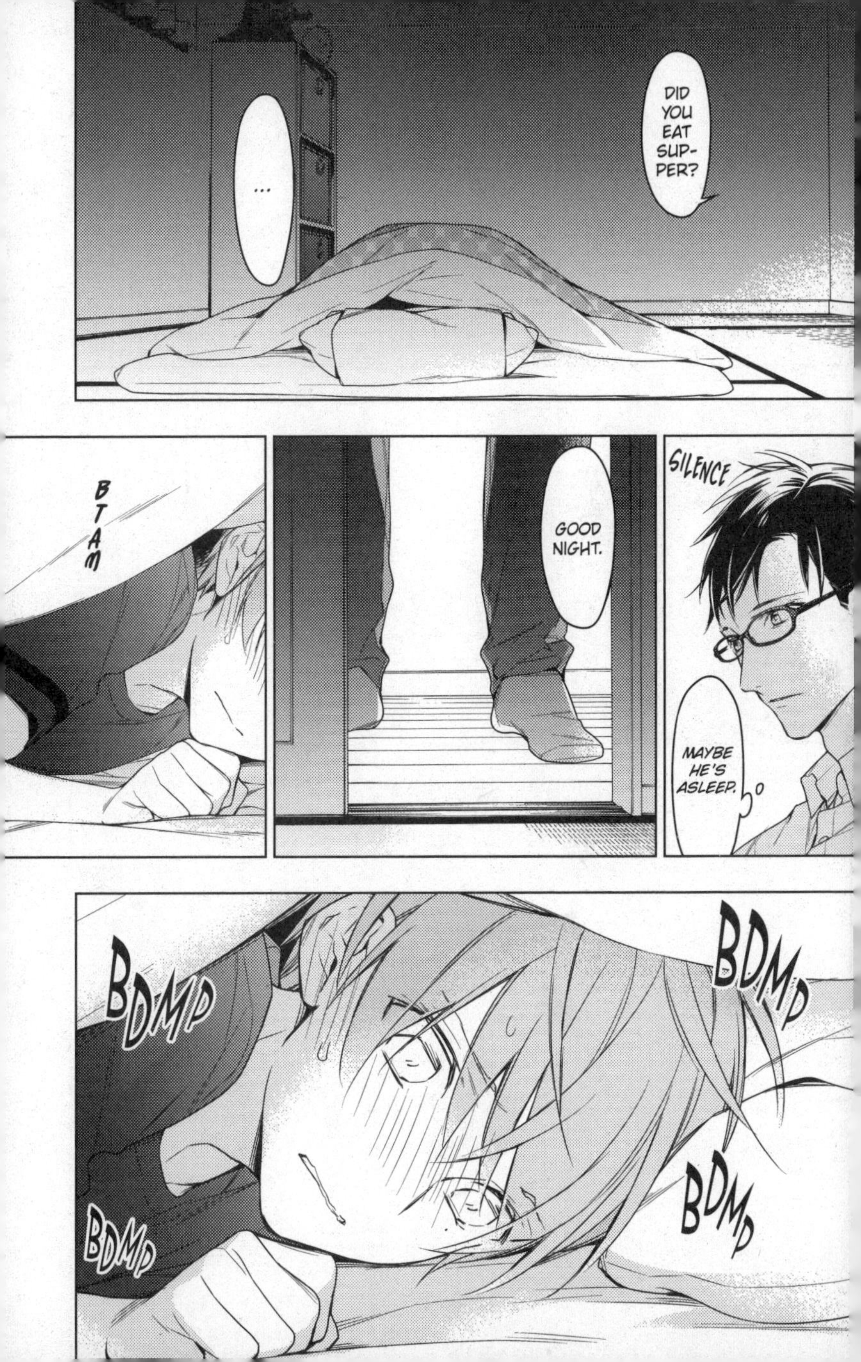
DID YOU EAT SUPPER?
...
SILENCE
MAYBE HE'S ASLEEP.
GOOD NIGHT.
BTAM
BDMP
BDMP
BDMP
BDMP

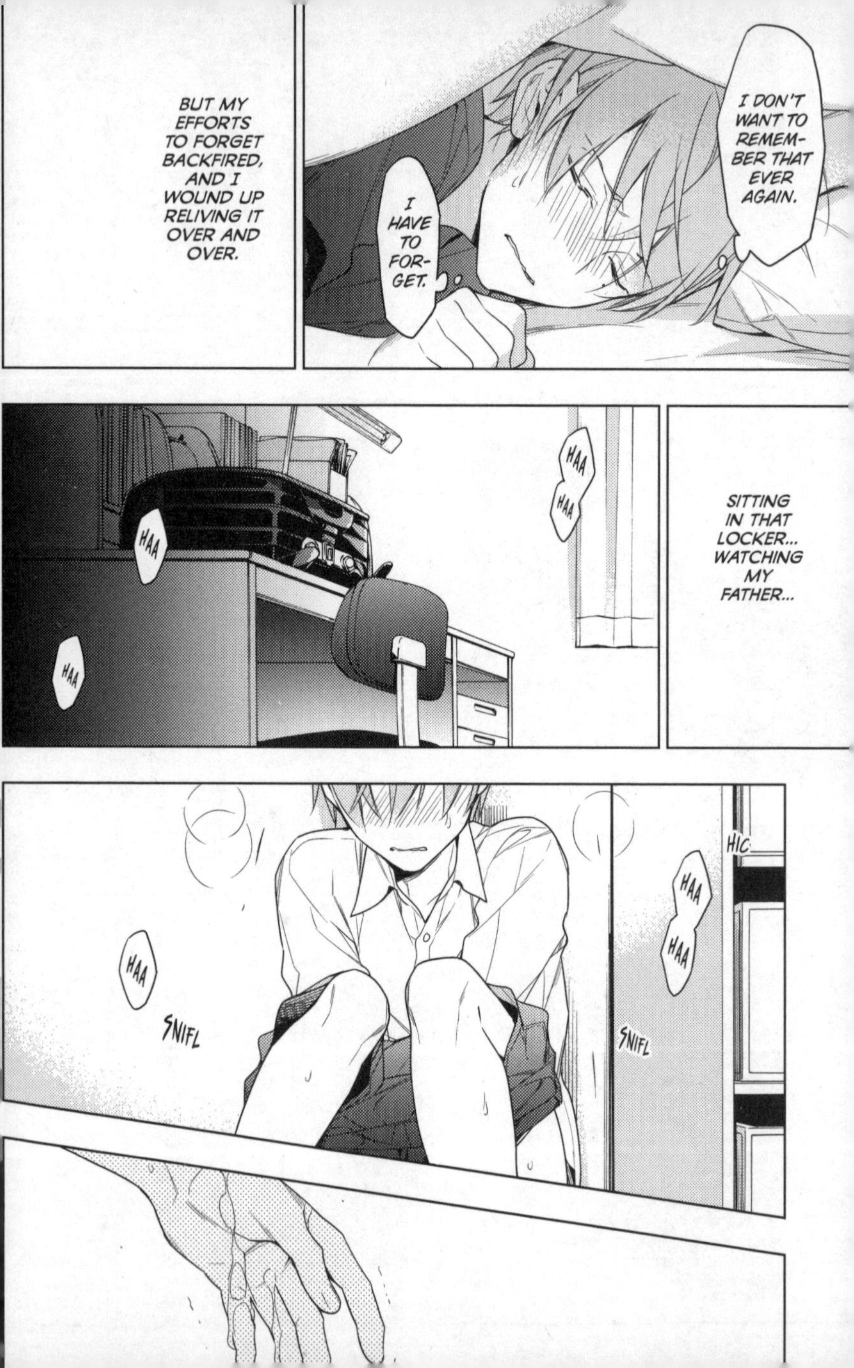
I DON'T WANT TO REMEMBER THAT EVER AGAIN.
I HAVE TO FORGET.
BUT MY EFFORTS TO FORGET BACKFIRED, AND I WOUND UP RELIVING IT OVER AND OVER.
SITTING IN THAT LOCKER... WATCHING MY FATHER...
HAA
HAA
HAA
HAA
HIC
HAA
HAA
SNIFL
HAA
SNIFL

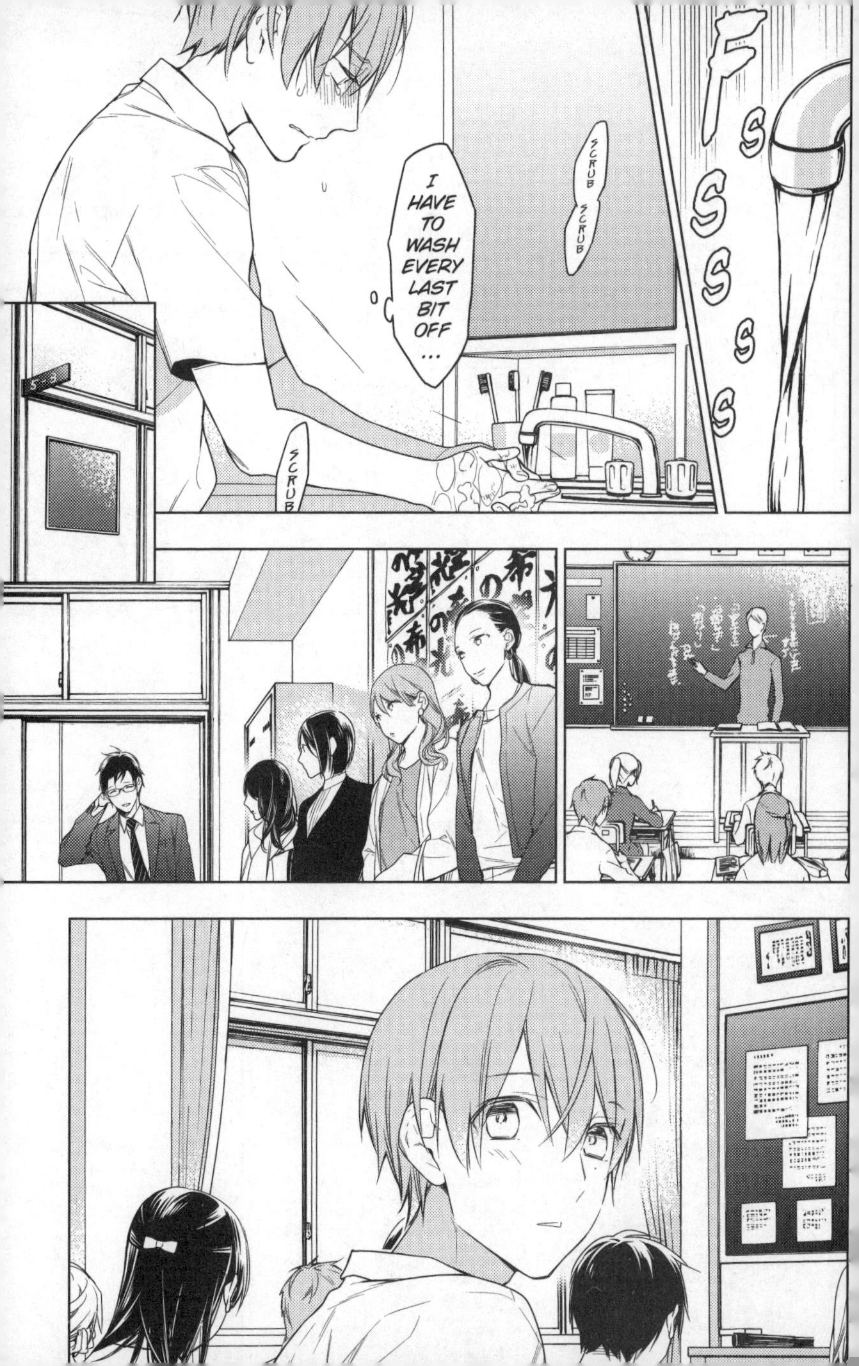
FSSSSS
SCRUB SCRUB
I HAVE TO WASH EVERY LAST BIT OFF...
SCRUB

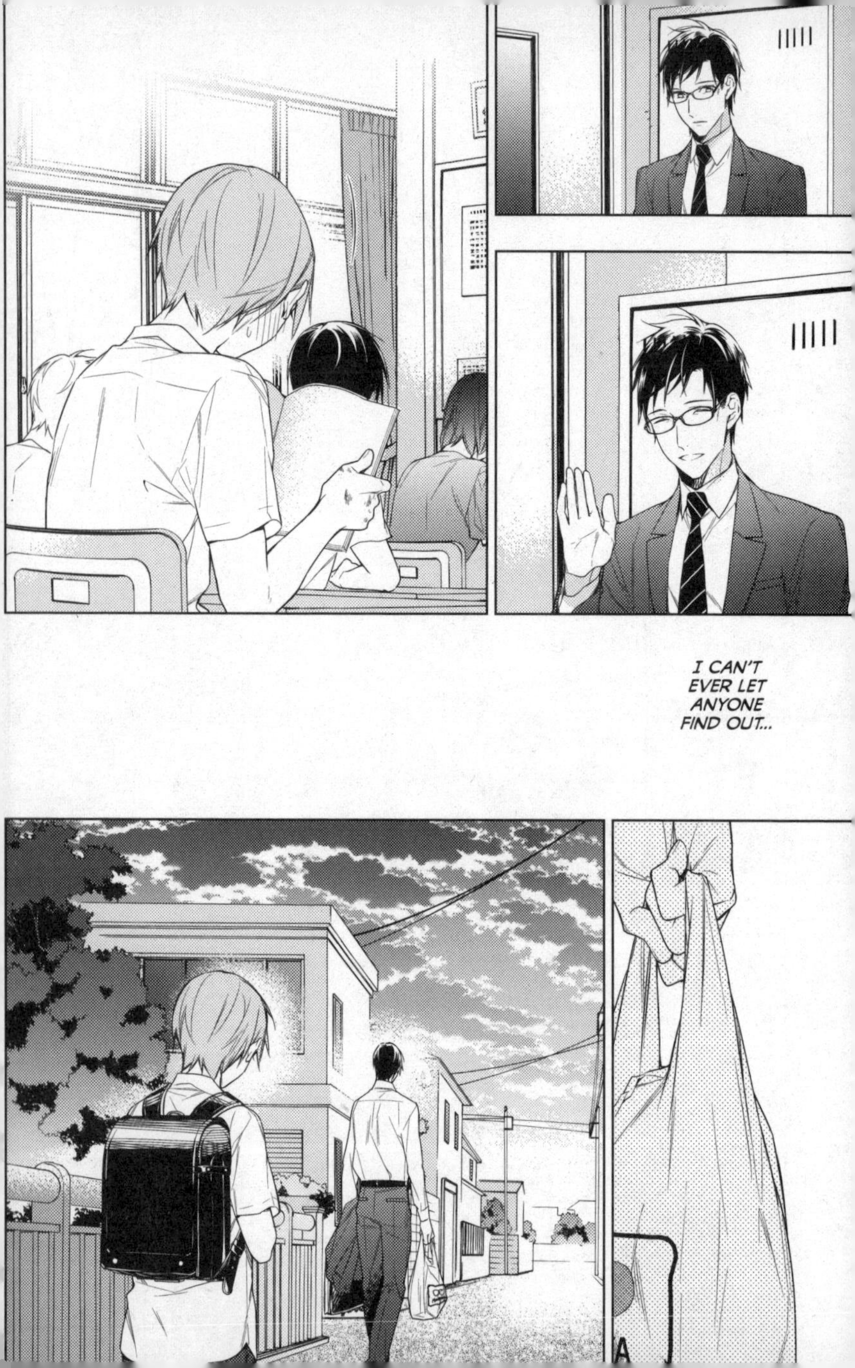
I CAN'T EVER LET ANYONE FIND OUT...

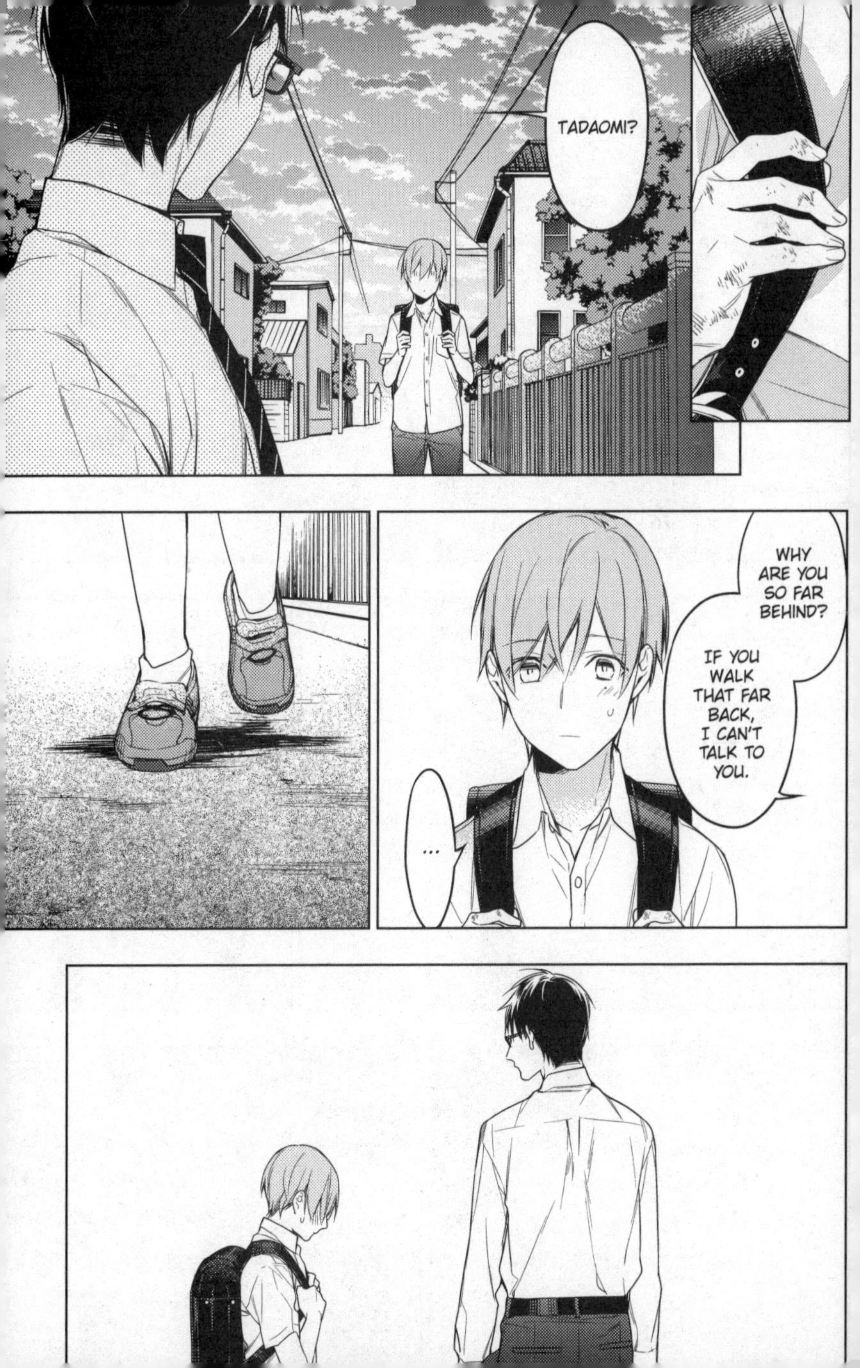
TADAOMI?
WHY ARE YOU SO FAR BEHIND?
IF YOU WALK THAT FAR BACK, I CAN'T TALK TO YOU.
...

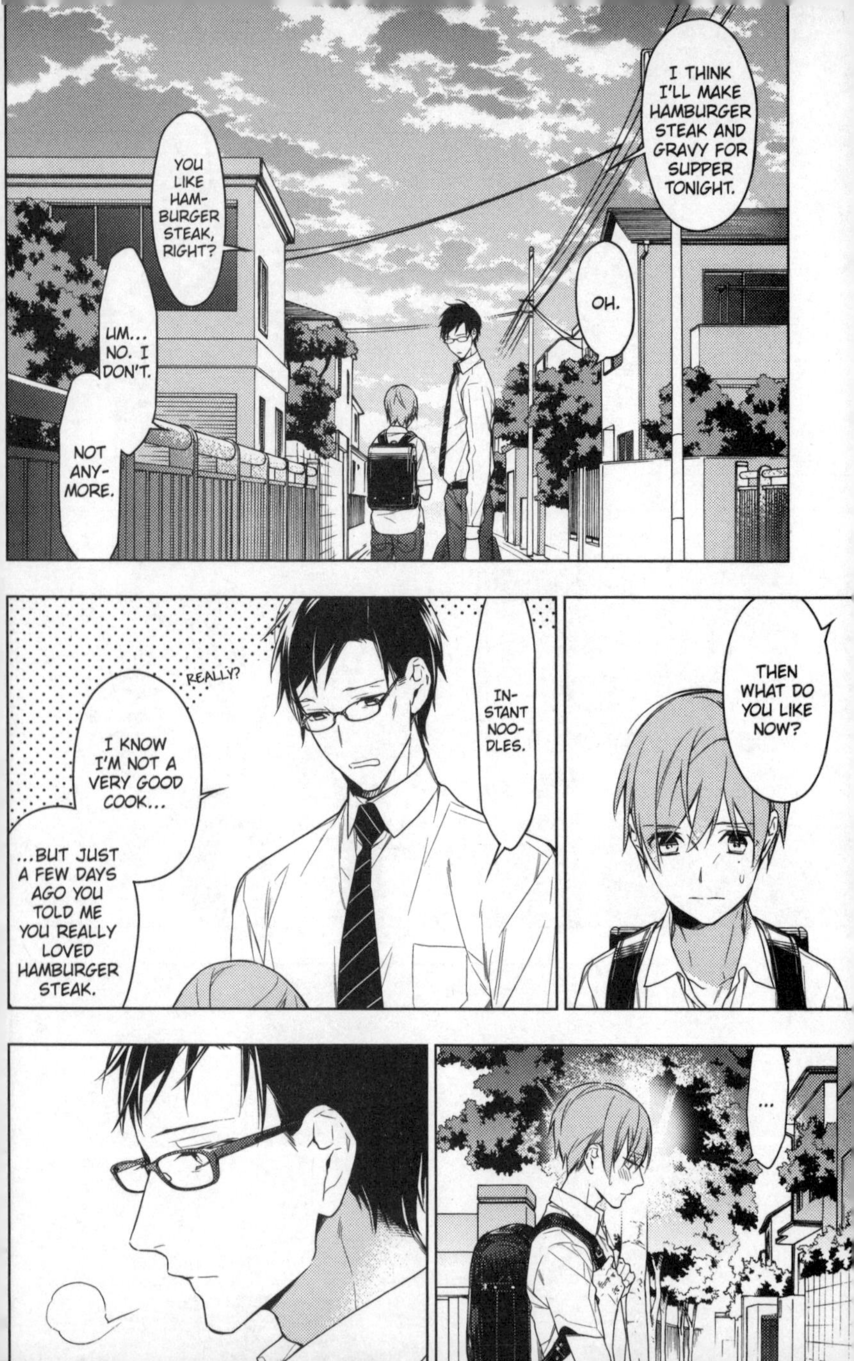
I THINK I'LL MAKE HAMBURGER STEAK AND GRAVY FOR SUPPER TONIGHT.
OH.
YOU LIKE HAM-BURGER STEAK, RIGHT?
UM... NO. I DON'T.
NOT ANY-MORE.
THEN WHAT DO YOU LIKE NOW?
IN-STANT NOO-DLES.
REALLY?
I KNOW I'M NOT A VERY GOOD COOK...
...BUT JUST A FEW DAYS AGO YOU TOLD ME YOU REALLY LOVED HAMBURGER STEAK.
...

YOU KNOW, ON SCHOOL VISITATION DAYS LIKE THIS...

...I CAN'T HELP BUT THINK YOU'D BE MUCH HAPPIER IF YOU HAD A YOUNG AND PRETTY MOTHER YOU COULD BRAG ABOUT TO YOUR FRIENDS.

ER... NEVER MIND.

NO, I WOULDN'T.

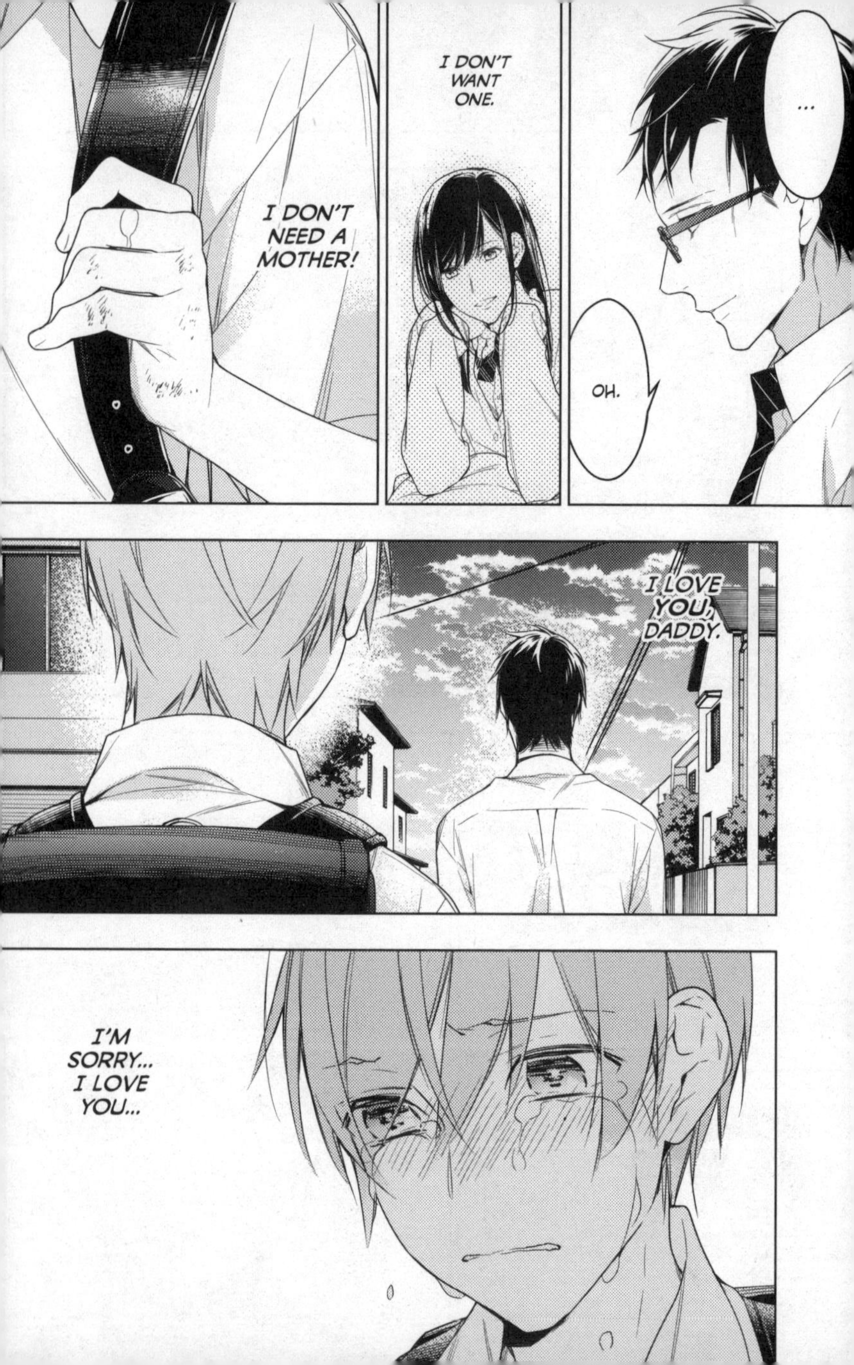
...
OH.
I DON'T WANT ONE.
I DON'T NEED A MOTHER!
I LOVE YOU, DADDY.
I'M SORRY... I LOVE YOU...

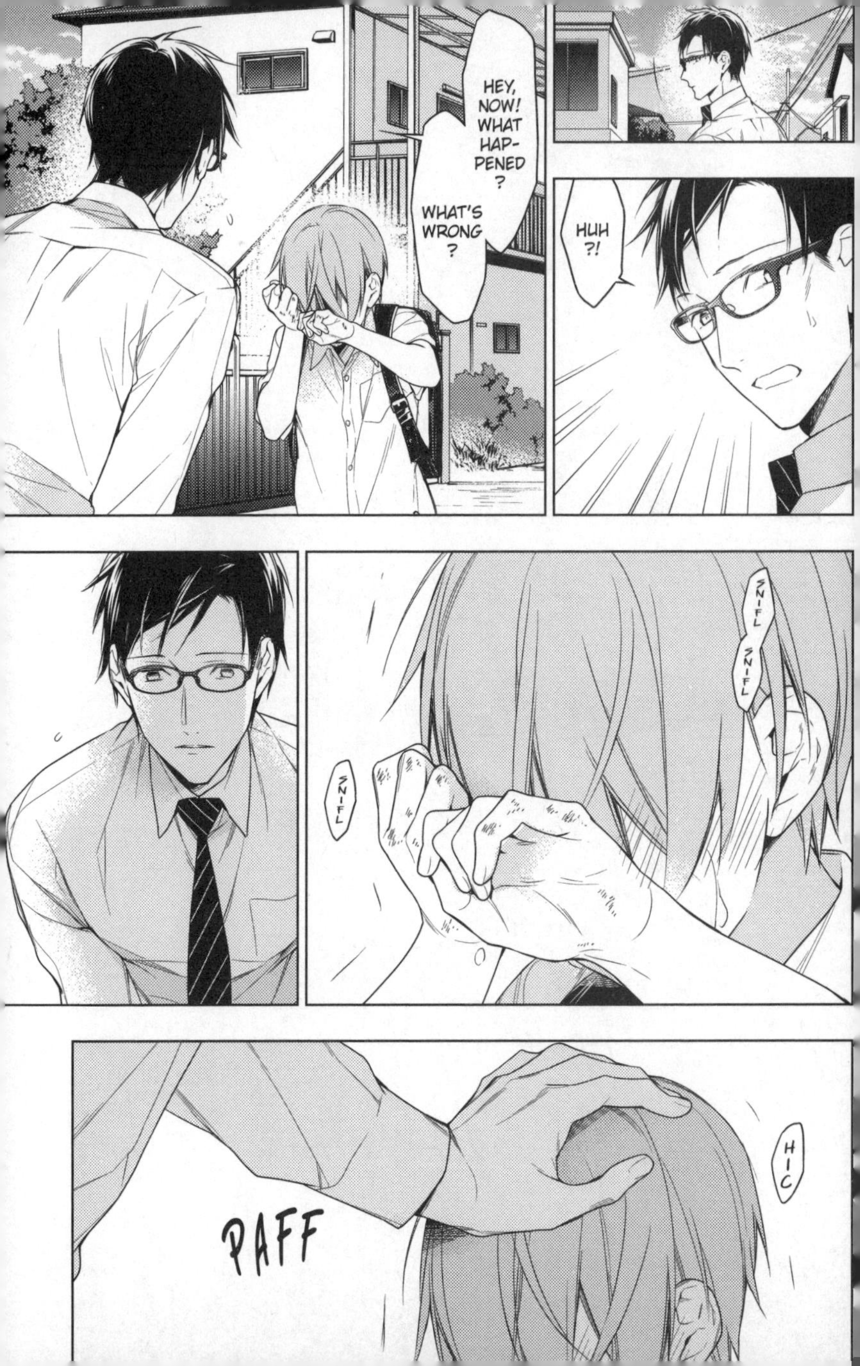
HUH ?!
HEY, NOW! WHAT HAP-PENED ?
WHAT'S WRONG ?
SNIFL
SNIFL
SNIFL
HIC
PAFF

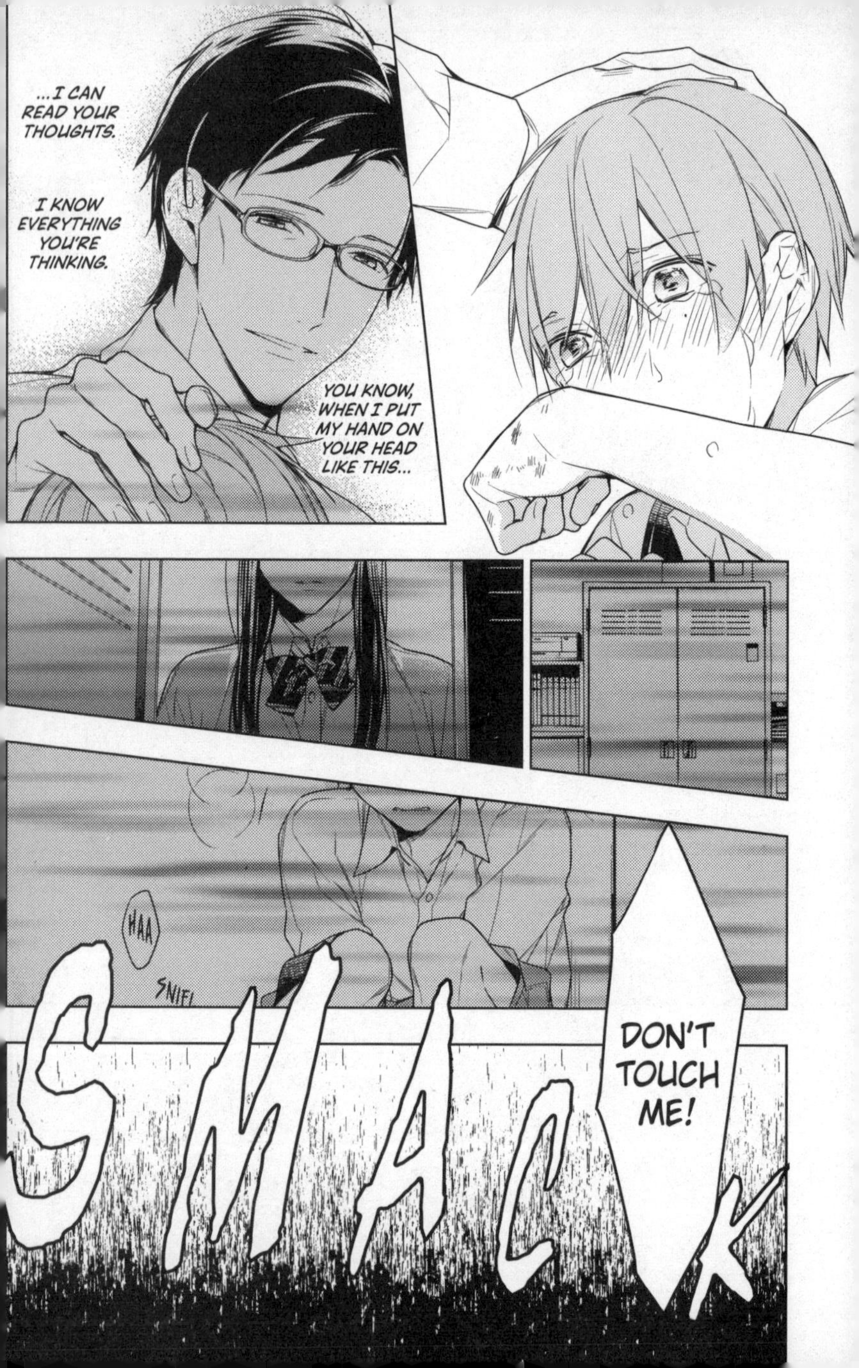
...I CAN READ YOUR THOUGHTS.
I KNOW EVERYTHING YOU'RE THINKING.
YOU KNOW, WHEN I PUT MY HAND ON YOUR HEAD LIKE THIS...
HAA
SNIFF
DON'T TOUCH ME!
SMACK

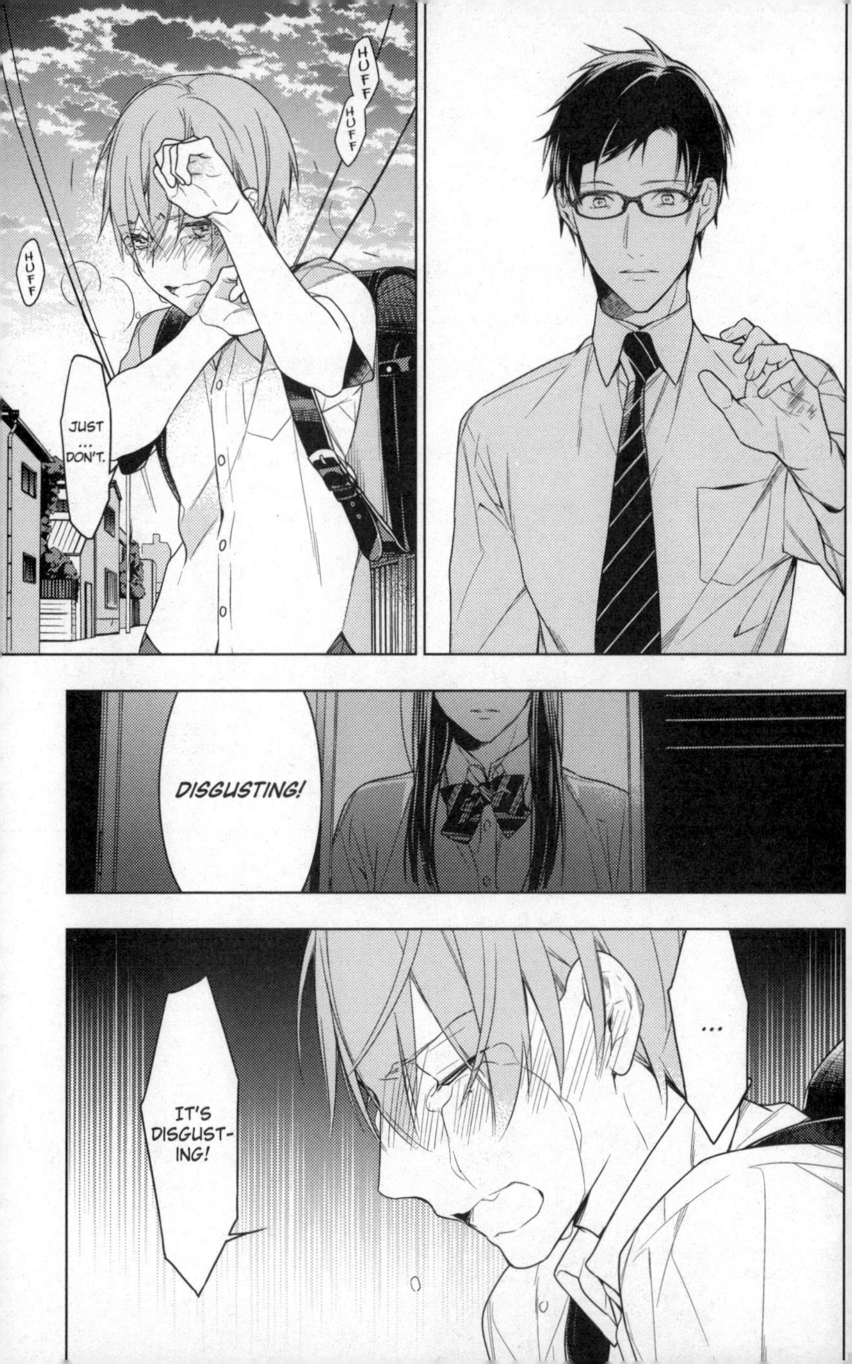
HUFF HUFF
HUFF
JUST ... DON'T.
DISGUSTING!
...
IT'S DISGUST-ING!

I'M DISGUSTING INSIDE.

DON'T TOUCH ME...

DASH

TADA-OMI!

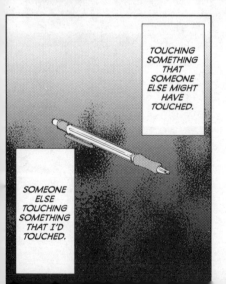

TOUCHING SOMETHING THAT SOMEONE ELSE MIGHT HAVE TOUCHED.

SOMEONE ELSE TOUCHING SOMETHING THAT I'D TOUCHED.

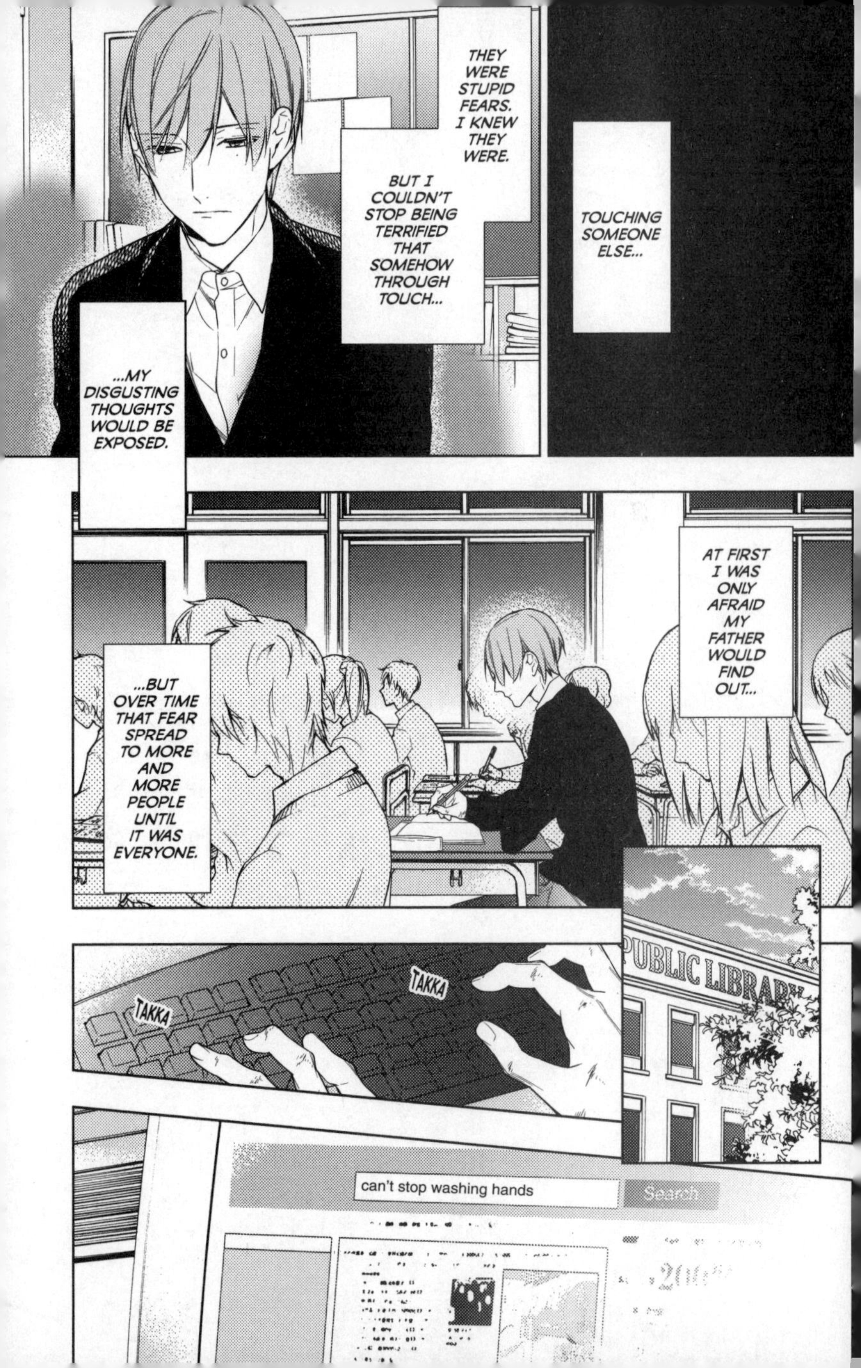
TOUCHING SOMEONE ELSE...
THEY WERE STUPID FEARS. I KNEW THEY WERE.
BUT I COULDN'T STOP BEING TERRIFIED THAT SOMEHOW THROUGH TOUCH...
...MY DISGUSTING THOUGHTS WOULD BE EXPOSED.
AT FIRST I WAS ONLY AFRAID MY FATHER WOULD FIND OUT...
...BUT OVER TIME THAT FEAR SPREAD TO MORE AND MORE PEOPLE UNTIL IT WAS EVERYONE.
PUBLIC LIBRAR
TAKKA
TAKKA
can't stop washing hands
Search

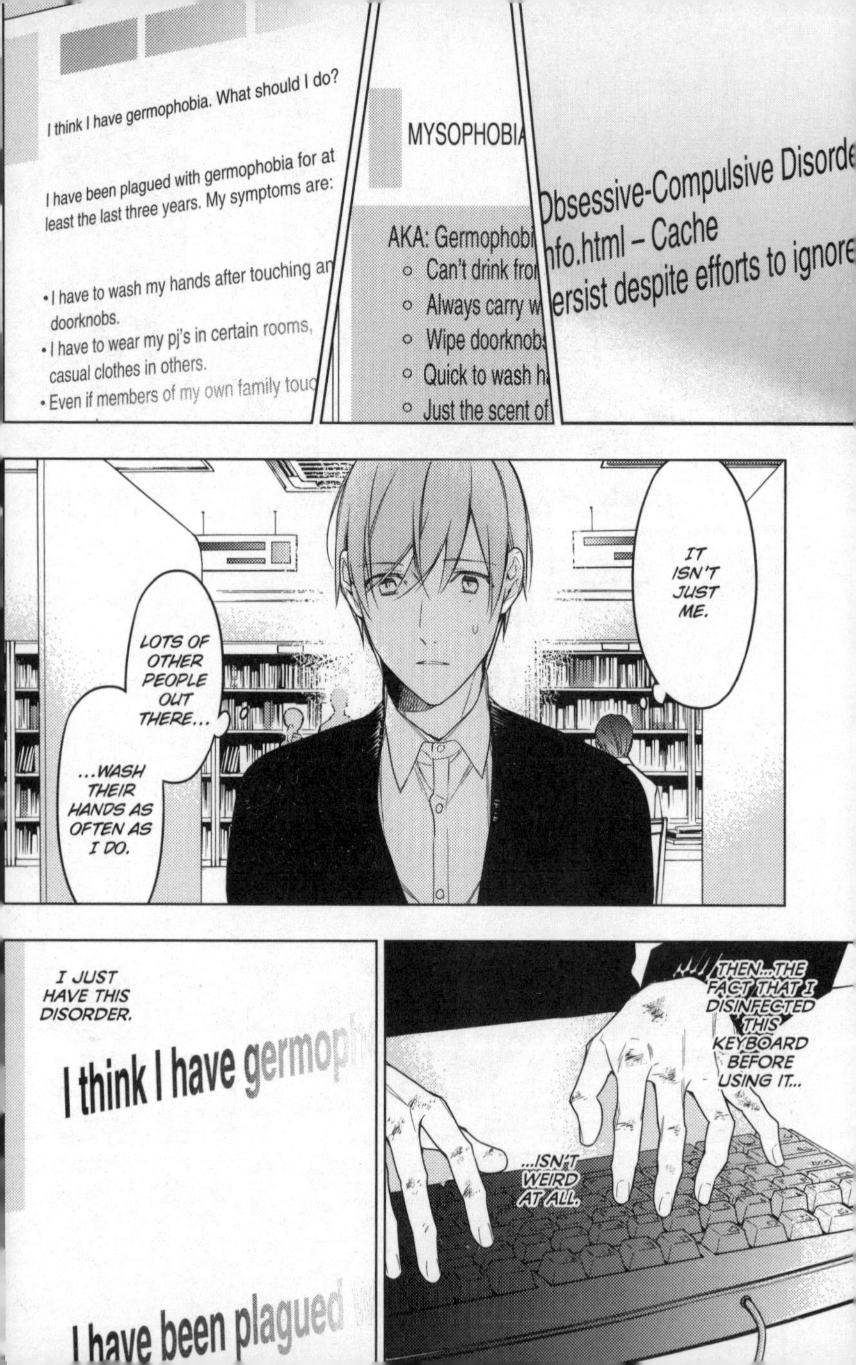
Obsessive-Compulsive Disorde
nfo.html – Cache
ersist despite efforts to ignore
MYSOPHOBIA
AKA: Germophobi
Can't drink fro
Always carry w
Wipe doorknob
Quick to wash h
Just the scent of
I think I have germophobia. What should I do?
I have been plagued with germophobia for at least the last three years. My symptoms are:
• I have to wash my hands after touching an doorknobs.
• I have to wear my pj's in certain rooms, casual clothes in others.
• Even if members of my own family touc
IT ISN'T JUST ME.
LOTS OF OTHER PEOPLE OUT THERE...
...WASH THEIR HANDS AS OFTEN AS I DO.
THEN...THE FACT THAT I DISINFECTED THIS KEYBOARD BEFORE USING IT...
...ISN'T WEIRD AT ALL.
I JUST HAVE THIS DISORDER.
I think I have germop
I have been plagued

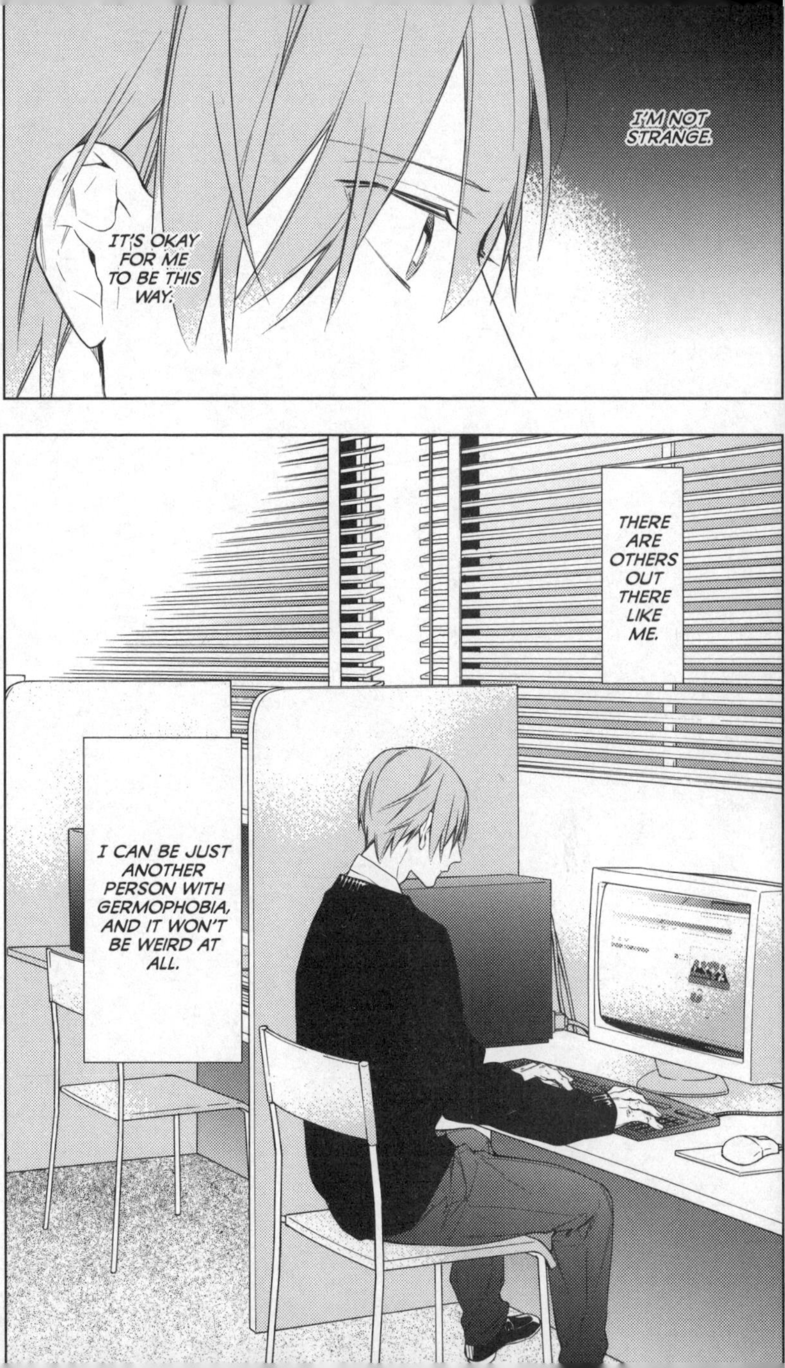
I'M NOT STRANGE.
IT'S OKAY FOR ME TO BE THIS WAY.
THERE ARE OTHERS OUT THERE LIKE ME.
I CAN BE JUST ANOTHER PERSON WITH GERMOPHOBIA, AND IT WON'T BE WEIRD AT ALL.

ten count by rihito takarai

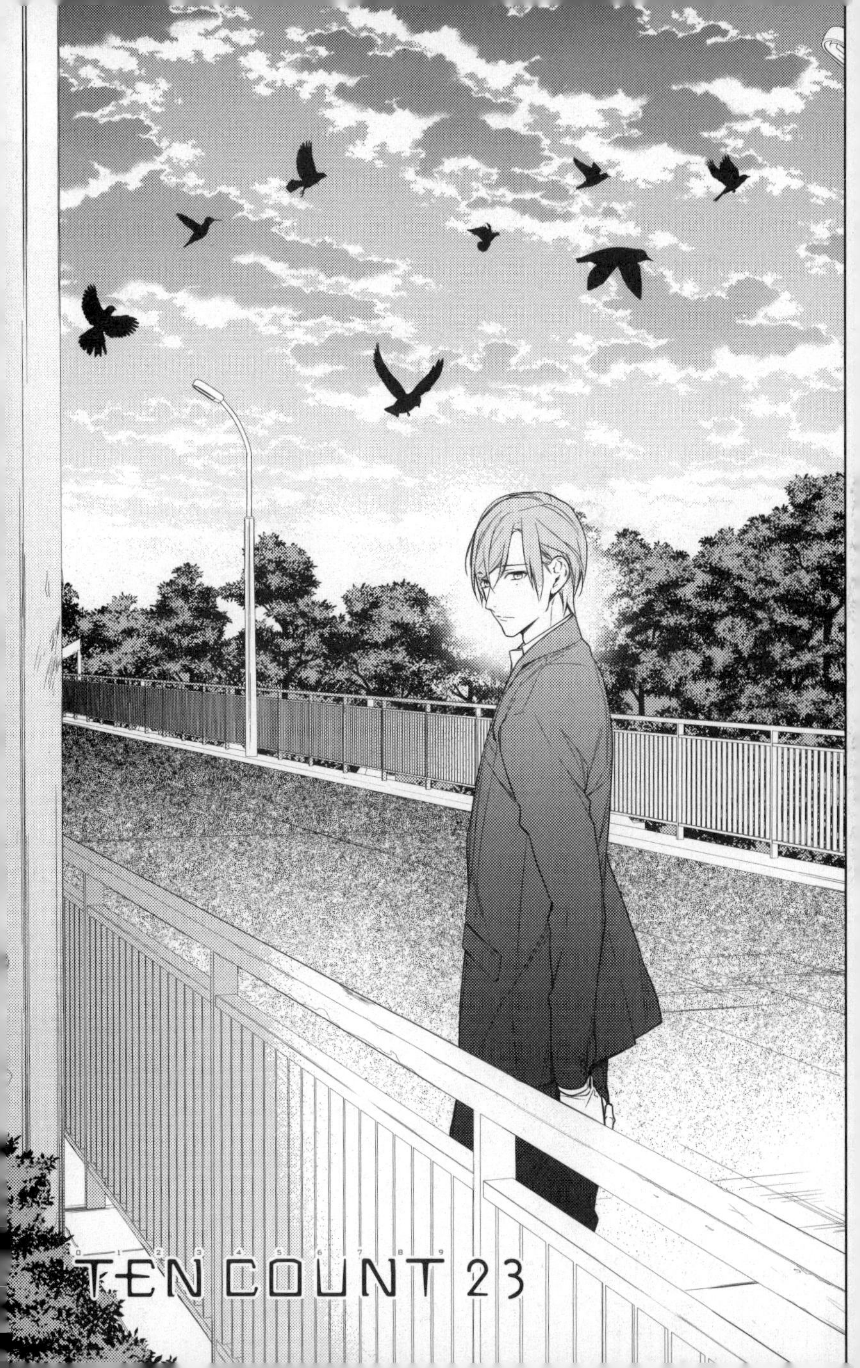
0 1 2 3 4 5 6 7 8 9
TEN COUNT 23

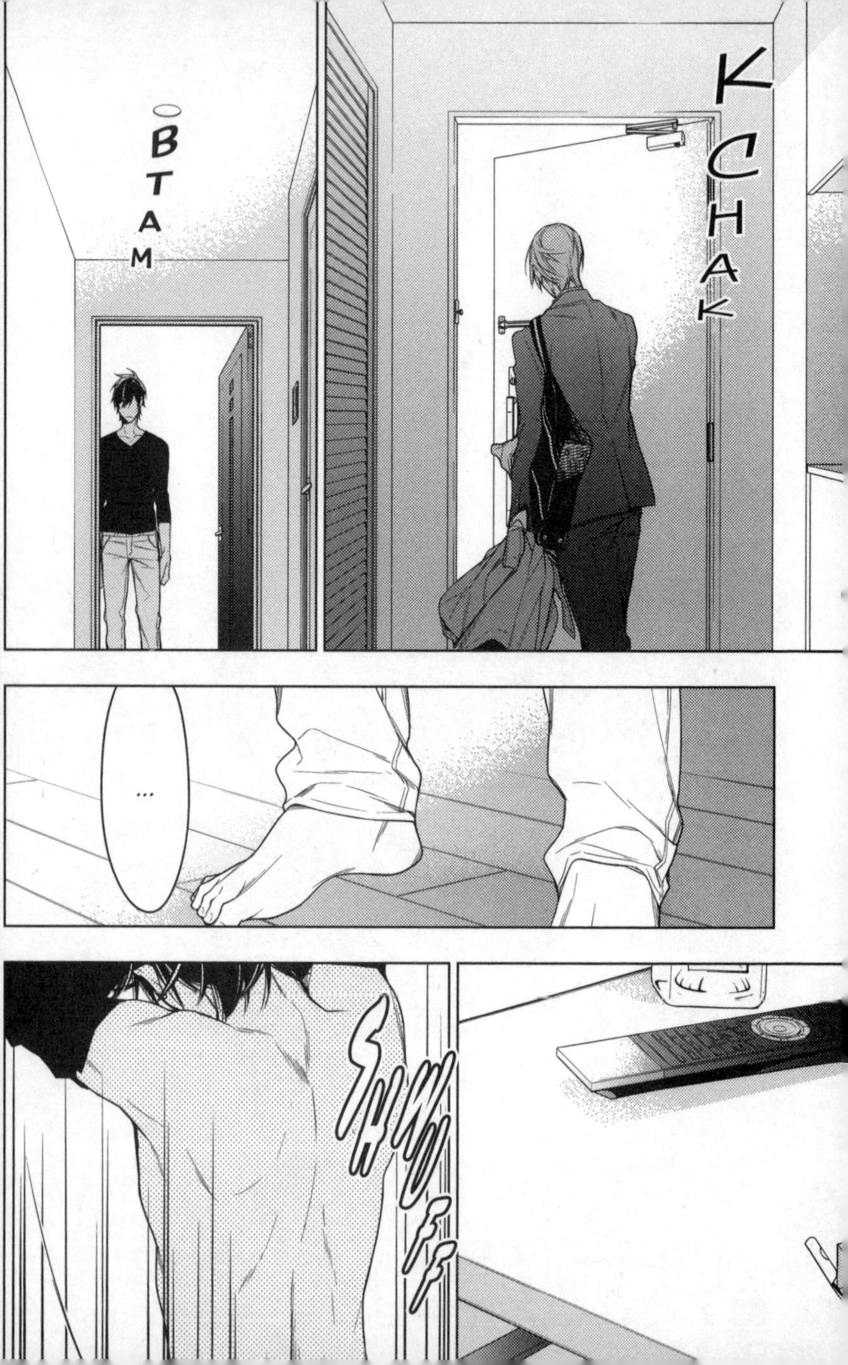
KCHAK
BTAM
...
SHWFF

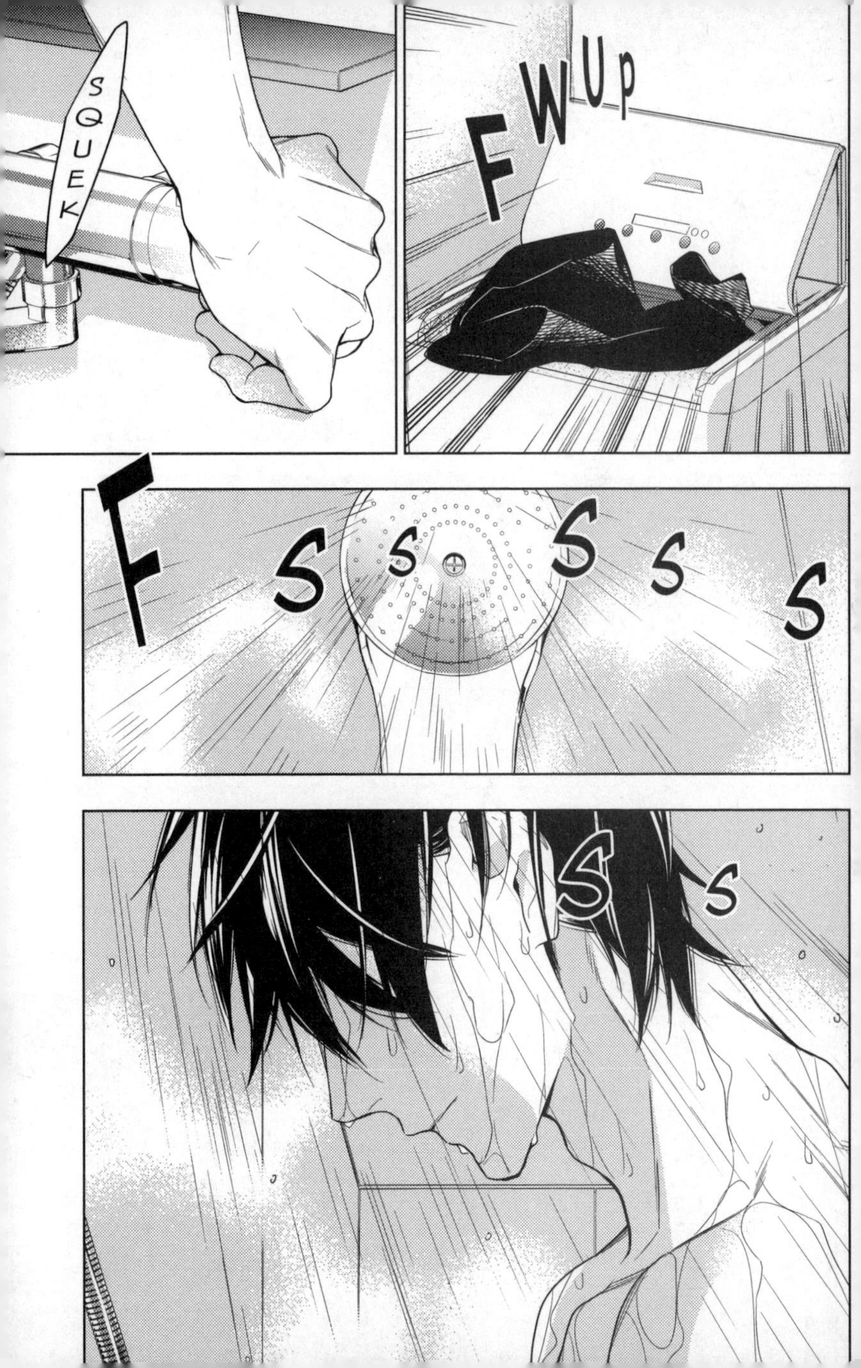
FWUP
SQUEK
FSSSSS
SS

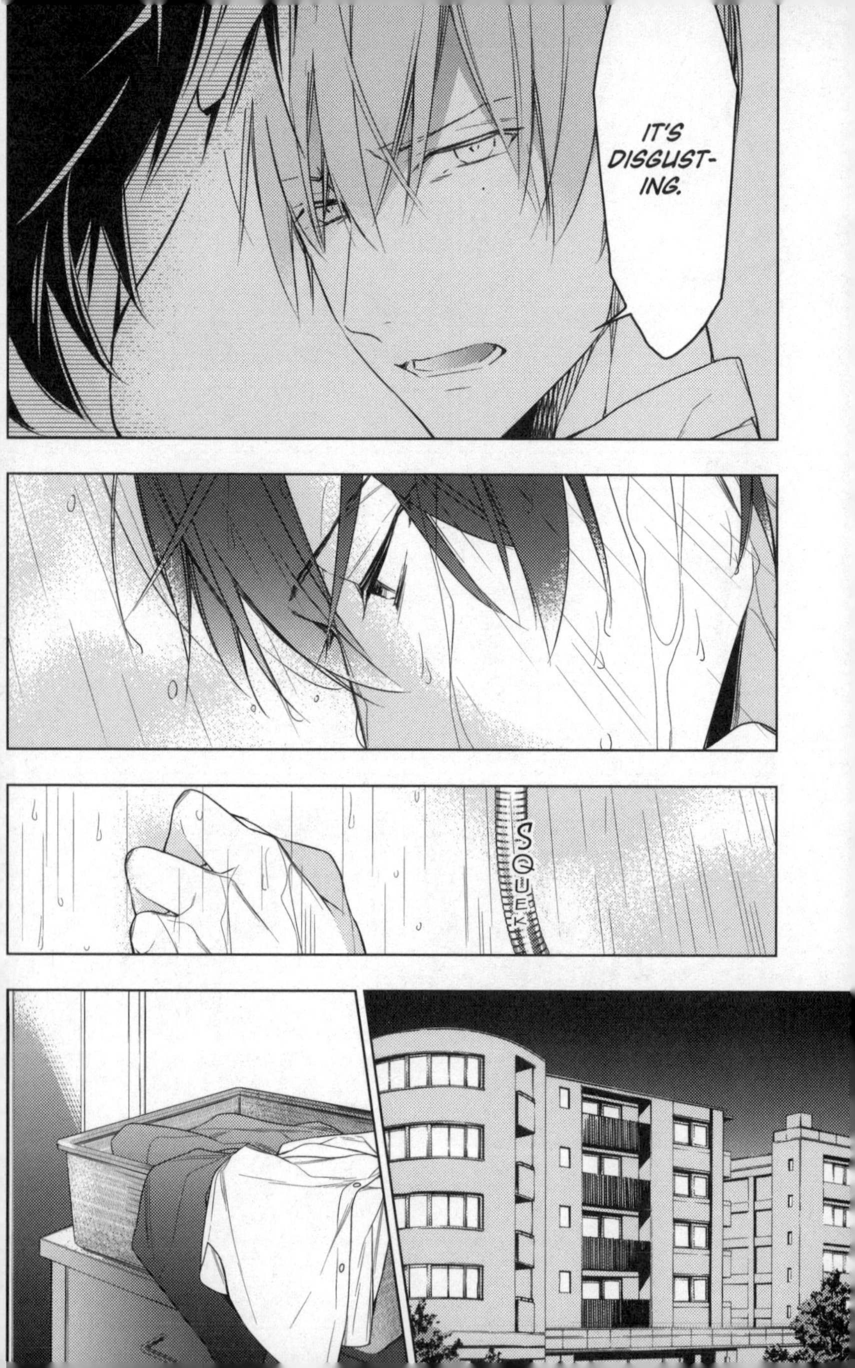
IT'S DISGUST-ING.
SQUEK

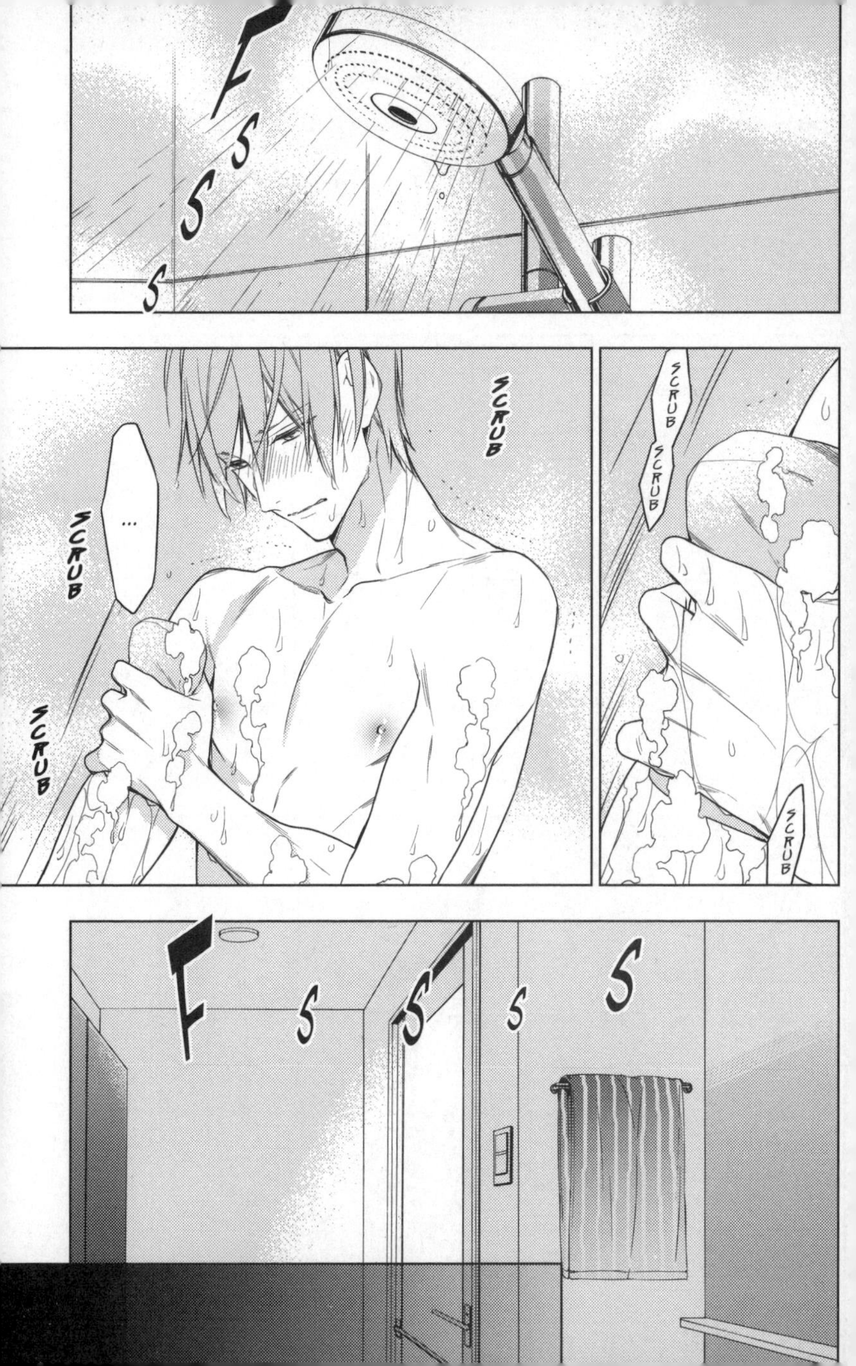
FSSSS
SCRUB SCRUB
SCRUB
SCRUB
...
SCRUB
SCRUB
FSSSS

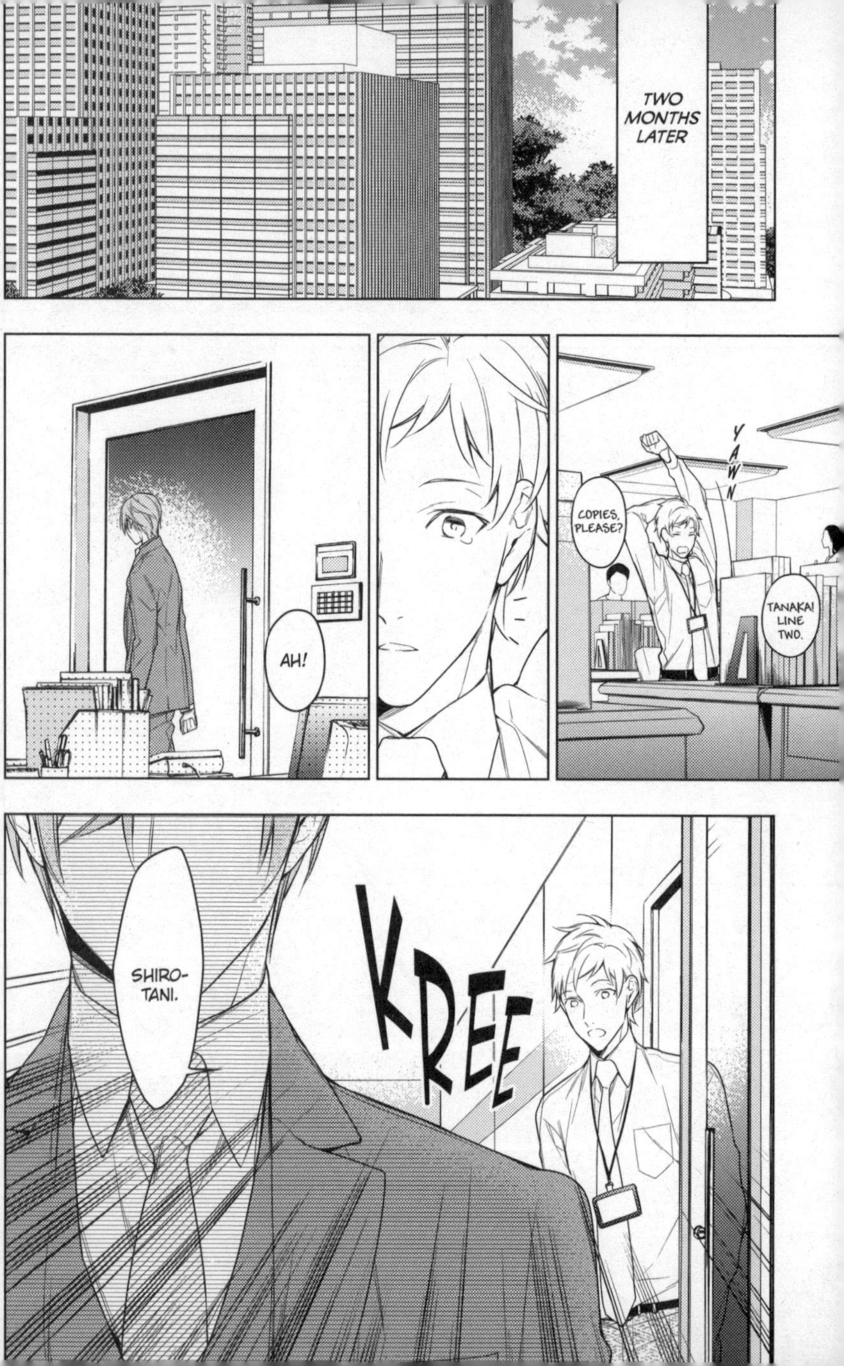
TWO MONTHS LATER
YAWN
TANAKA! LINE TWO.
COPIES, PLEASE?
AH!
KREE
SHIRO-TANI.

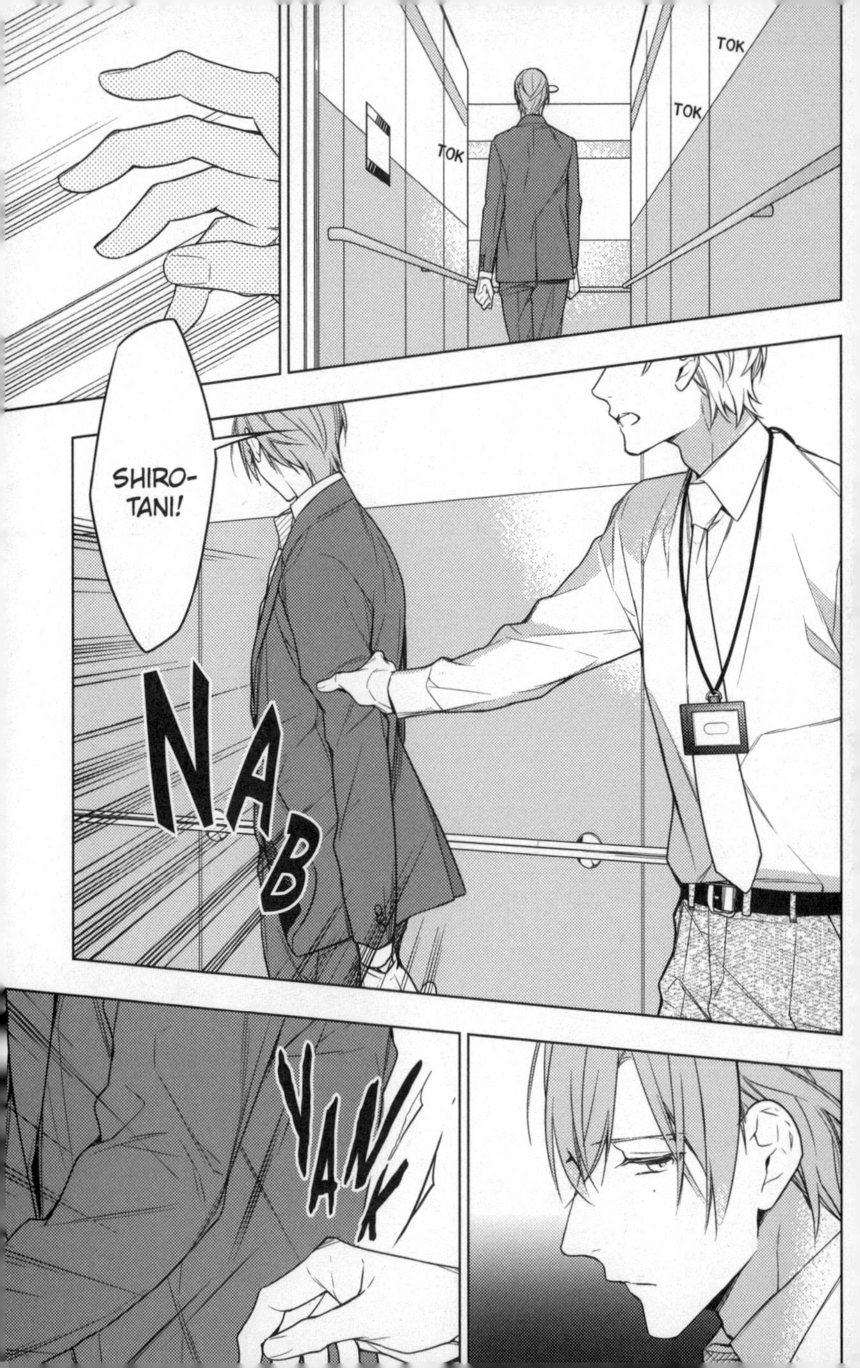
TOK
TOK
TOK
SHIRO-TANI!
NAB
YANK

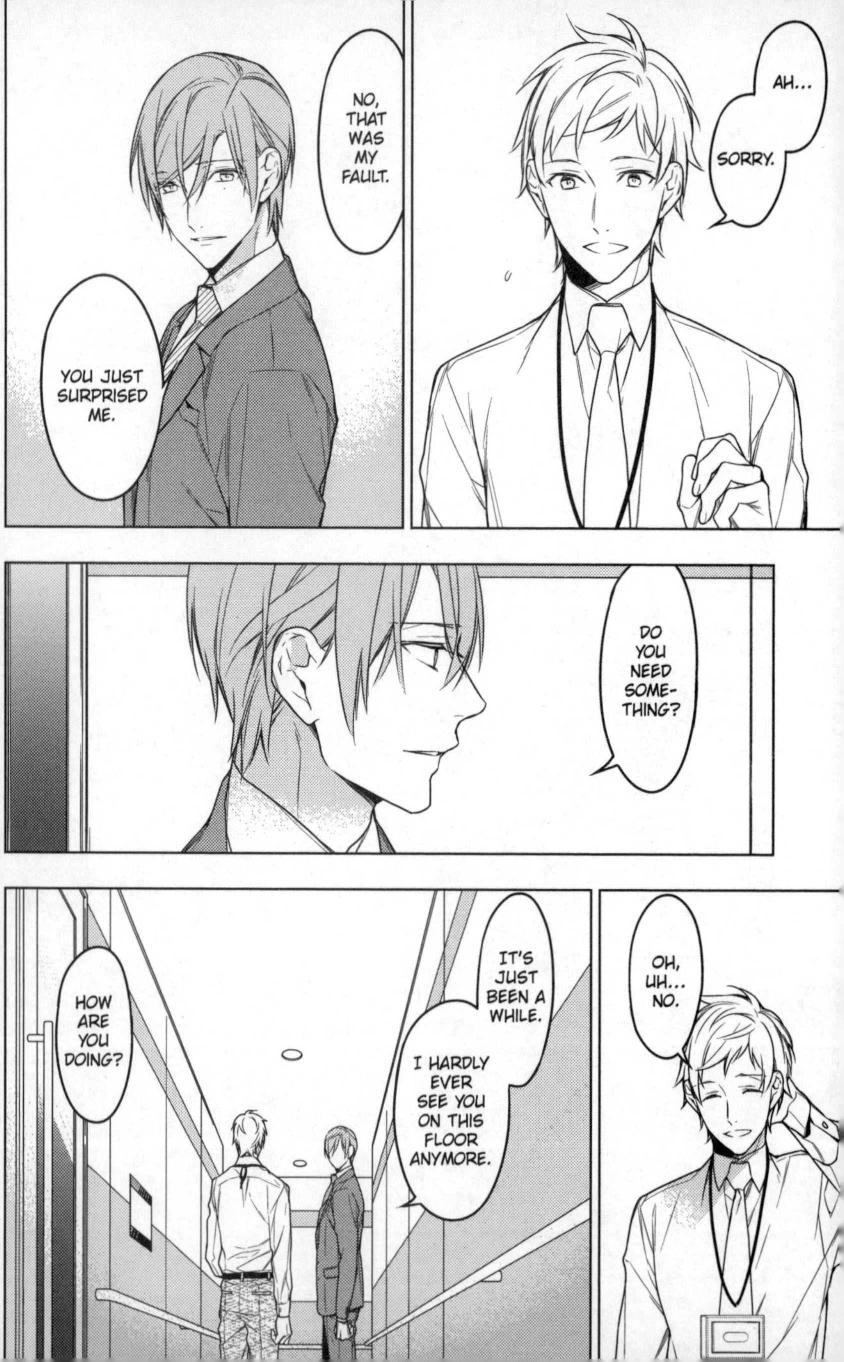
AH...
SORRY.
NO, THAT WAS MY FAULT.
YOU JUST SURPRISED ME.
DO YOU NEED SOME-THING?
OH, UH... NO.
IT'S JUST BEEN A WHILE.
I HARDLY EVER SEE YOU ON THIS FLOOR ANYMORE.
HOW ARE YOU DOING?

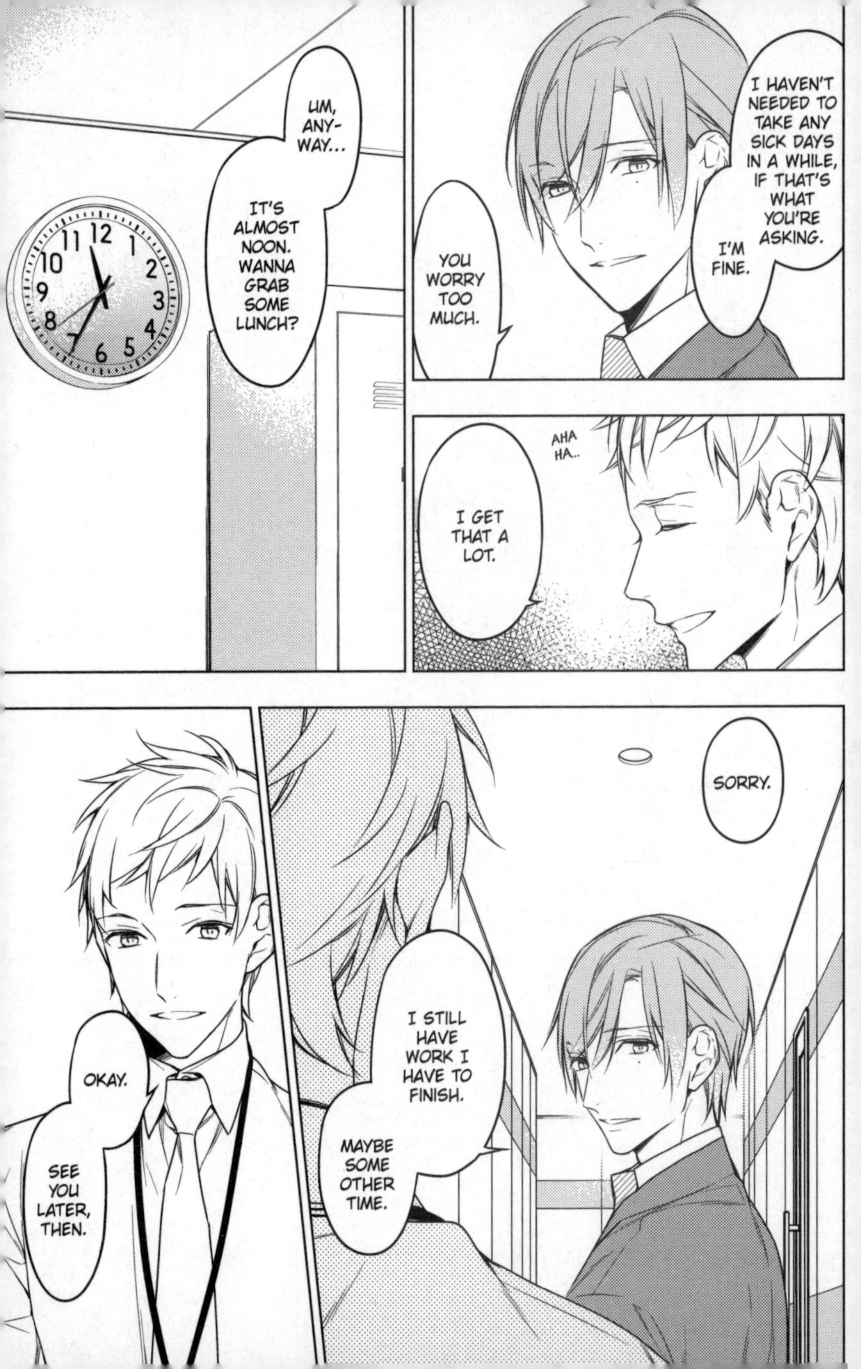
I HAVEN'T NEEDED TO TAKE ANY SICK DAYS IN A WHILE, IF THAT'S WHAT YOU'RE ASKING.
I'M FINE.
YOU WORRY TOO MUCH.
AHA HA..
I GET THAT A LOT.
UM, ANY-WAY...
IT'S ALMOST NOON. WANNA GRAB SOME LUNCH?
SORRY.
I STILL HAVE WORK I HAVE TO FINISH.
MAYBE SOME OTHER TIME.
OKAY.
SEE YOU LATER, THEN.

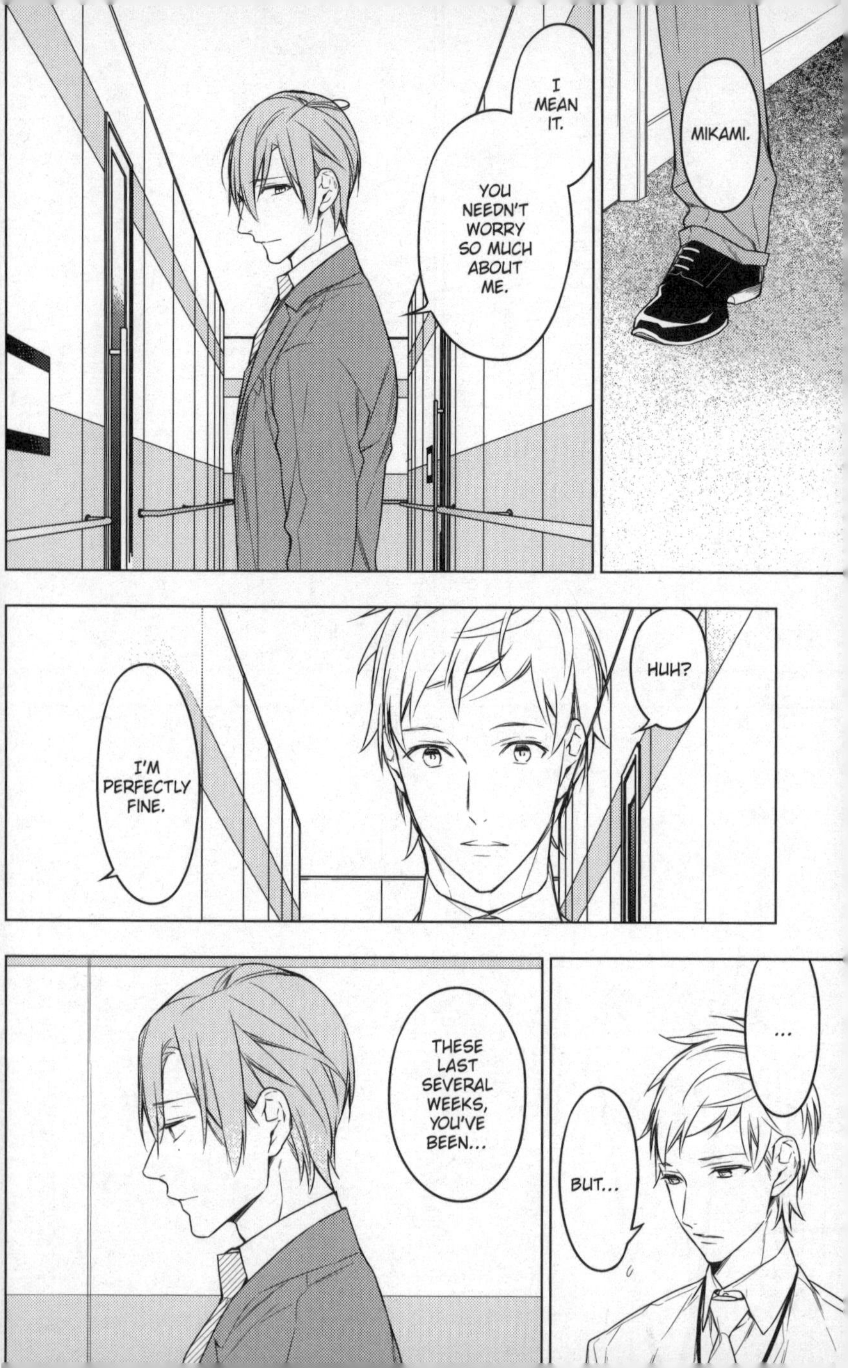
MIKAMI.
I MEAN IT.
YOU NEEDN'T WORRY SO MUCH ABOUT ME.
HUH?
I'M PERFECTLY FINE.
...
BUT...
THESE LAST SEVERAL WEEKS, YOU'VE BEEN...

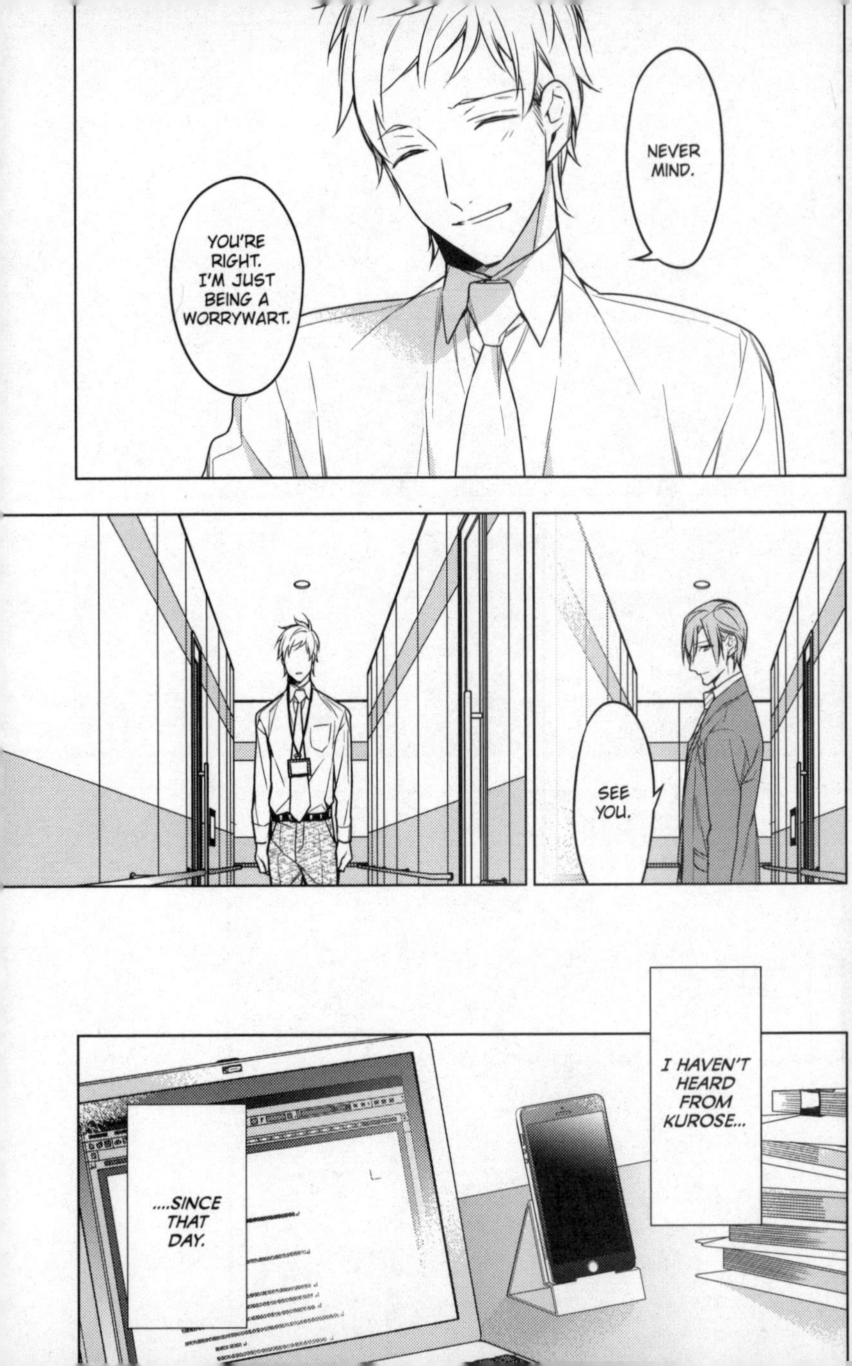
NEVER MIND.
YOU'RE RIGHT. I'M JUST BEING A WORRYWART.
SEE YOU.
I HAVEN'T HEARD FROM KUROSE...
....SINCE THAT DAY.

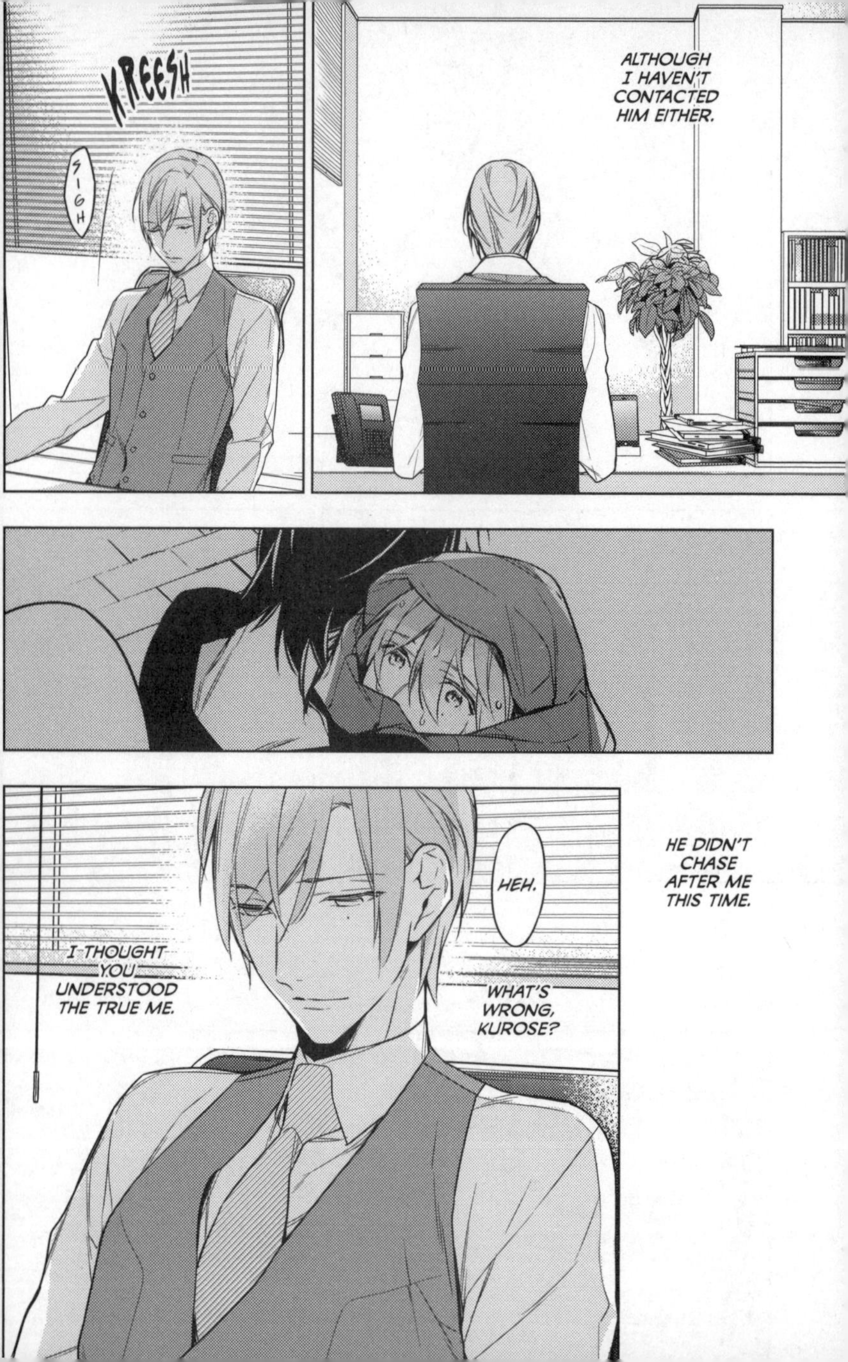
ALTHOUGH I HAVEN'T CONTACTED HIM EITHER.
KREESH
SIGH
HE DIDN'T CHASE AFTER ME THIS TIME.
HEH.
WHAT'S WRONG, KUROSE?
I THOUGHT YOU UNDERSTOOD THE TRUE ME.

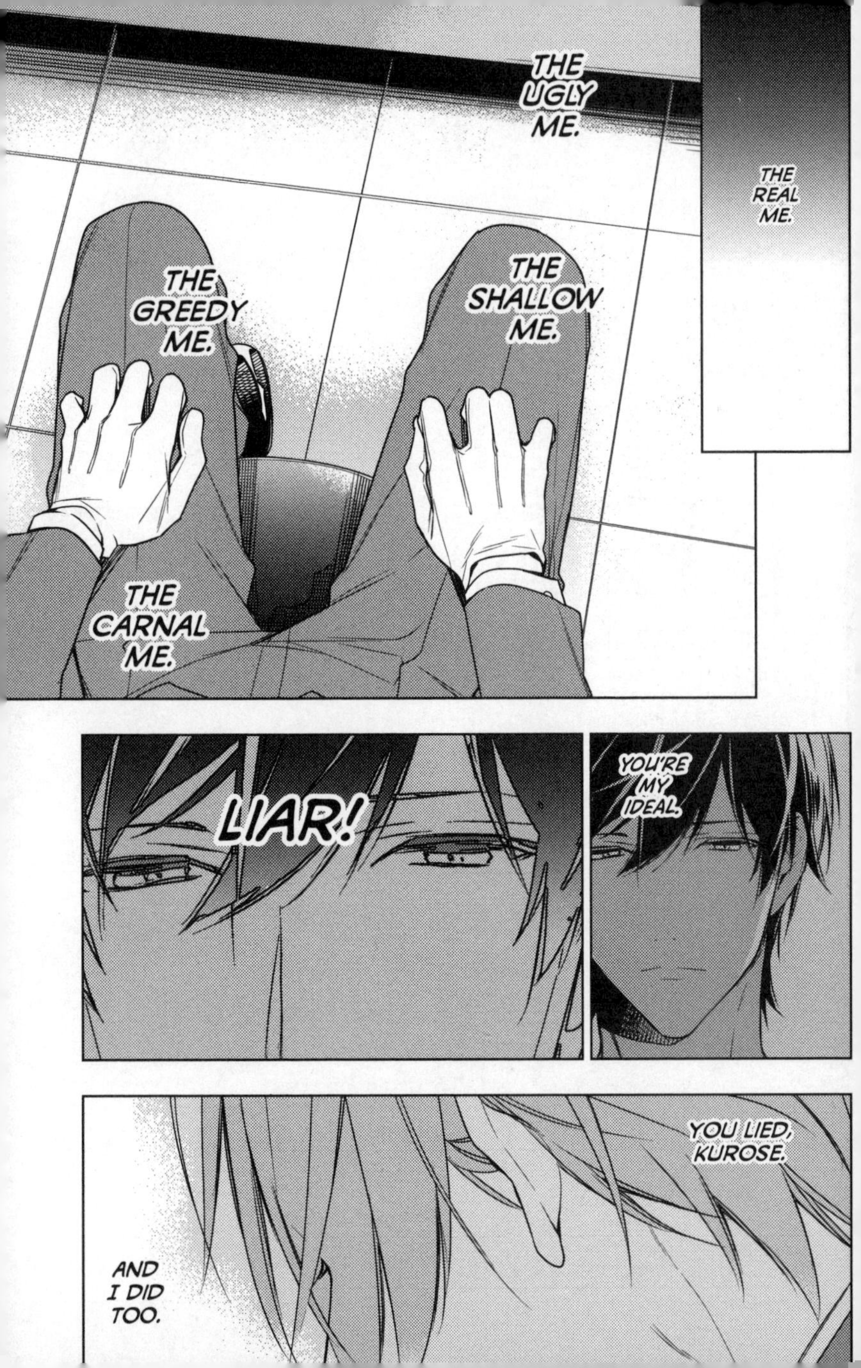
THE REAL ME.
THE UGLY ME.
THE SHALLOW ME.
THE GREEDY ME.
THE CARNAL ME.
YOU'RE MY IDEAL.
LIAR!
YOU LIED, KUROSE.
AND I DID TOO.

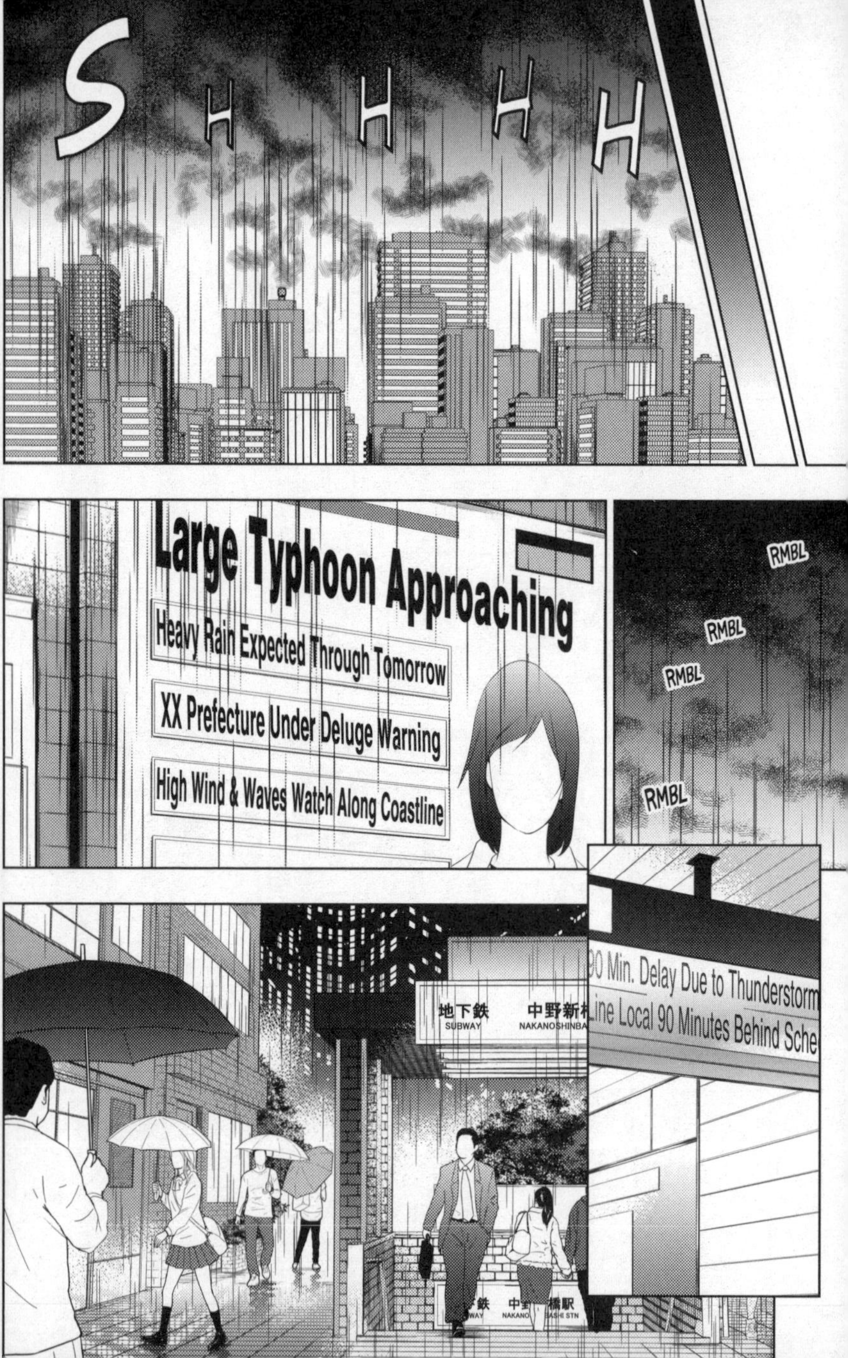
SHHH
RMBL
RMBL
RMBL
RMBL
Large Typhoon Approaching
Heavy Rain Expected Through Tomorrow
XX Prefecture Under Deluge Warning
High Wind & Waves Watch Along Coastline
90 Min. Delay Due to Thunderstorm
Line Local 90 Minutes Behind Sche
地下鉄
SUBWAY
中野新
NAKANOSHINBA

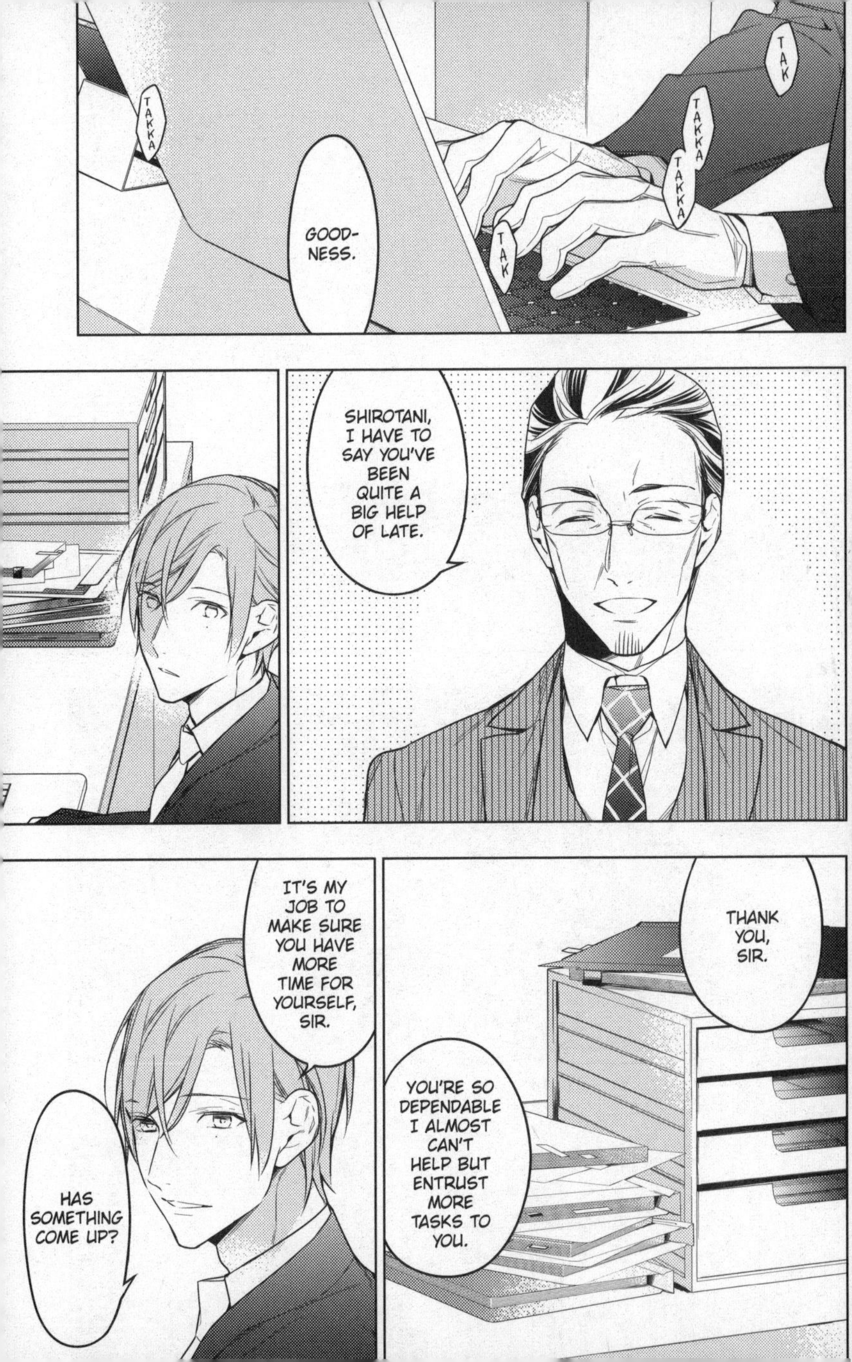
TAK
TAKKA
TAKKA
TAK
TAKKA
GOOD-NESS.
SHIROTANI, I HAVE TO SAY YOU'VE BEEN QUITE A BIG HELP OF LATE.
THANK YOU, SIR.
YOU'RE SO DEPENDABLE I ALMOST CAN'T HELP BUT ENTRUST MORE TASKS TO YOU.
IT'S MY JOB TO MAKE SURE YOU HAVE MORE TIME FOR YOURSELF, SIR.
HAS SOMETHING COME UP?

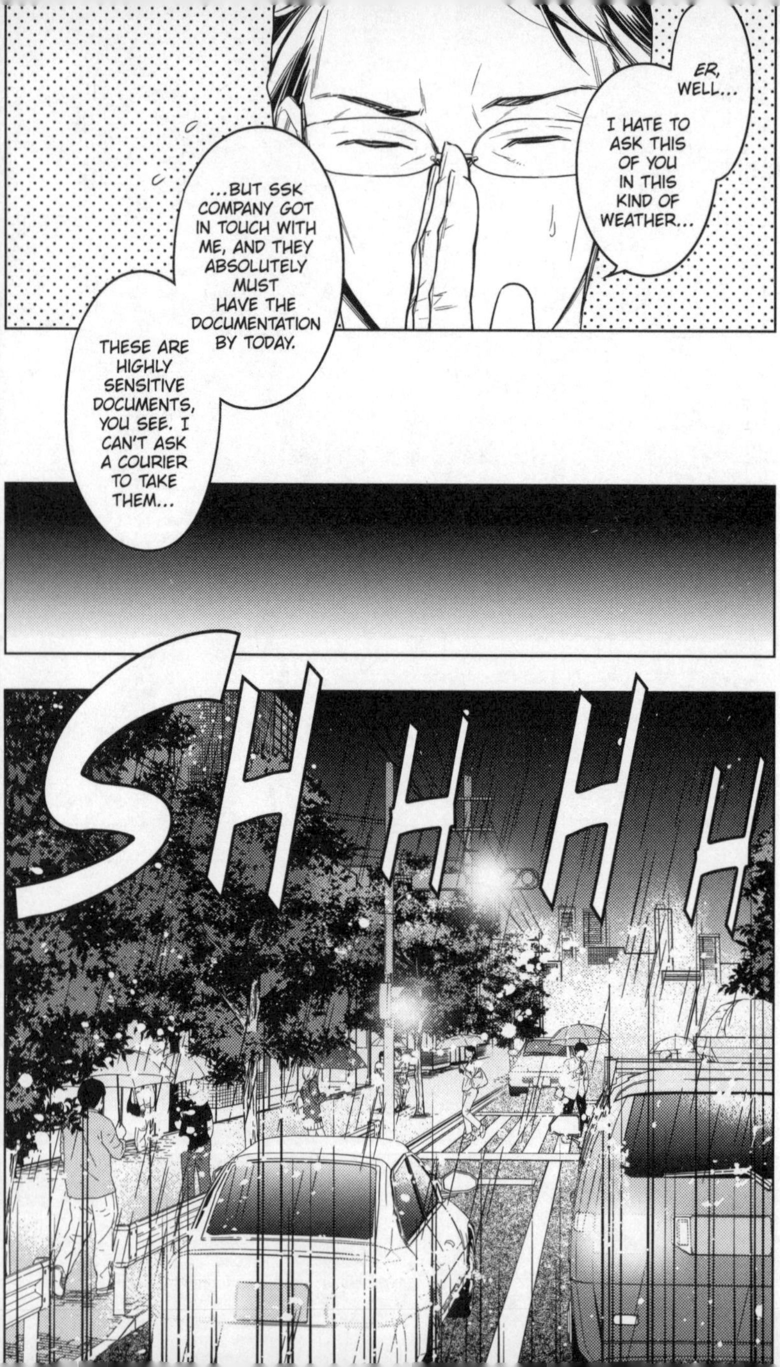
ER, WELL...
I HATE TO ASK THIS OF YOU IN THIS KIND OF WEATHER...
...BUT SSK COMPANY GOT IN TOUCH WITH ME, AND THEY ABSOLUTELY MUST HAVE THE DOCUMENTATION BY TODAY.
THESE ARE HIGHLY SENSITIVE DOCUMENTS, YOU SEE. I CAN'T ASK A COURIER TO TAKE THEM...
SHHHH

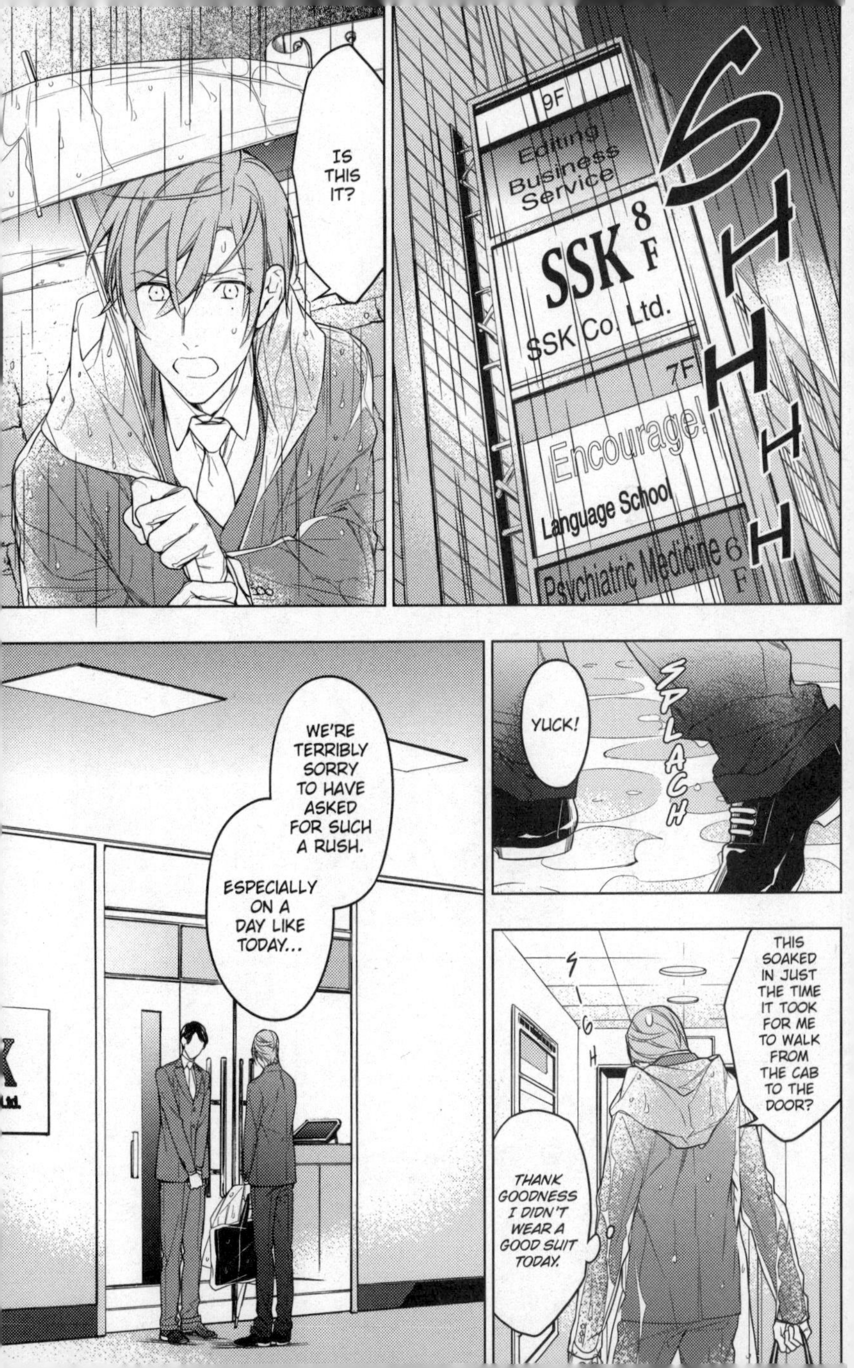
SHHHHH
9F
Editing Business Service
SSK 8F
SSK Co. Ltd.
7F
Encourage!
Language School
Psychiatric Medicine 6F
IS THIS IT?
SPLACH
YUCK!
SIGH
THIS SOAKED IN JUST THE TIME IT TOOK FOR ME TO WALK FROM THE CAB TO THE DOOR?
THANK GOODNESS I DIDN'T WEAR A GOOD SUIT TODAY.
WE'RE TERRIBLY SORRY TO HAVE ASKED FOR SUCH A RUSH.
ESPECIALLY ON A DAY LIKE TODAY...

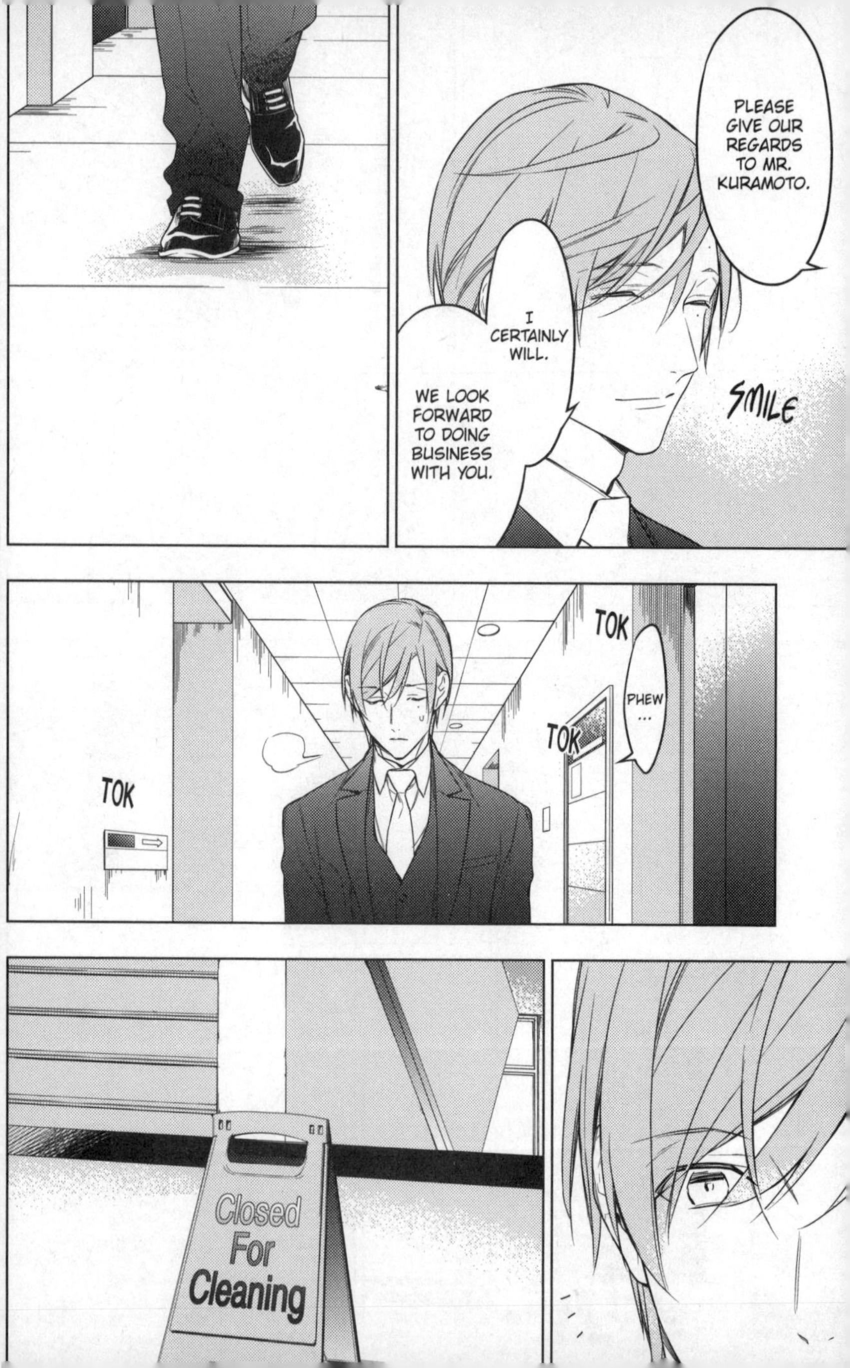
PLEASE GIVE OUR REGARDS TO MR. KURAMOTO.
SMILE
I CERTAINLY WILL.
WE LOOK FORWARD TO DOING BUSINESS WITH YOU.
TOK
PHEW ...
TOK
TOK
Closed For Cleaning

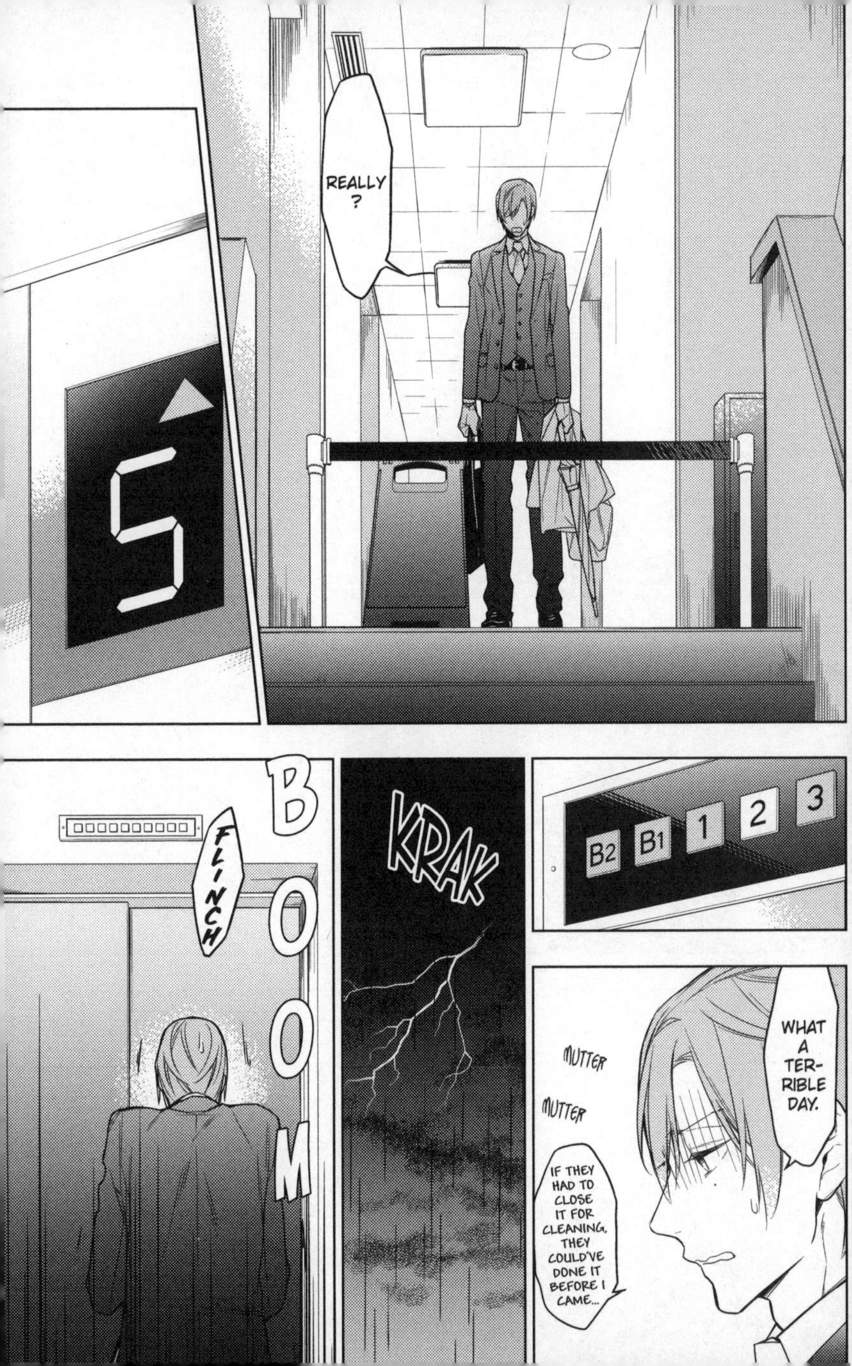
REALLY ?
B2 B1 1 2 3
WHAT A TER-RIBLE DAY.
MUTTER
MUTTER
IF THEY HAD TO CLOSE IT FOR CLEANING, THEY COULD'VE DONE IT BEFORE I CAME...
KRAK
BOOM
FLINCH

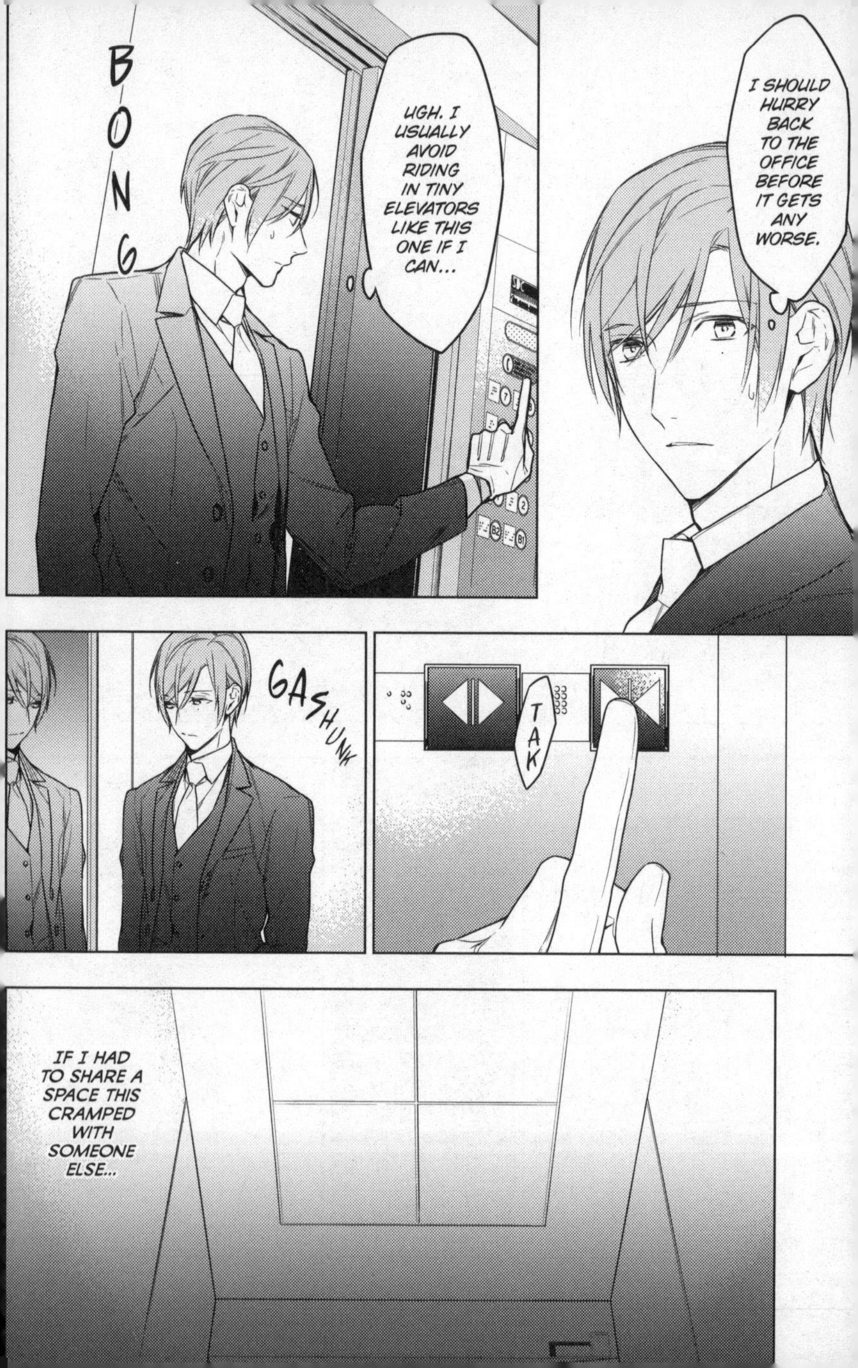
I SHOULD HURRY BACK TO THE OFFICE BEFORE IT GETS ANY WORSE.
BONG
UGH. I USUALLY AVOID RIDING IN TINY ELEVATORS LIKE THIS ONE IF I CAN...
TAK
GASHUNK
IF I HAD TO SHARE A SPACE THIS CRAMPED WITH SOMEONE ELSE...

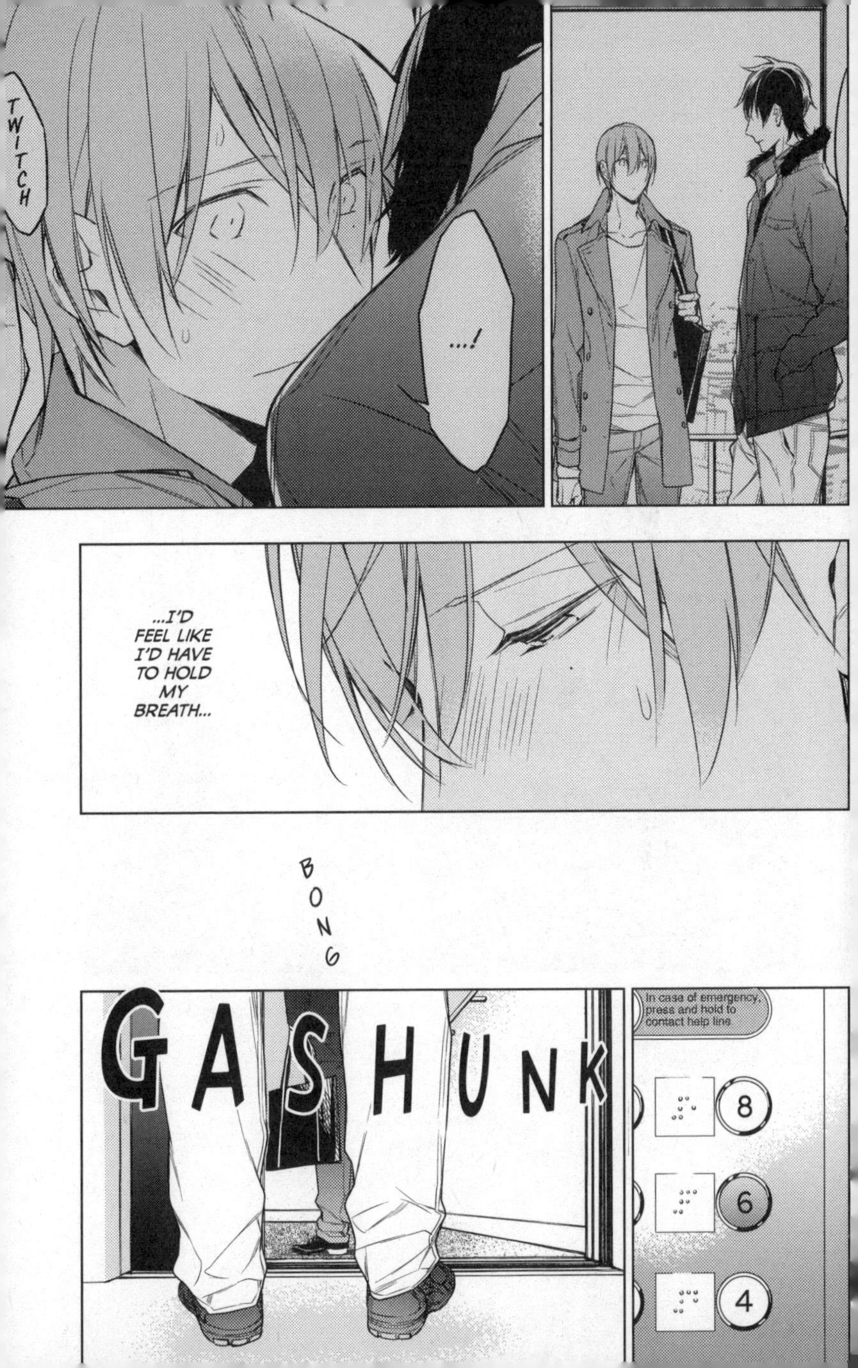
...!
TWITCH
...I'D FEEL LIKE I'D HAVE TO HOLD MY BREATH...
BONG
In case of emergency, press and hold to contact help line
8
6
4
GASHUNK

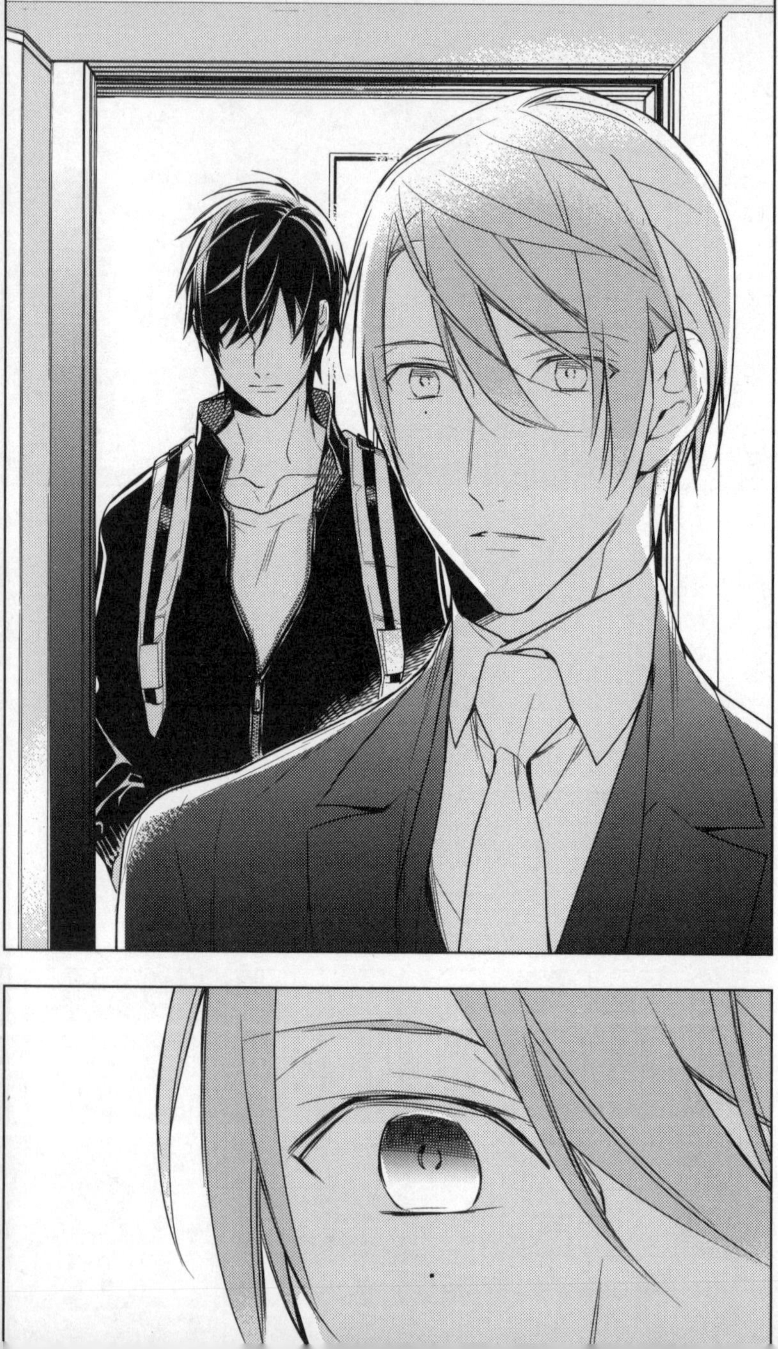

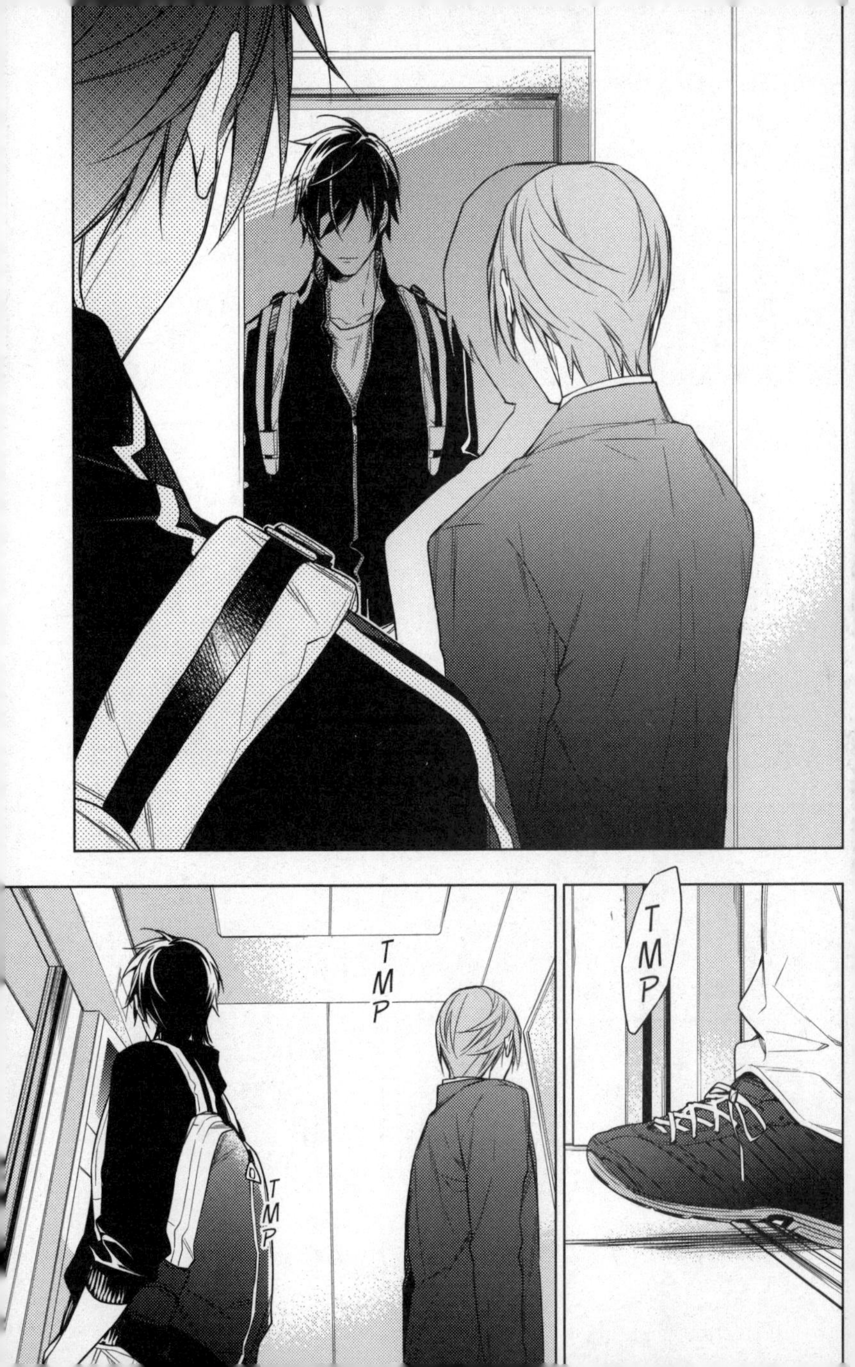
TMP
TMP
TMP

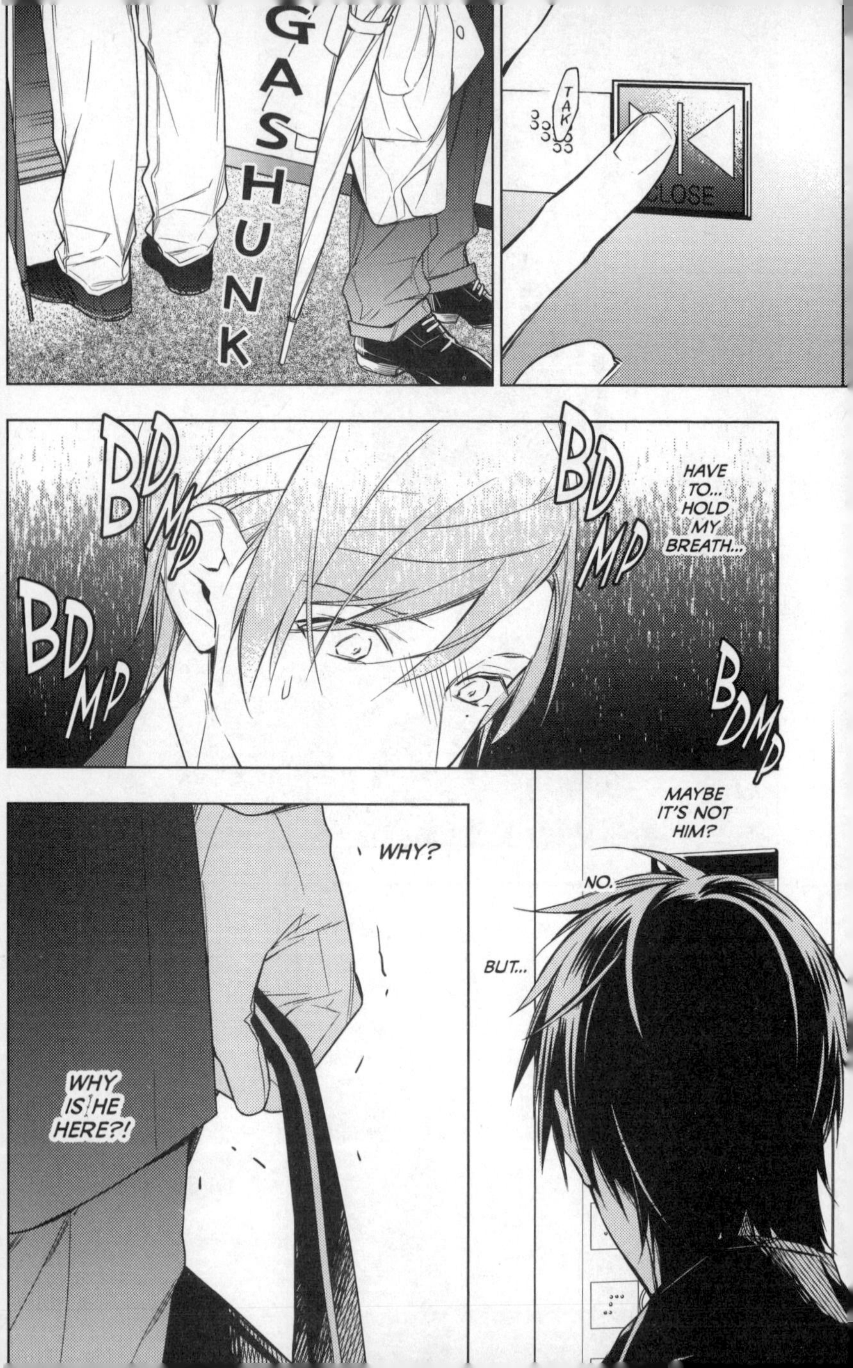
TAK
CLOSE
GASHUNK
BDMP
HAVE TO... HOLD MY BREATH...
BDMP
BDMP
BDMP
MAYBE IT'S NOT HIM?
NO.
BUT...
WHY?
WHY IS HE HERE?!

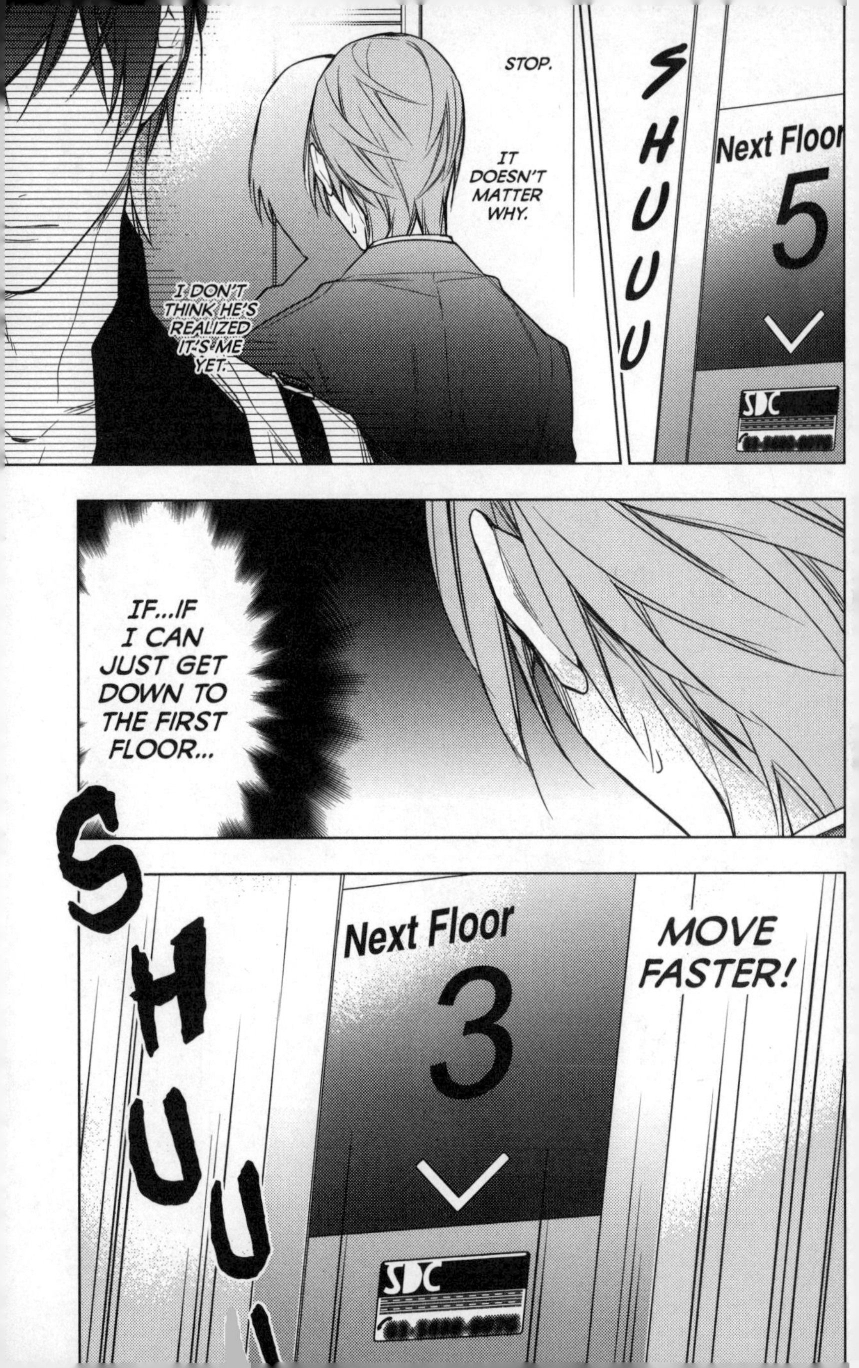
Next Floor
5
SDC
SHUUU
STOP.
IT DOESN'T MATTER WHY.
I DON'T THINK HE'S REALIZED IT'S ME YET.
IF...IF I CAN JUST GET DOWN TO THE FIRST FLOOR...
MOVE FASTER!
Next Floor
3
SDC
SHUU

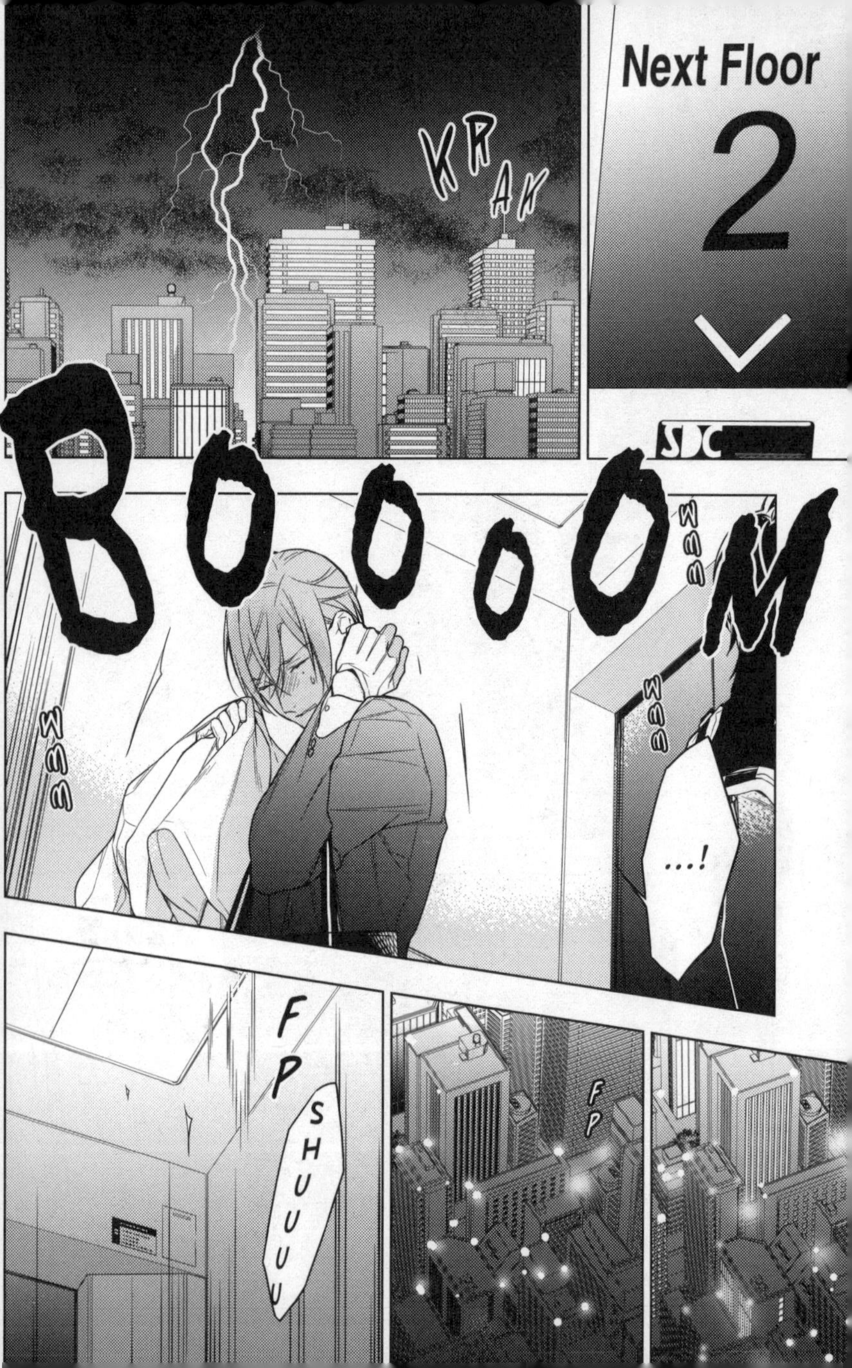
Next Floor
2
SDC
KRAK
BOOOOM
WMM
WMM
...!
WMM
FP
FP
FP
SHUUUUU

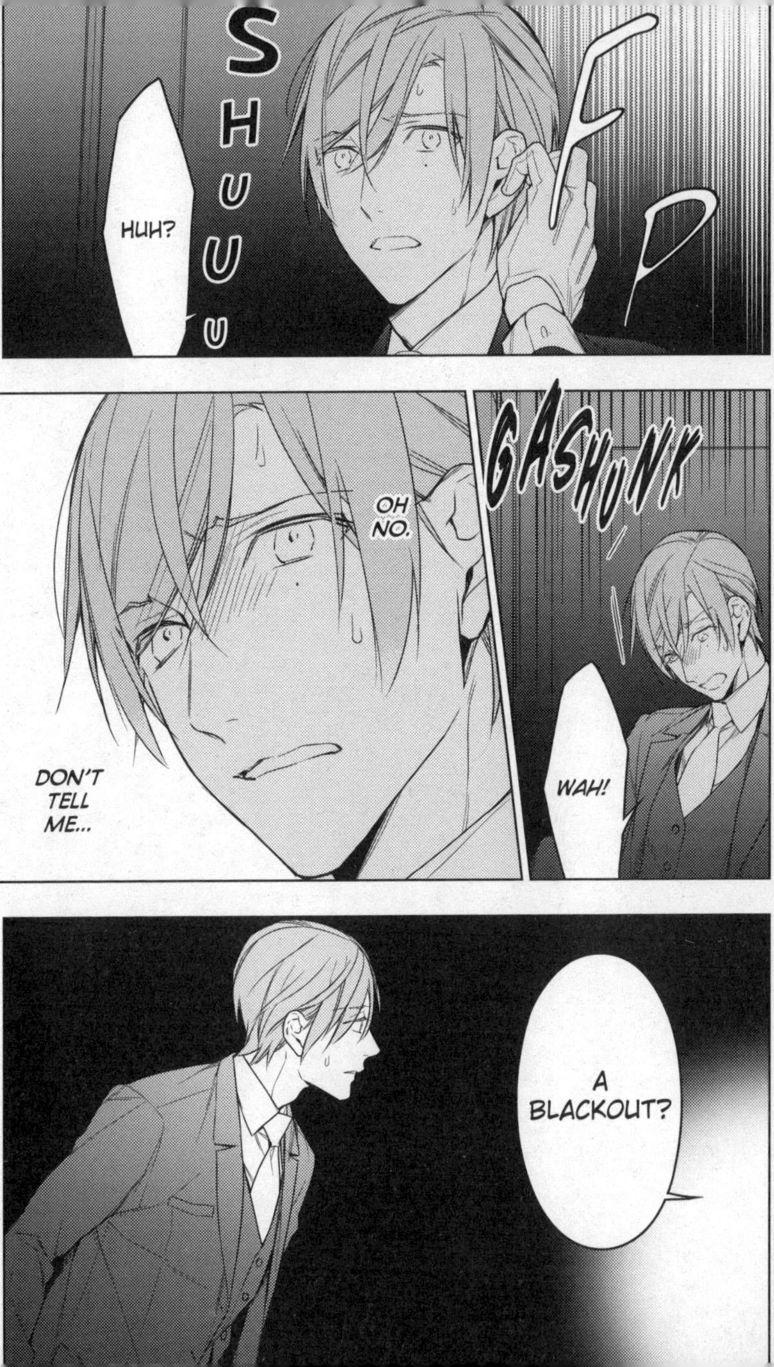
FP
SHUUUU
HUH?
GASHUNK
WAH!
OH NO.
DON'T TELL ME...
A BLACKOUT?

t
e
n

c
o
u
n
t

b
y

r
i
h
i
t
o

t
a
k
a
r
a
i

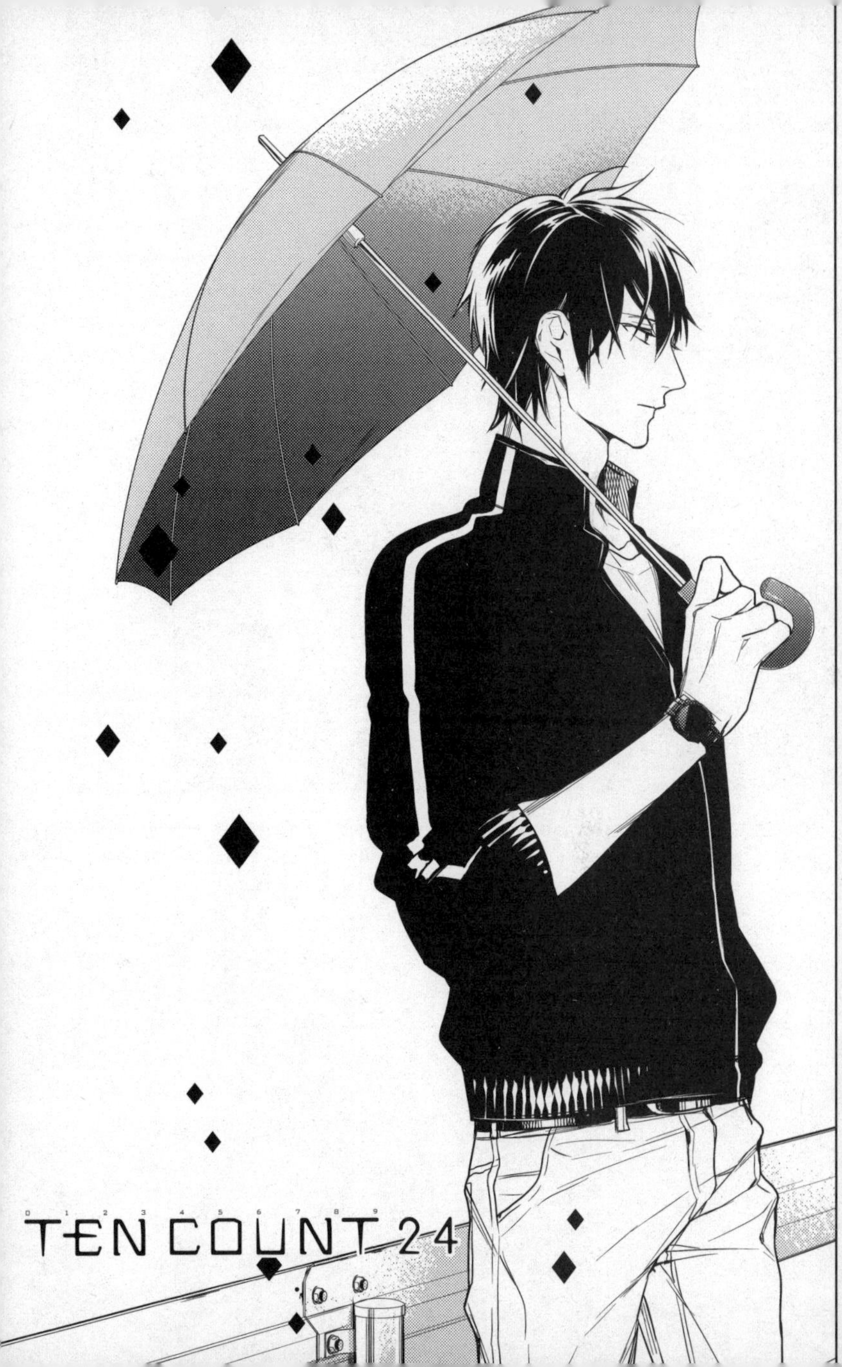
0 1 2 3 4 5 6 7 8 9
TEN COUNT 24

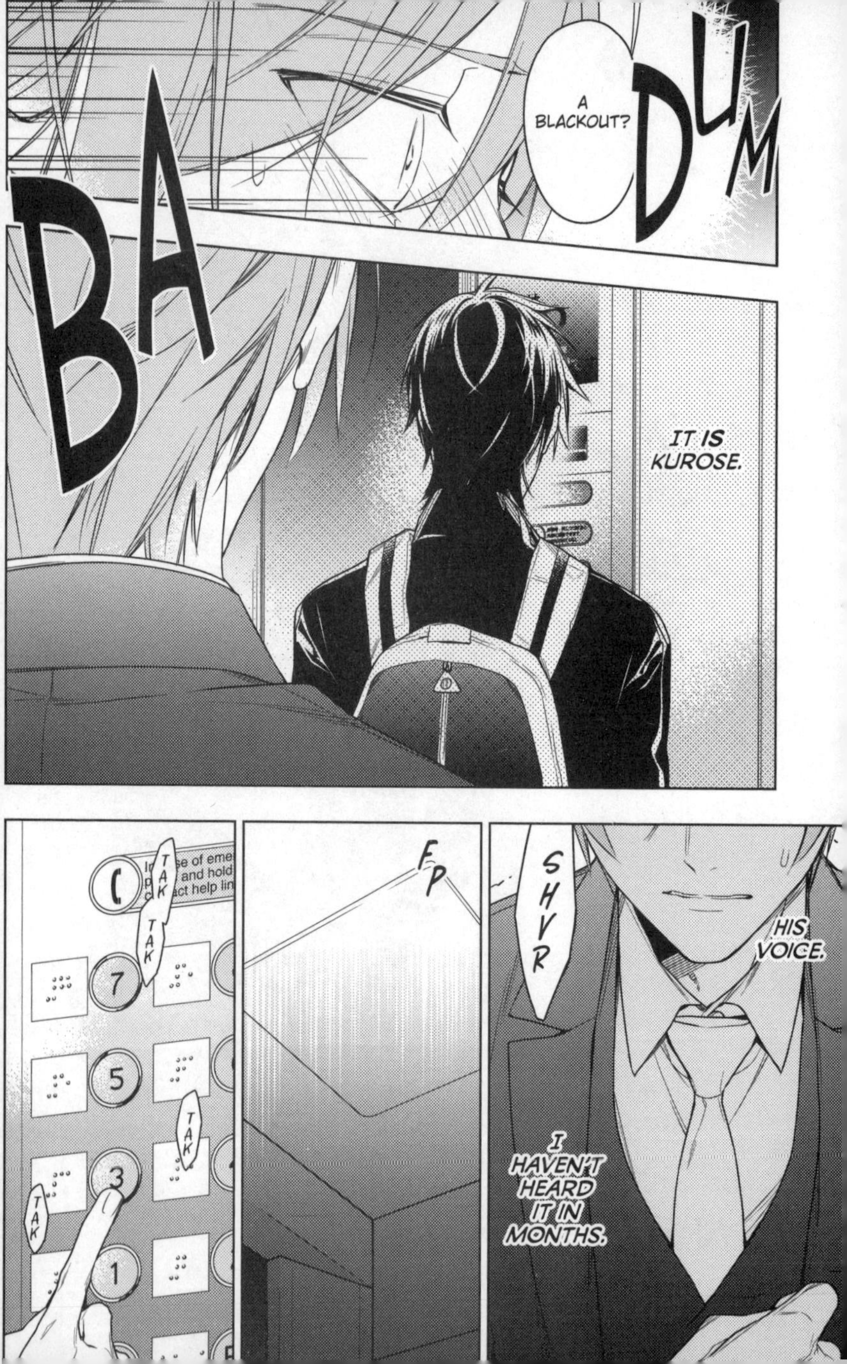
A BLACKOUT?
BA DUM
IT IS KUROSE.
SHVR
HIS VOICE.
I HAVEN'T HEARD IT IN MONTHS.
FP
TAK
TAK
TAK
TAK

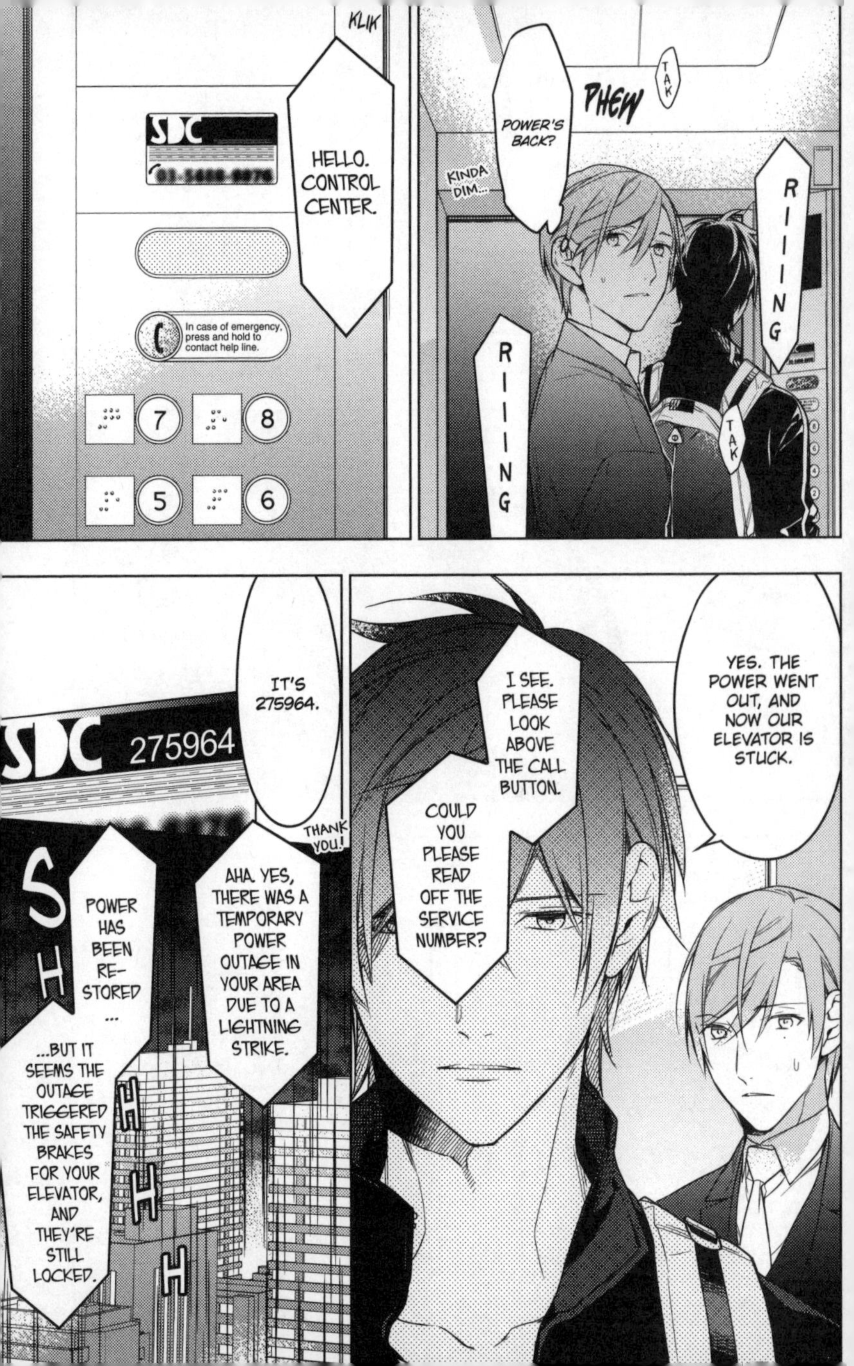

TAK
PHEW
POWER'S BACK?
KINDA DIM...
RIIING
TAK
RIIING
KLIK
HELLO. CONTROL CENTER.
SDC
In case of emergency, press and hold to contact help line.
7
8
5
6
YES. THE POWER WENT OUT, AND NOW OUR ELEVATOR IS STUCK.
I SEE. PLEASE LOOK ABOVE THE CALL BUTTON.
COULD YOU PLEASE READ OFF THE SERVICE NUMBER?
IT'S 275964.
SDC 275964
THANK YOU!
AHA. YES, THERE WAS A TEMPORARY POWER OUTAGE IN YOUR AREA DUE TO A LIGHTNING STRIKE.
POWER HAS BEEN RE-STORED...
...BUT IT SEEMS THE OUTAGE TRIGGERED THE SAFETY BRAKES FOR YOUR ELEVATOR, AND THEY'RE STILL LOCKED.
SHHHHH

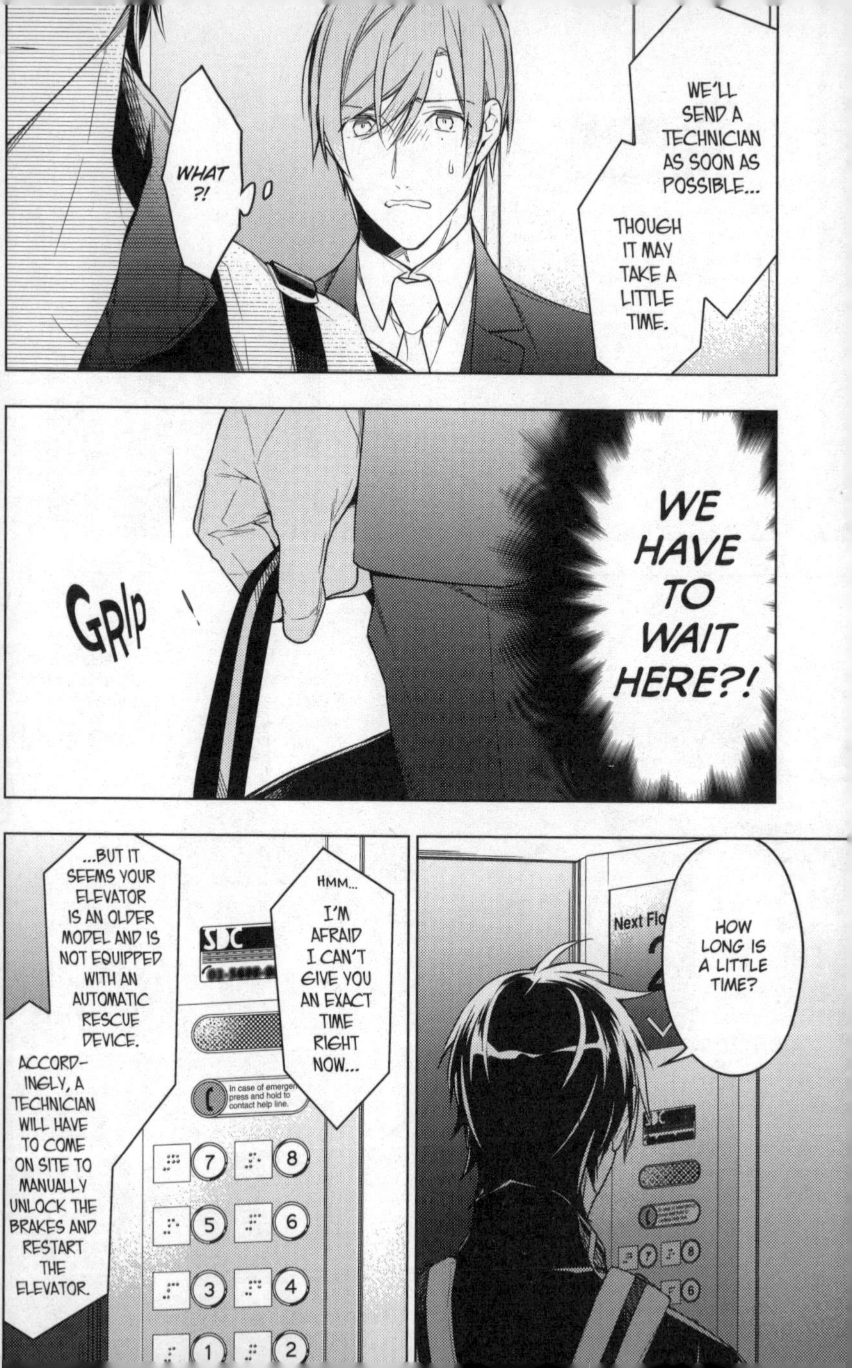
WE'LL SEND A TECHNICIAN AS SOON AS POSSIBLE...
THOUGH IT MAY TAKE A LITTLE TIME.
WHAT ?!
WE HAVE TO WAIT HERE?!
GRIP
Next Flo
HOW LONG IS A LITTLE TIME?
HMM... I'M AFRAID I CAN'T GIVE YOU AN EXACT TIME RIGHT NOW...
...BUT IT SEEMS YOUR ELEVATOR IS AN OLDER MODEL AND IS NOT EQUIPPED WITH AN AUTOMATIC RESCUE DEVICE.
ACCORD-INGLY, A TECHNICIAN WILL HAVE TO COME ON SITE TO MANUALLY UNLOCK THE BRAKES AND RESTART THE ELEVATOR.
SDC
In case of emergen press and hold to contact help line.

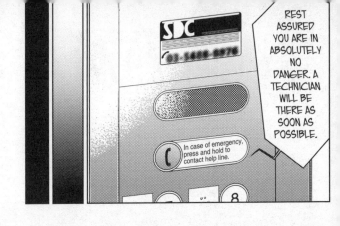

REST ASSURED YOU ARE IN ABSOLUTELY NO DANGER. A TECHNICIAN WILL BE THERE AS SOON AS POSSIBLE.

In case of emergency, press and hold to contact help line.

SHHHH

RMBL

RMBL

RMBL

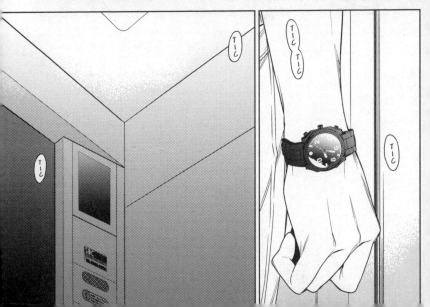

TIC

TIC

TIC TIC

TIC

TIC

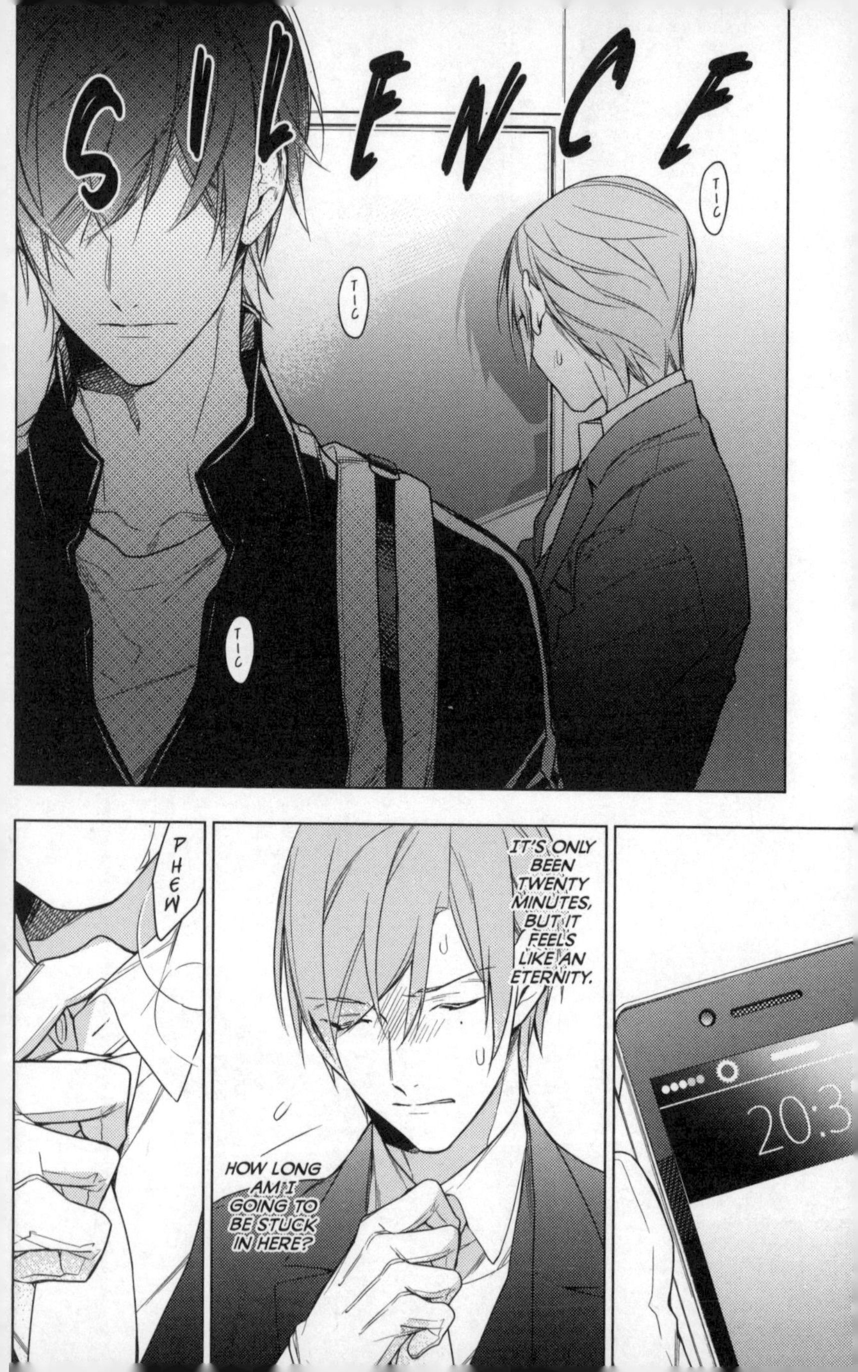
SILENCE
TIC
TIC
TIC
20:3
IT'S ONLY BEEN TWENTY MINUTES, BUT IT FEELS LIKE AN ETERNITY.
HOW LONG AM I GOING TO BE STUCK IN HERE?
PHEW

FLINCH

! BOOOM

RMBL
RMBL
RMBL

KRAK

HUFF

IT'S STARTING TO GET WARM.

AND STUFFY TOO. I THINK.

HUFF

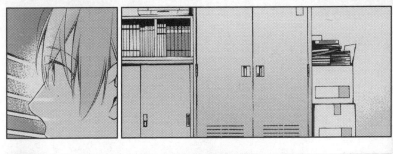

HUFF

...SHIRO-TANI?

HUFF

HUFF

ARE YOU ALL RIGHT...

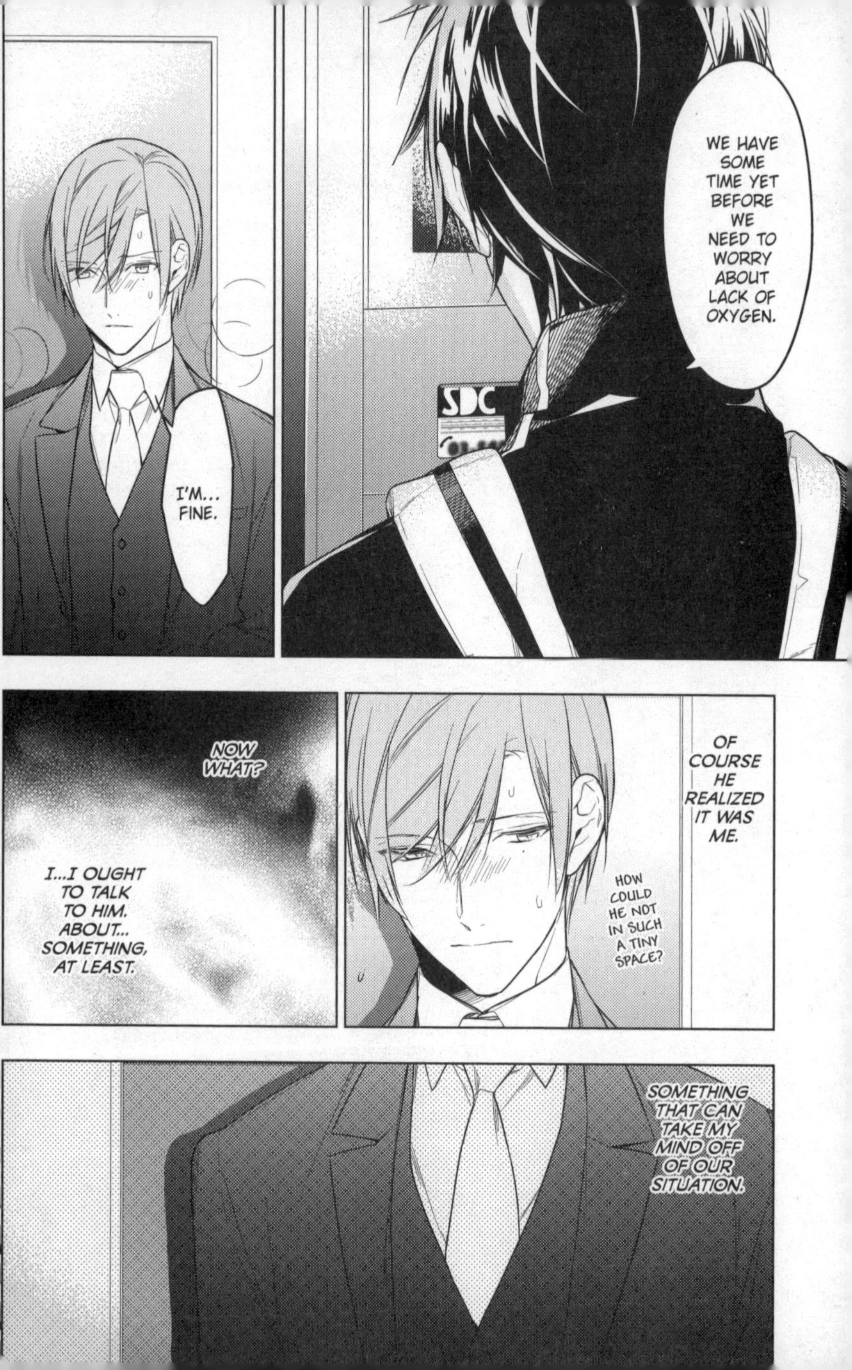
WE HAVE SOME TIME YET BEFORE WE NEED TO WORRY ABOUT LACK OF OXYGEN.
I'M... FINE.
OF COURSE HE REALIZED IT WAS ME.
HOW COULD HE NOT IN SUCH A TINY SPACE?
NOW WHAT?
I...I OUGHT TO TALK TO HIM. ABOUT... SOMETHING, AT LEAST.
SOMETHING THAT CAN TAKE MY MIND OFF OF OUR SITUATION.

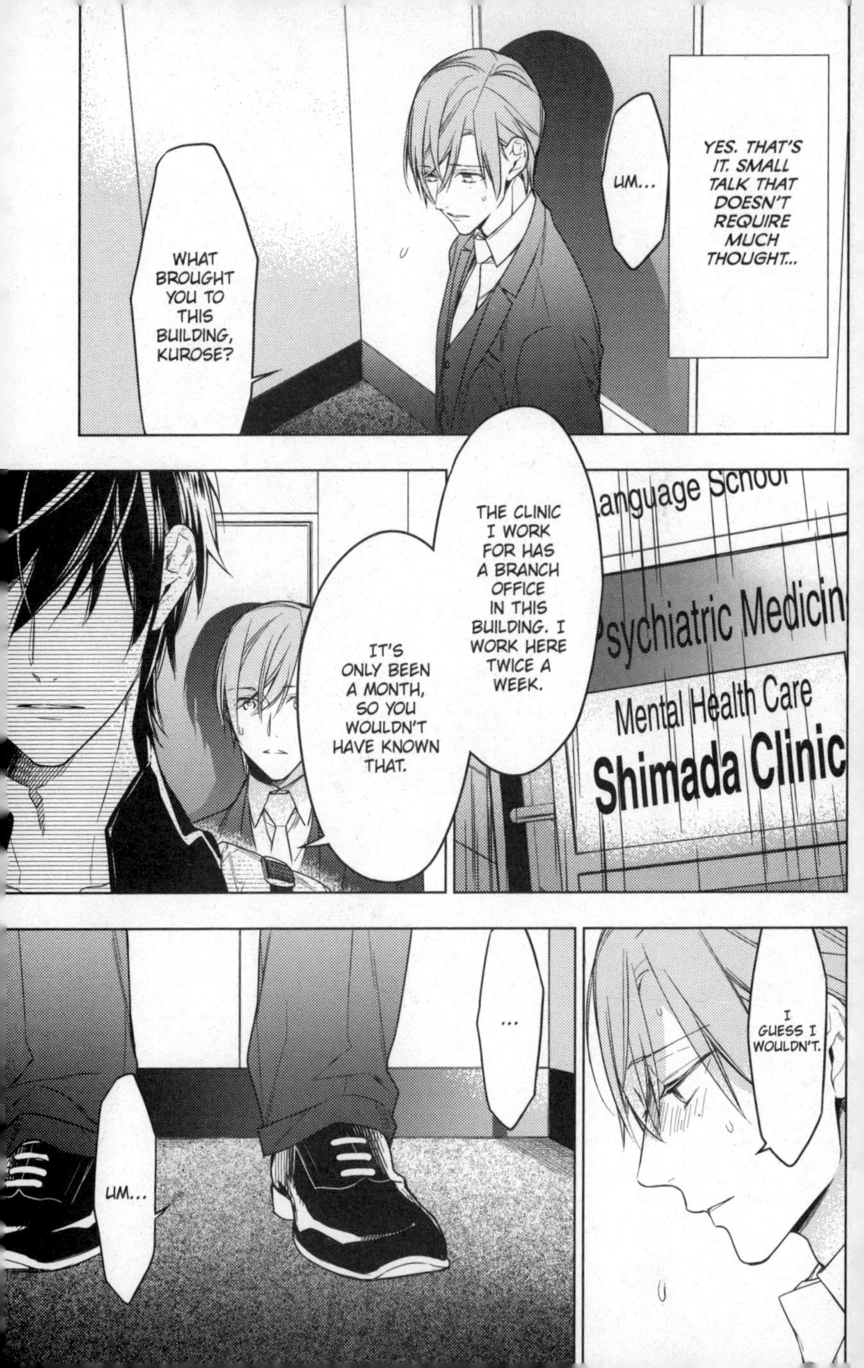
YES. THAT'S IT. SMALL TALK THAT DOESN'T REQUIRE MUCH THOUGHT...
UM...
WHAT BROUGHT YOU TO THIS BUILDING, KUROSE?
Language School
Psychiatric Medicin
Mental Health Care
Shimada Clinic
THE CLINIC I WORK FOR HAS A BRANCH OFFICE IN THIS BUILDING. I WORK HERE TWICE A WEEK.
IT'S ONLY BEEN A MONTH, SO YOU WOULDN'T HAVE KNOWN THAT.
I GUESS I WOULDN'T.
...
UM...

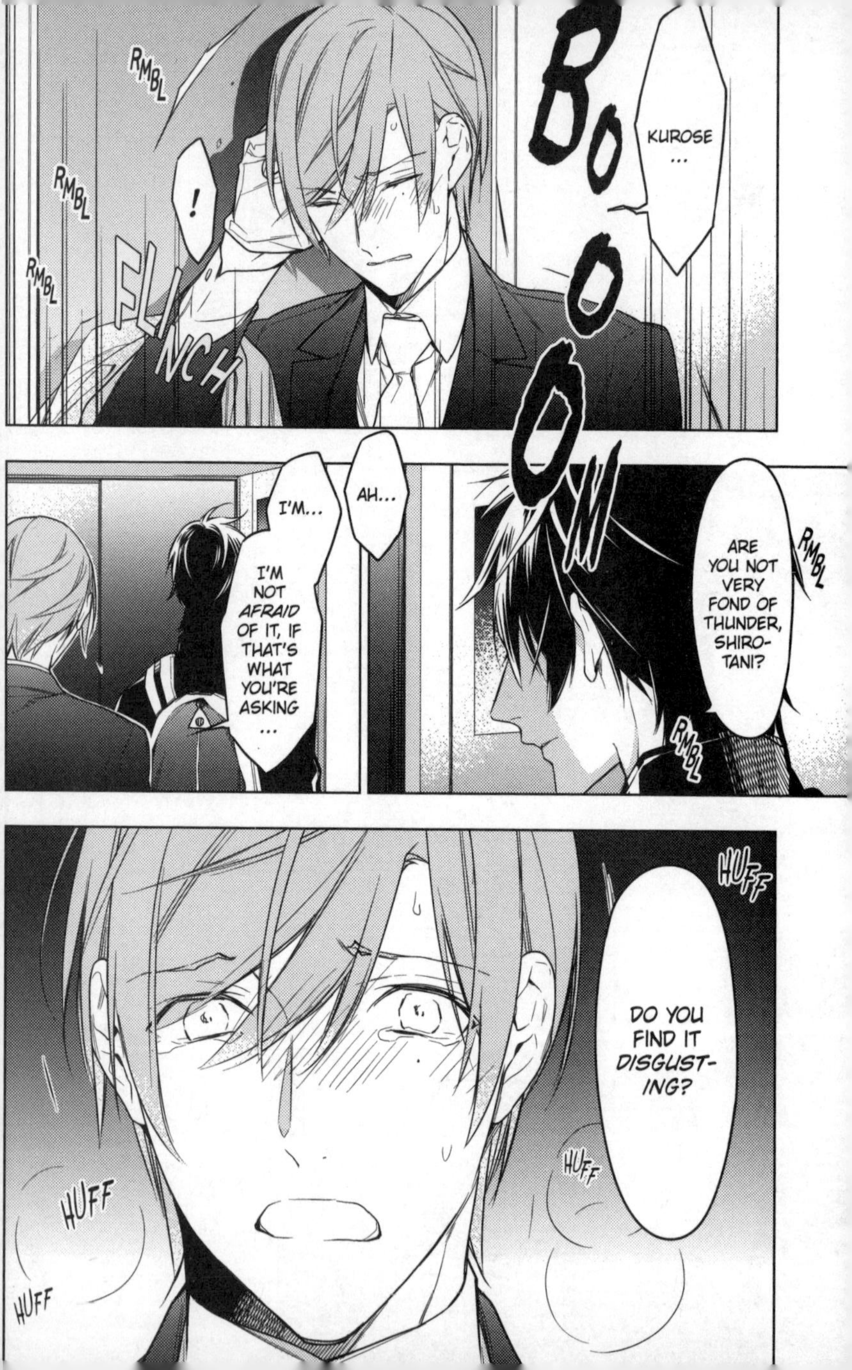
KUROSE ...
BOOOOM
!
FLINCH
RMBL
RMBL
RMBL
ARE YOU NOT VERY FOND OF THUNDER, SHIRO-TANI?
RMBL
RMBL
AH...
I'M...
I'M NOT AFRAID OF IT, IF THAT'S WHAT YOU'RE ASKING ...
HUFF
DO YOU FIND IT DISGUST-ING?
HUFF
HUFF
HUFF

KU-ROSE
...

KU
...

KU-RO
...

UM
...

I-I'M SORRY, BUT...

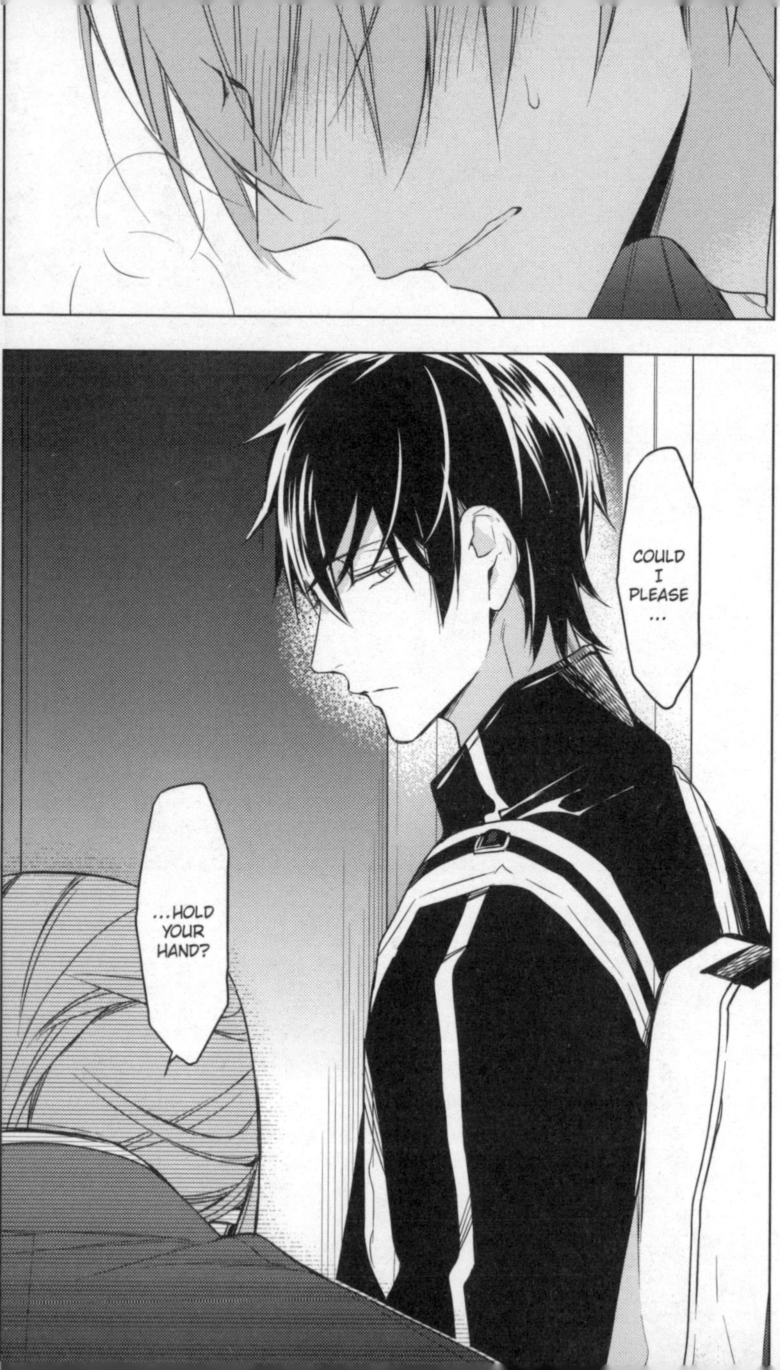
COULD I PLEASE ...
...HOLD YOUR HAND?

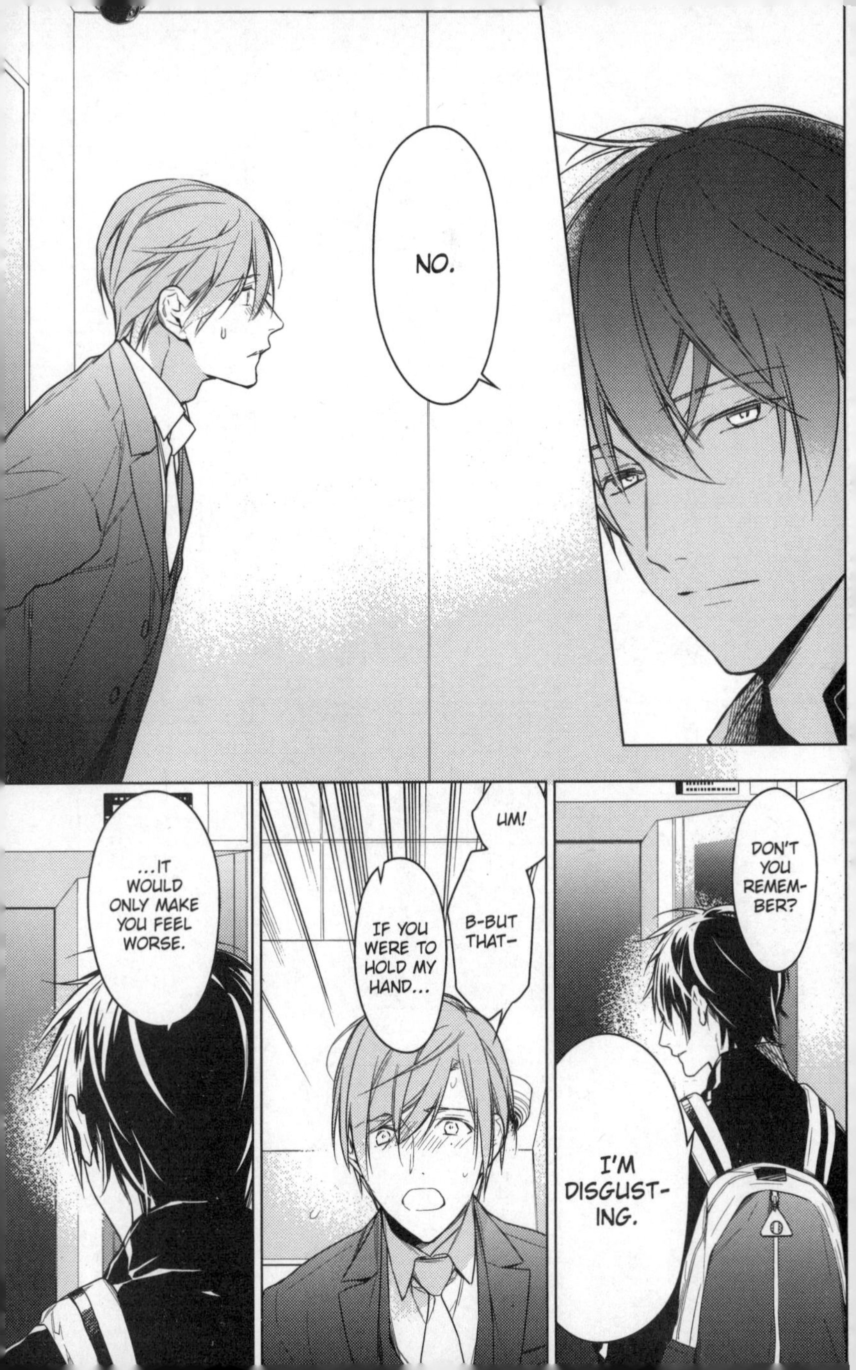
NO.
DON'T YOU REMEMBER?
I'M DISGUST-ING.
UM!
B-BUT THAT-
IF YOU WERE TO HOLD MY HAND...
...IT WOULD ONLY MAKE YOU FEEL WORSE.

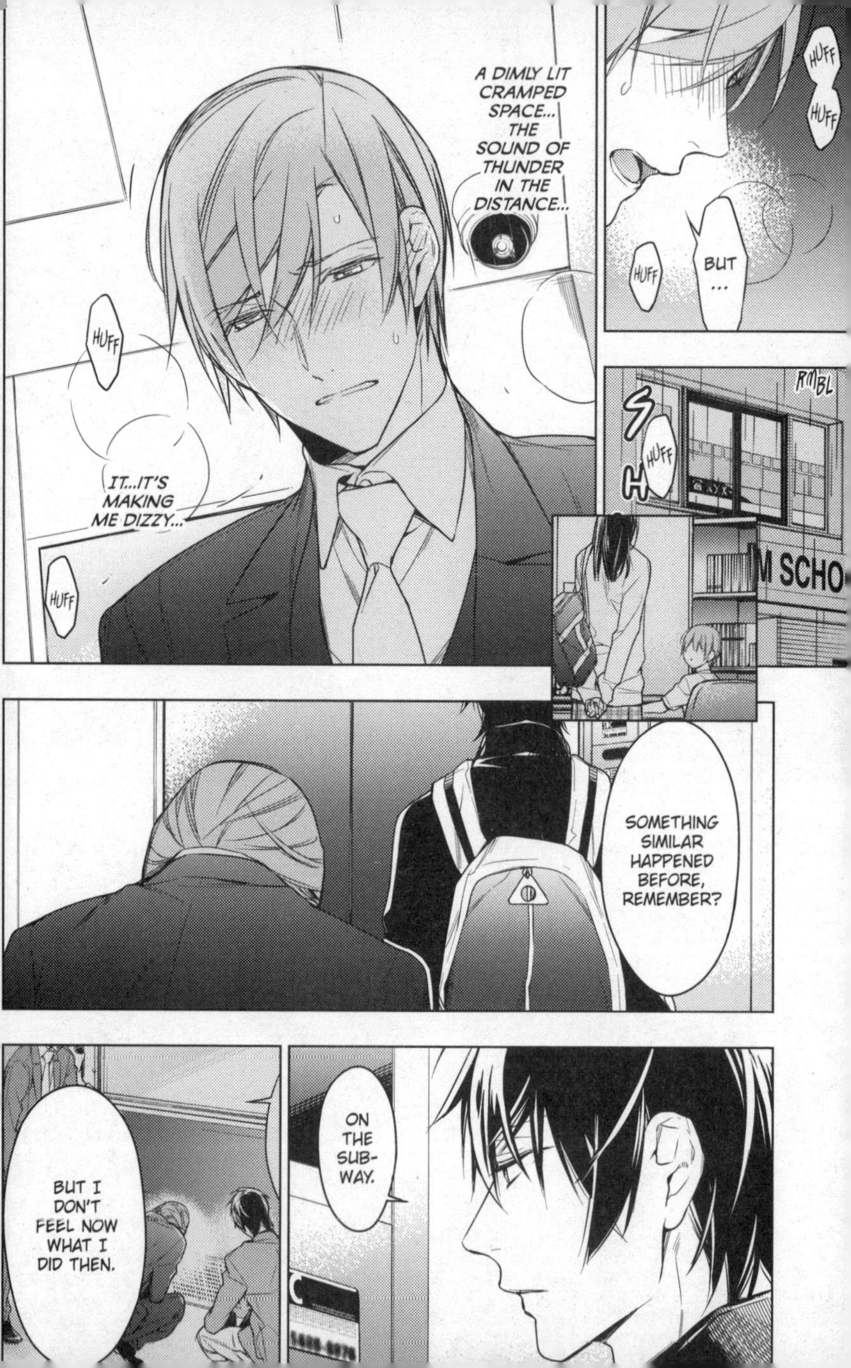
HUFF
HUFF
HUFF
BUT...
A DIMLY LIT CRAMPED SPACE... THE SOUND OF THUNDER IN THE DISTANCE...
HUFF
IT...IT'S MAKING ME DIZZY...
HUFF
RMBL
SH
HUFF
M SCHO
SOMETHING SIMILAR HAPPENED BEFORE, REMEMBER?
ON THE SUBWAY.
BUT I DON'T FEEL NOW WHAT I DID THEN.

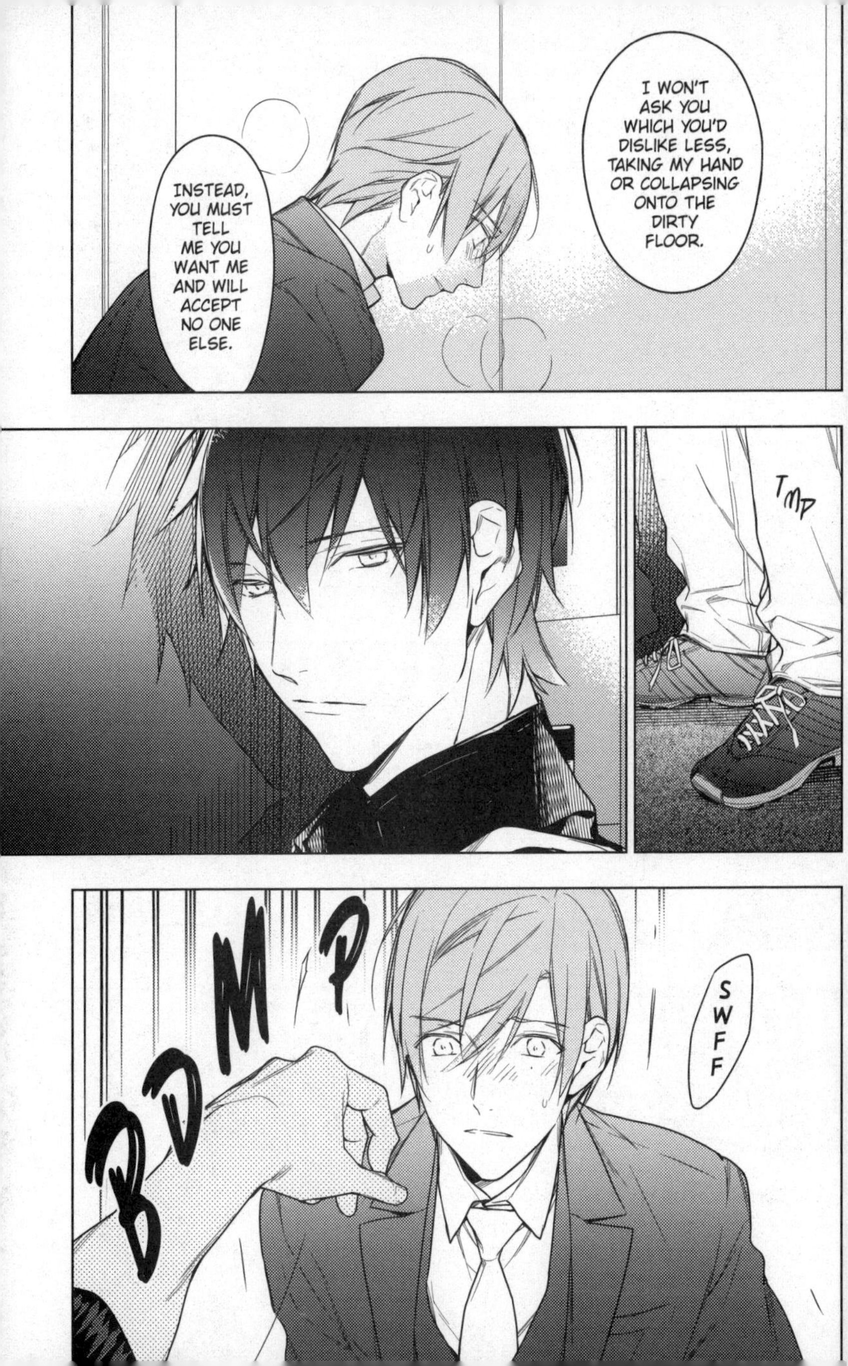
I WON'T ASK YOU WHICH YOU'D DISLIKE LESS, TAKING MY HAND OR COLLAPSING ONTO THE DIRTY FLOOR.
INSTEAD, YOU MUST TELL ME YOU WANT ME AND WILL ACCEPT NO ONE ELSE.
TMP
SWFF
BDMP

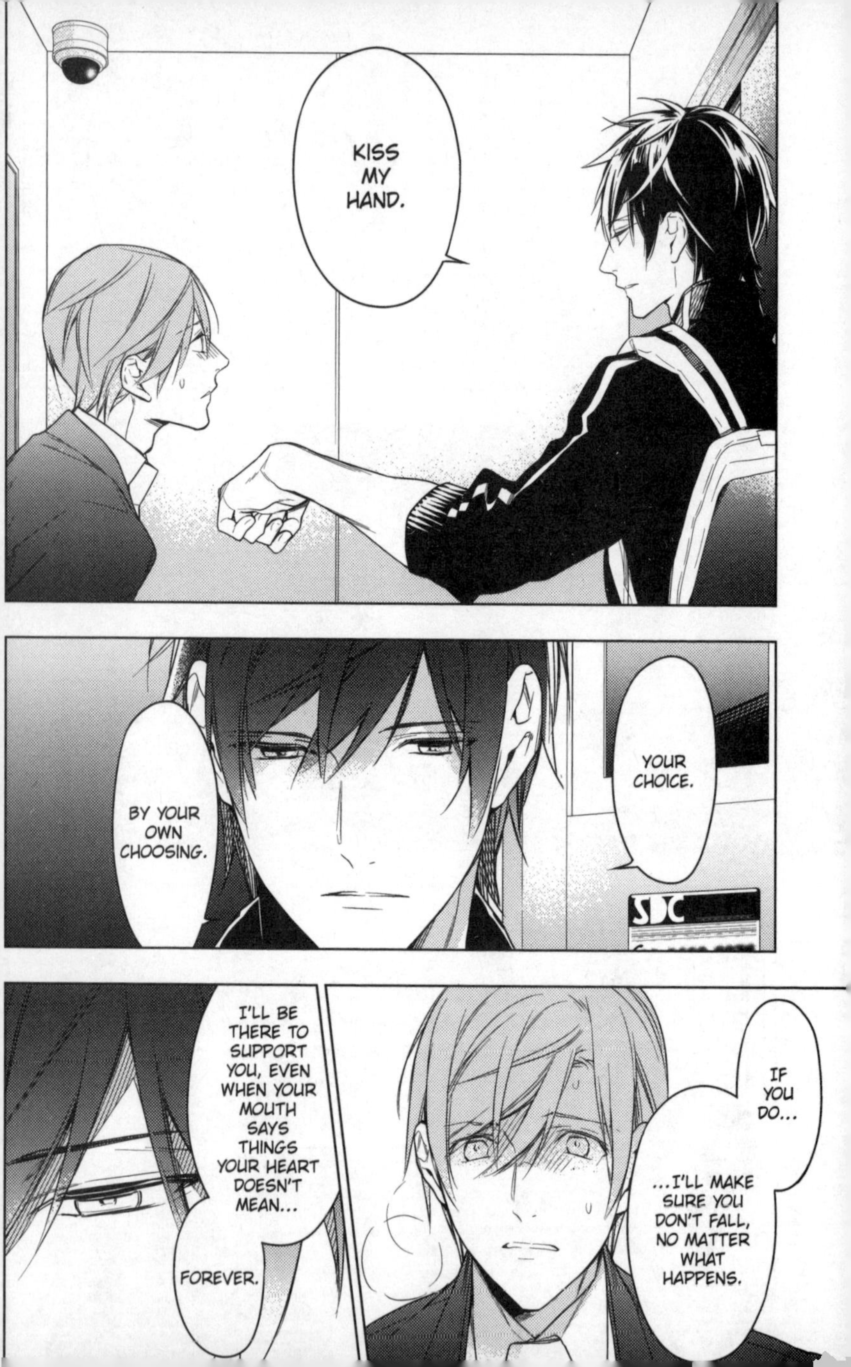
KISS MY HAND.
YOUR CHOICE.
SDC
BY YOUR OWN CHOOSING.
IF YOU DO...
...I'LL MAKE SURE YOU DON'T FALL, NO MATTER WHAT HAPPENS.
I'LL BE THERE TO SUPPORT YOU, EVEN WHEN YOUR MOUTH SAYS THINGS YOUR HEART DOESN'T MEAN...
FOREVER.

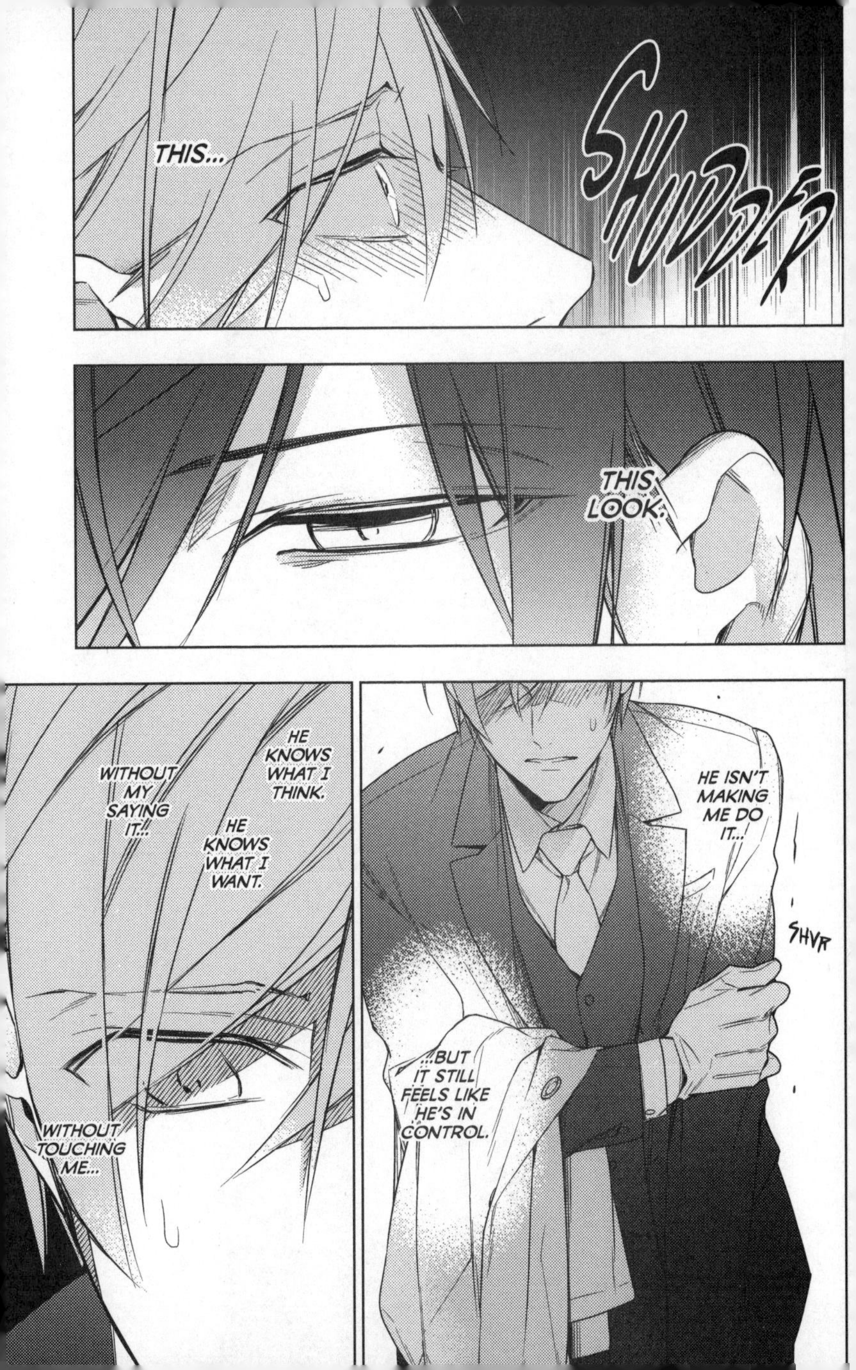
SHUDDER
THIS...
THIS LOOK.
HE ISN'T MAKING ME DO IT...
SHVR
...BUT IT STILL FEELS LIKE HE'S IN CONTROL.
HE KNOWS WHAT I THINK.
WITHOUT MY SAYING IT...
HE KNOWS WHAT I WANT.
WITHOUT TOUCHING ME...

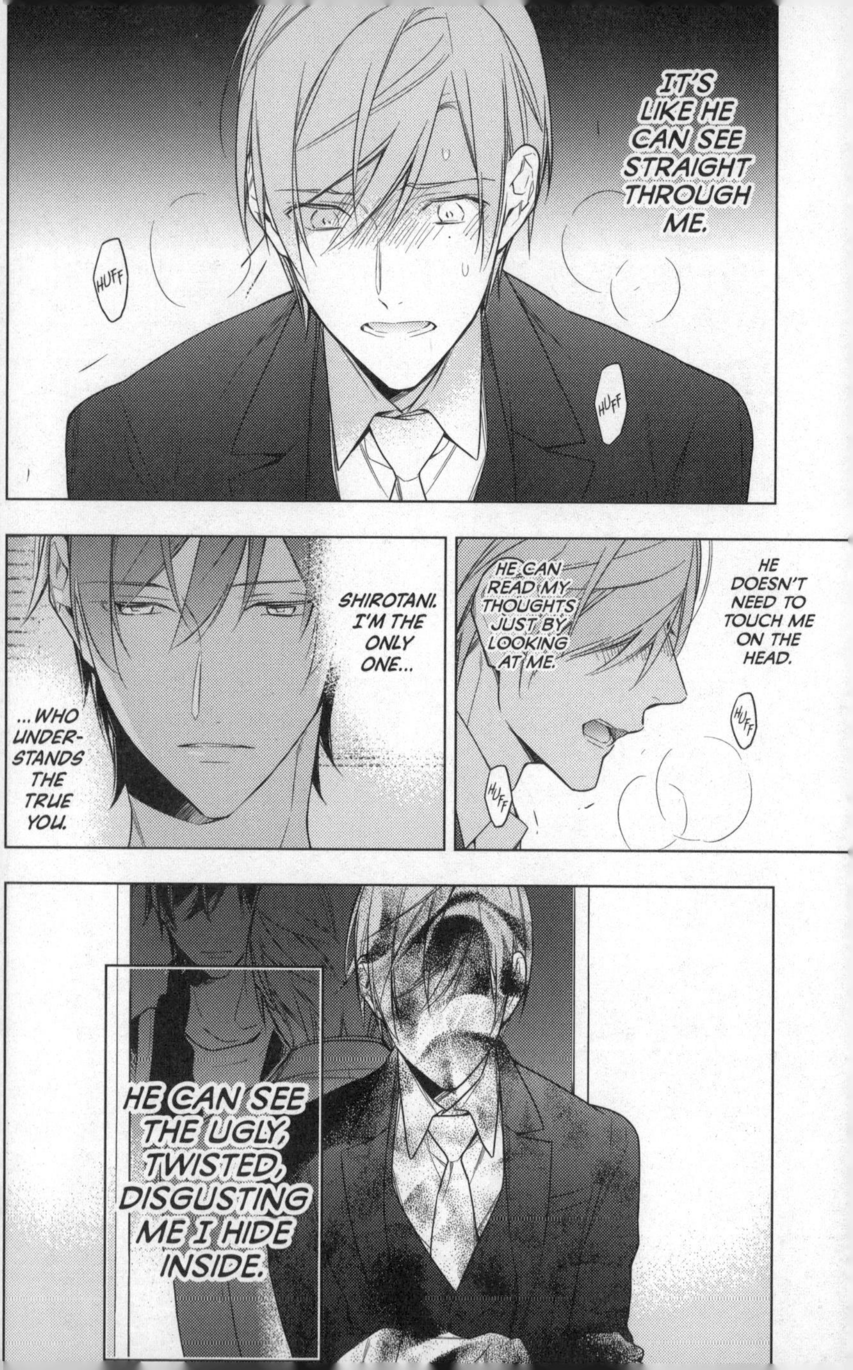
IT'S LIKE HE CAN SEE STRAIGHT THROUGH ME.
HUFF
HUFF
HE DOESN'T NEED TO TOUCH ME ON THE HEAD.
HE CAN READ MY THOUGHTS JUST BY LOOKING AT ME.
HUFF
HUFF
SHIROTANI. I'M THE ONLY ONE...
...WHO UNDER-STANDS THE TRUE YOU.
HE CAN SEE THE UGLY, TWISTED, DISGUSTING ME I HIDE INSIDE.

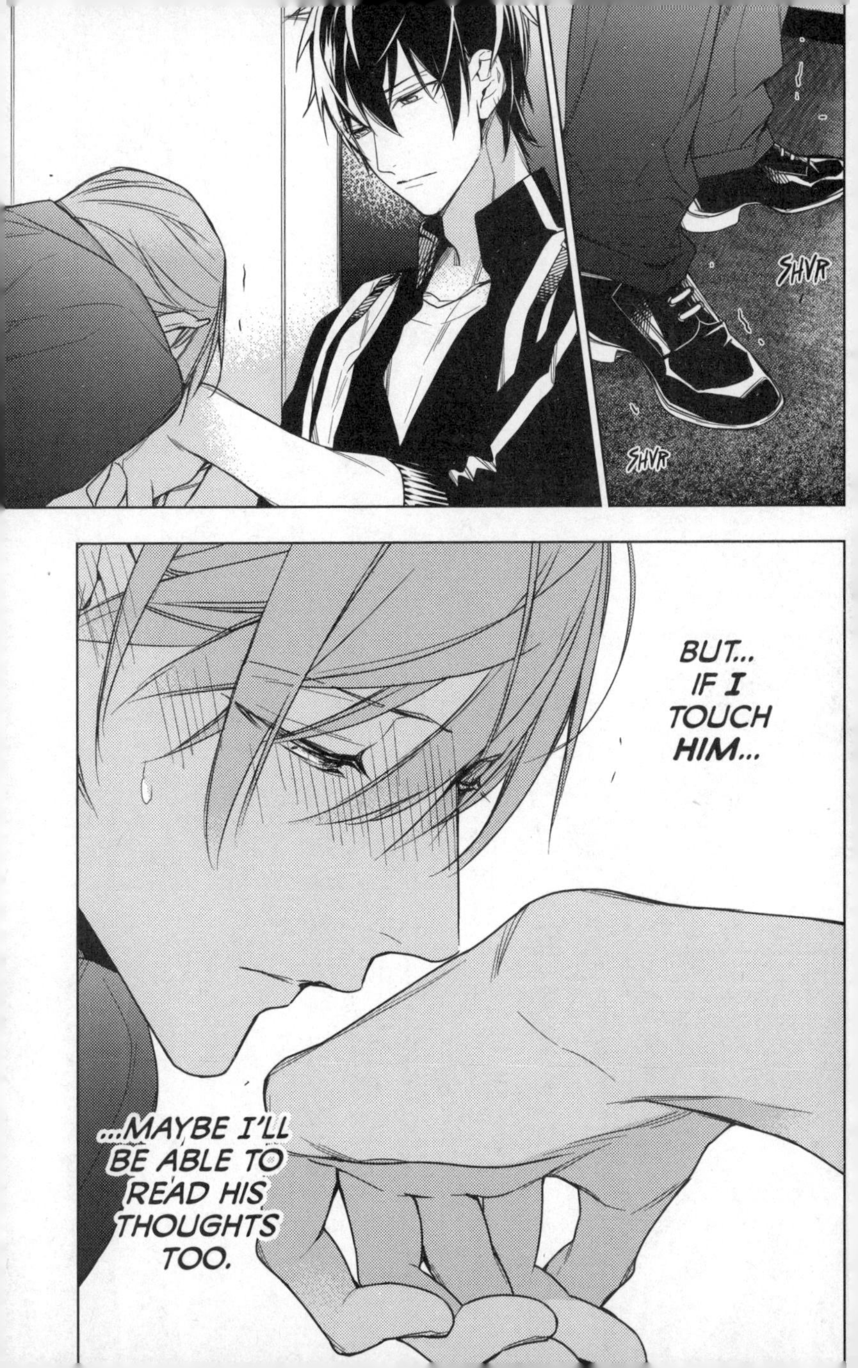
SHVR
SHVR
BUT... IF I TOUCH HIM...
...MAYBE I'LL BE ABLE TO READ HIS THOUGHTS TOO.

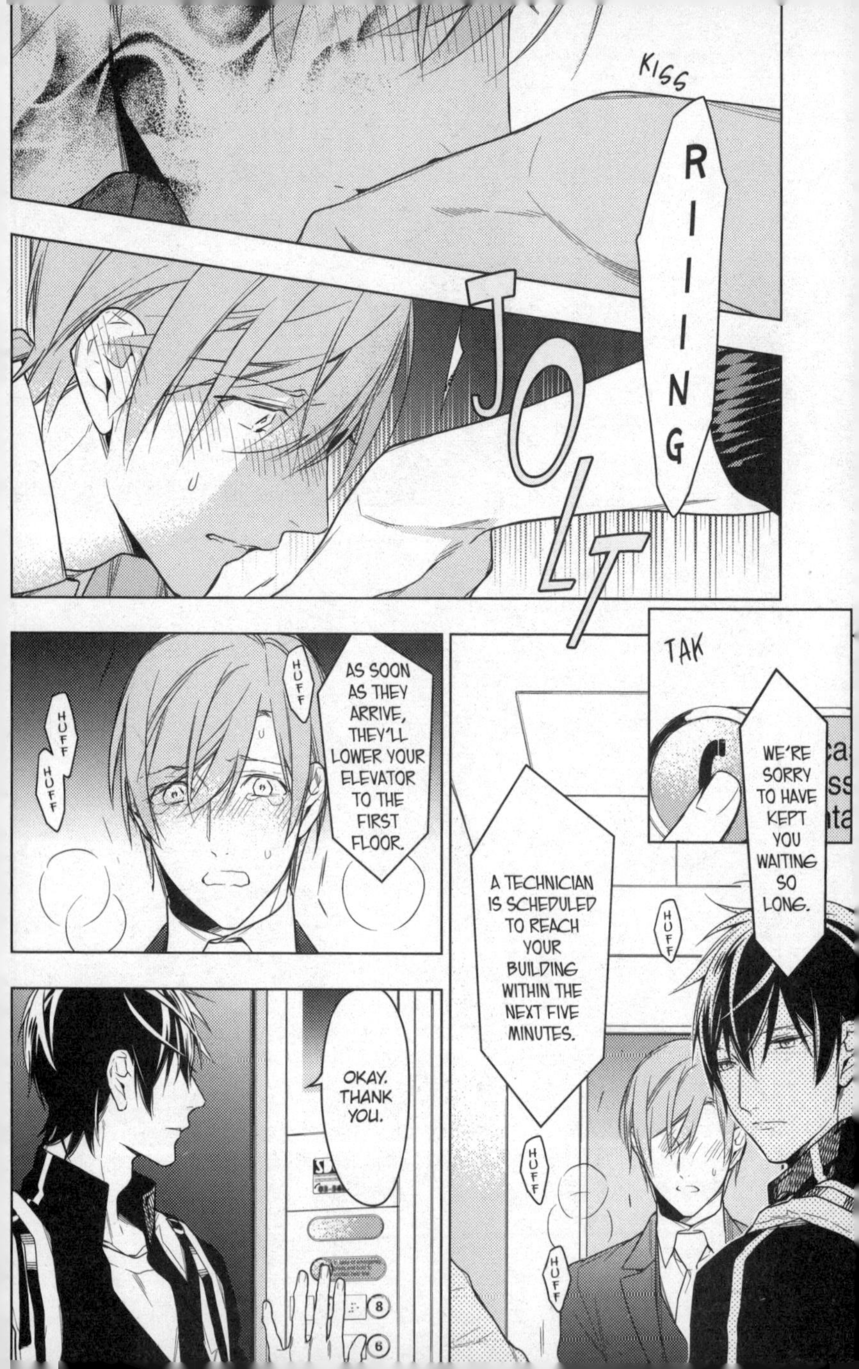
KISS
RIIING
JOLT
TAK
WE'RE SORRY TO HAVE KEPT YOU WAITING SO LONG.
A TECHNICIAN IS SCHEDULED TO REACH YOUR BUILDING WITHIN THE NEXT FIVE MINUTES.
HUFF
HUFF
HUFF
AS SOON AS THEY ARRIVE, THEY'LL LOWER YOUR ELEVATOR TO THE FIRST FLOOR.
HUFF
HUFF HUFF
OKAY. THANK YOU.

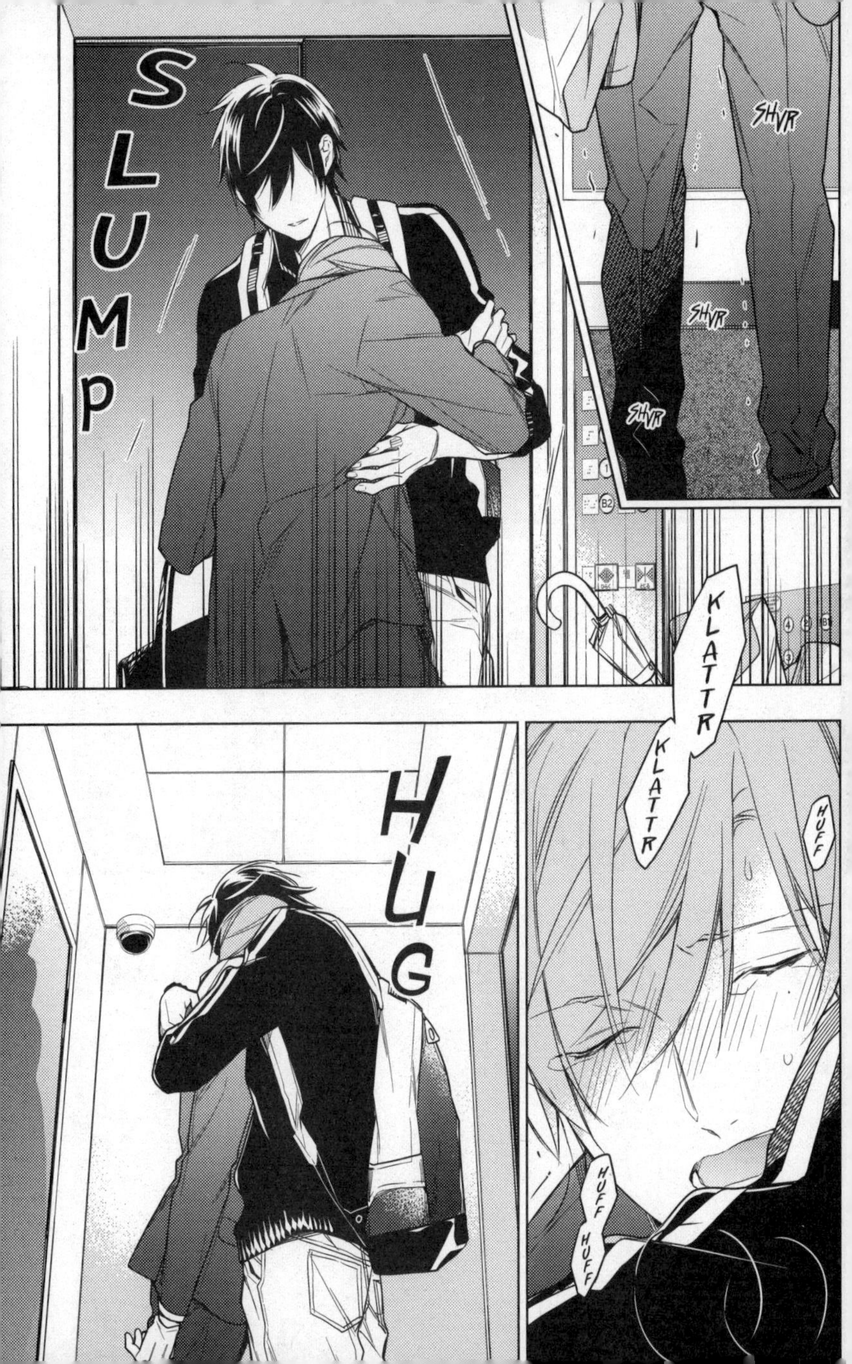
SHVR
SHVR
SHVR
KLATTR
KLATTR
SLUMP
HUFF
HUFF
HUFF
HUG

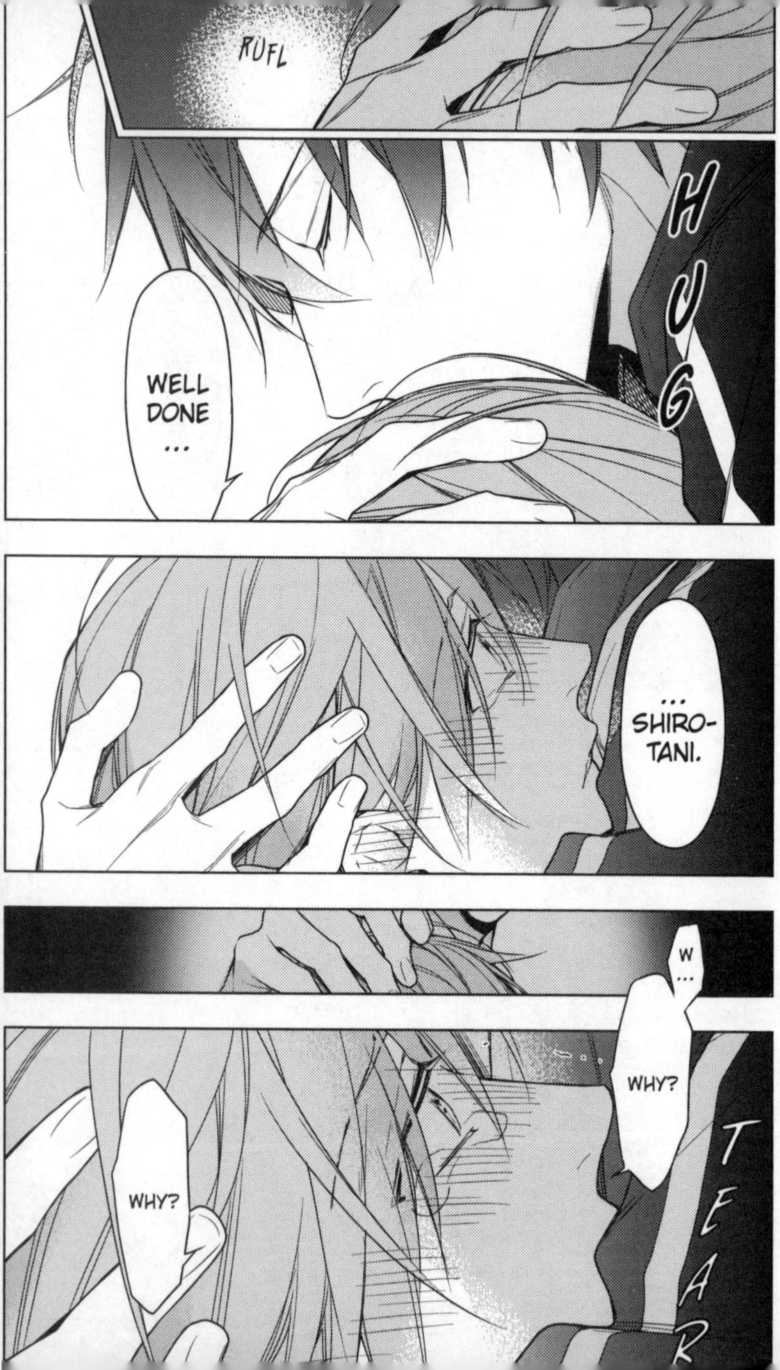
RUFL
HUG
WELL DONE ...
... SHIRO-TANI.
W ...
WHY?
TEAR
WHY?

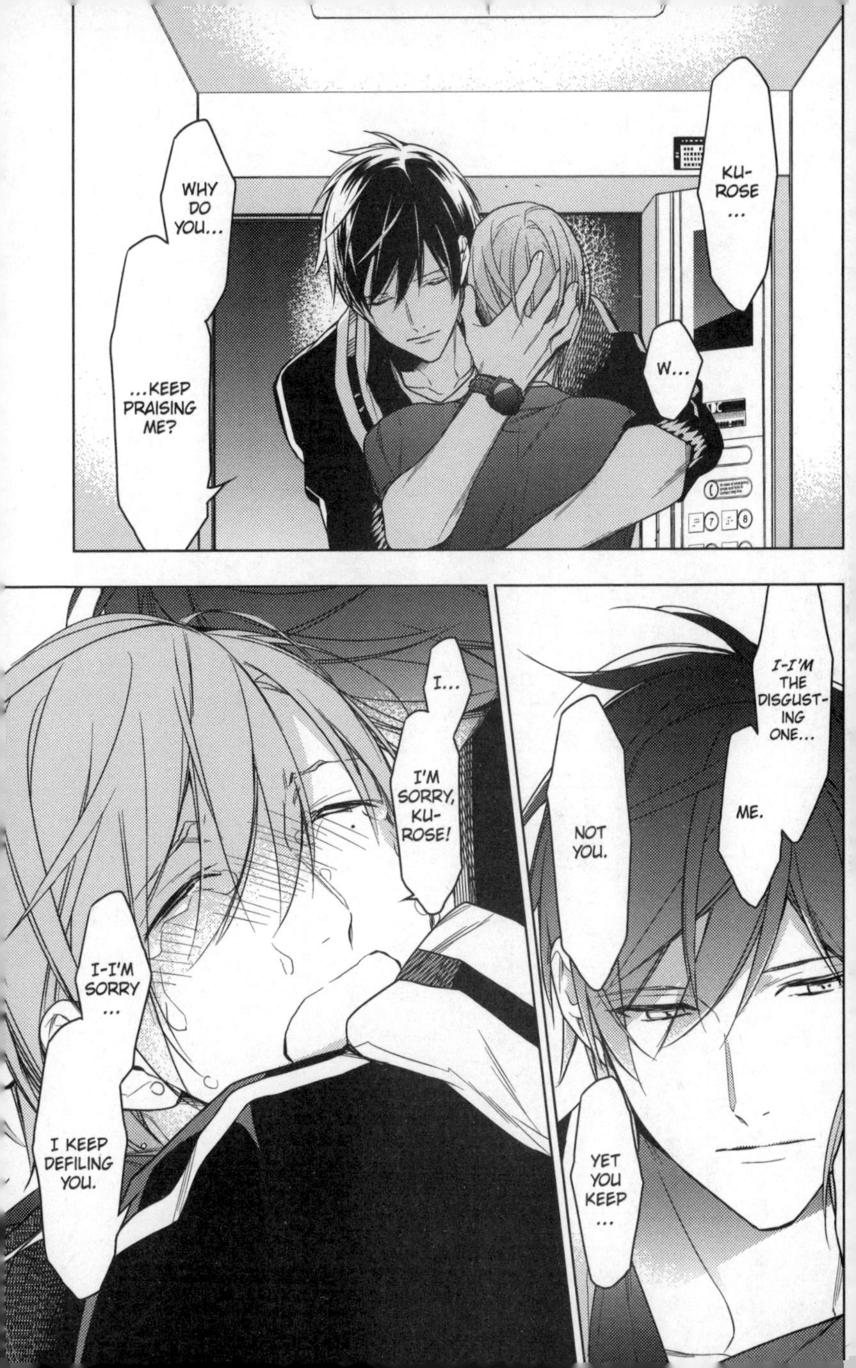
KU-ROSE...
W...
WHY DO YOU...
...KEEP PRAISING ME?
I-I'M THE DISGUST-ING ONE...
ME.
NOT YOU.
YET YOU KEEP...
I...
I'M SORRY, KU-ROSE!
I-I'M SORRY...
I KEEP DEFILING YOU.

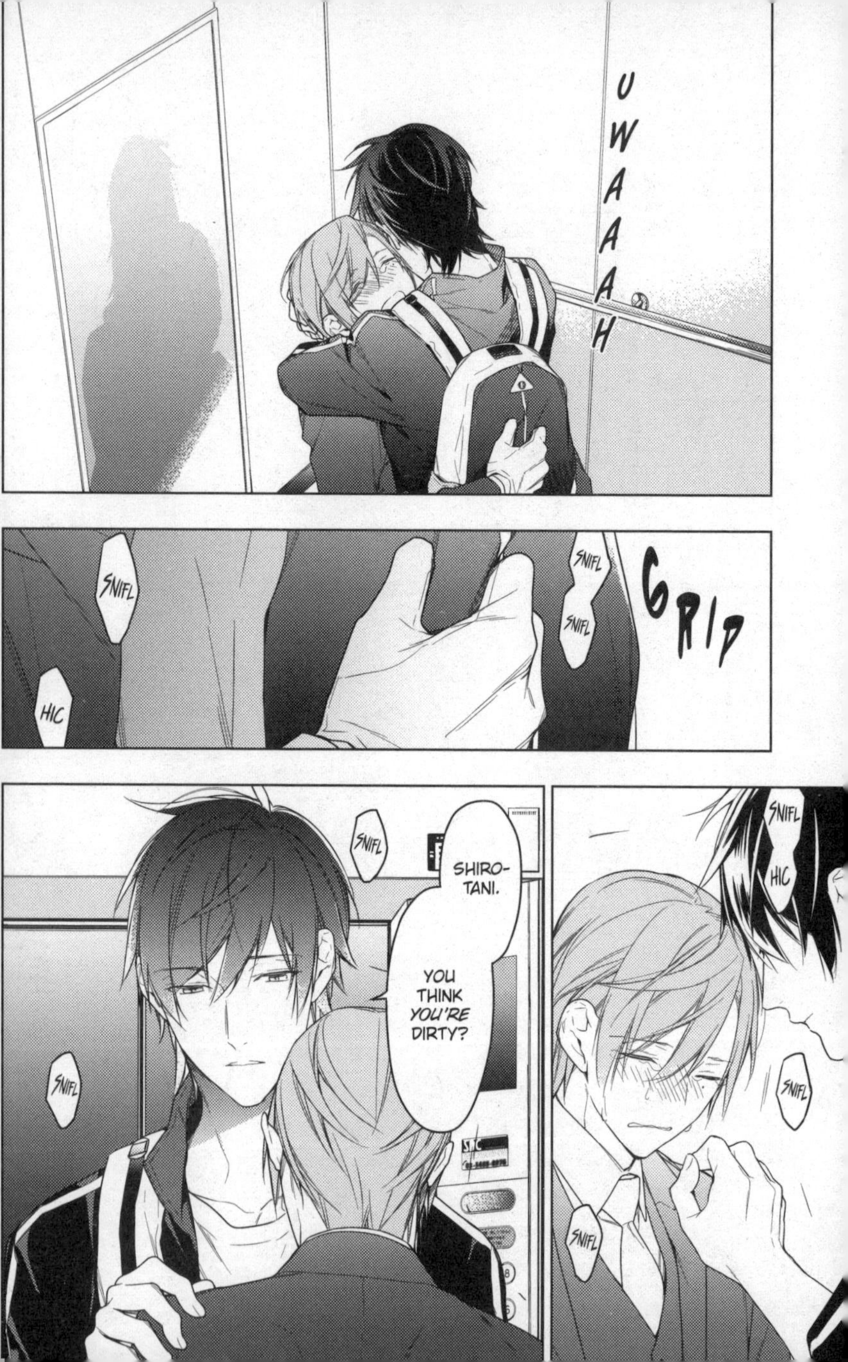
UWAAAAH
GRIP
SNIFL
SNIFL
SNIFL
HIC
SNIFL
HIC
SNIFL
SNIFL
SNIFL
SHIRO-TANI.
YOU THINK YOU'RE DIRTY?
SNIFL

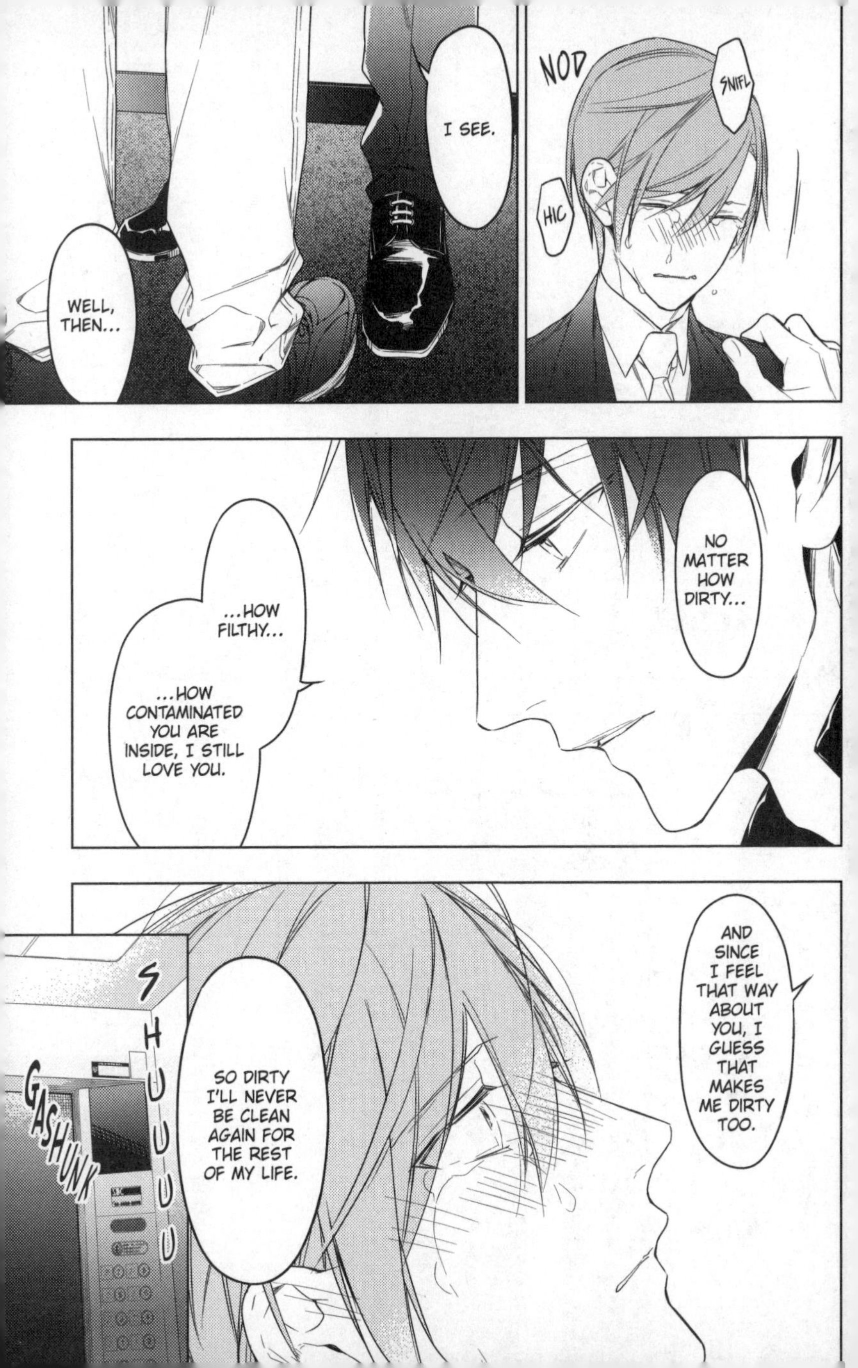
NOD
SNIFL
HIC
I SEE.
WELL, THEN...
NO MATTER HOW DIRTY...
...HOW FILTHY...
...HOW CONTAMINATED YOU ARE INSIDE, I STILL LOVE YOU.
AND SINCE I FEEL THAT WAY ABOUT YOU, I GUESS THAT MAKES ME DIRTY TOO.
SO DIRTY I'LL NEVER BE CLEAN AGAIN FOR THE REST OF MY LIFE.
SHUUUUU
GASHUNK

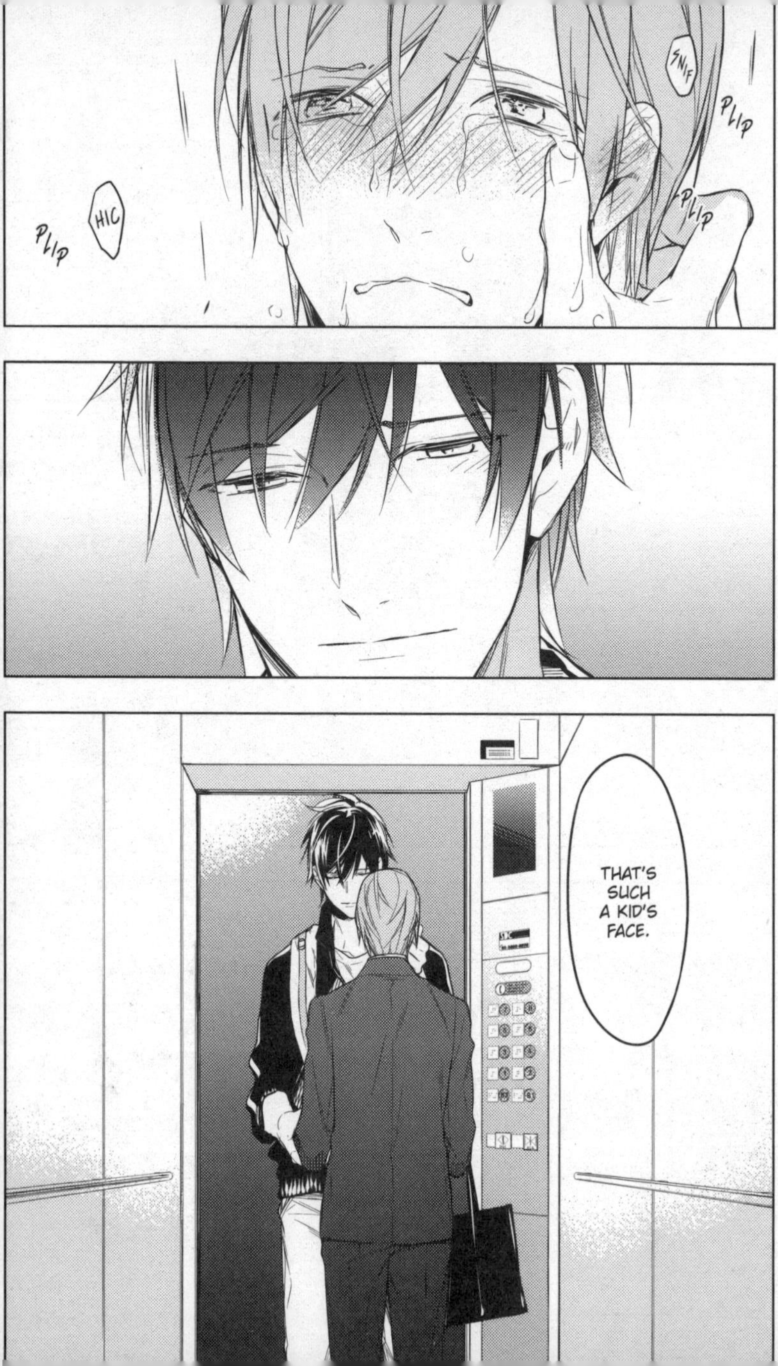
SNIF
PLIP
PLIP
HIC
PLIP
THAT'S SUCH A KID'S FACE.

ten count

by

rihito takarai

ten count by rihito takarai

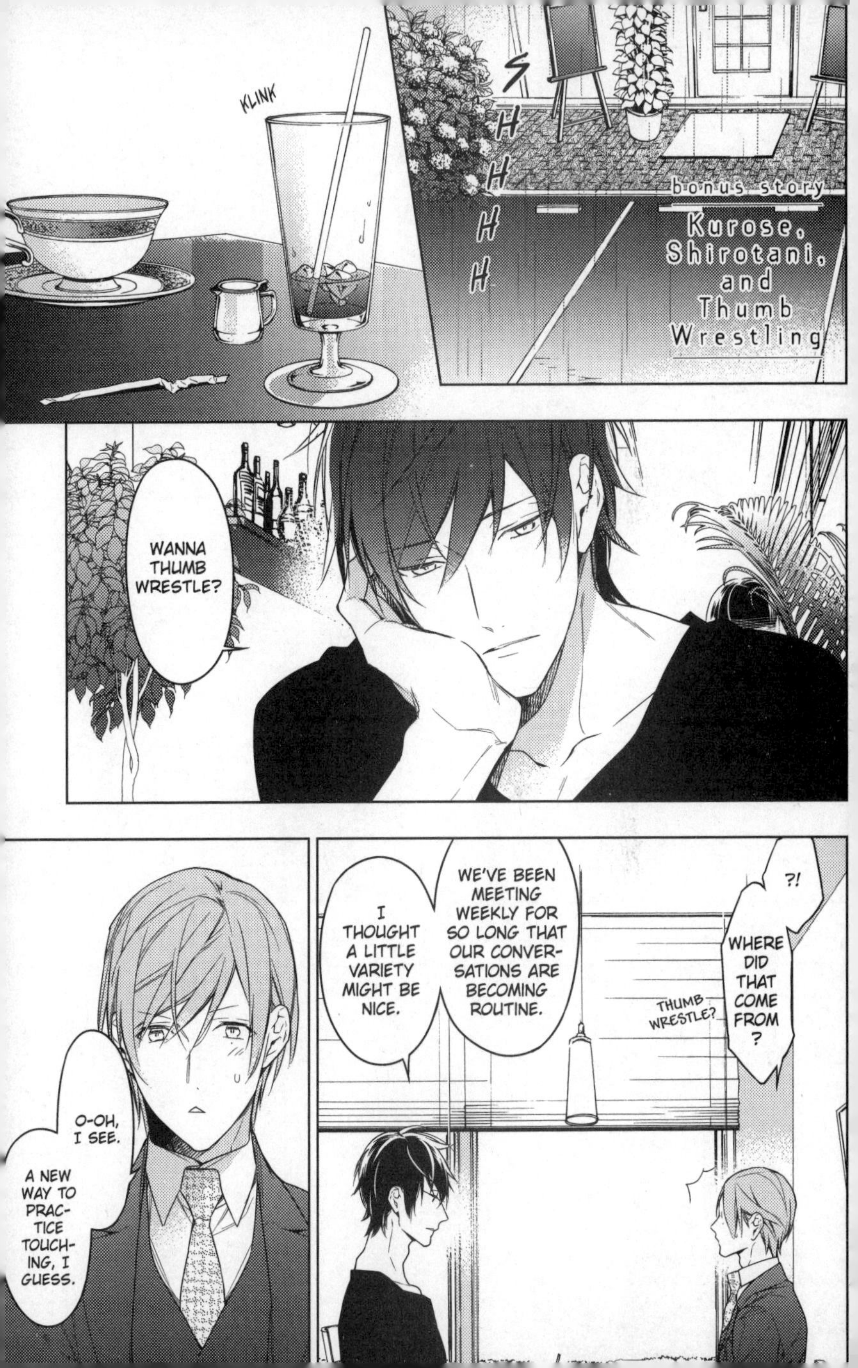
bonus story
Kurose, Shirotani, and Thumb Wrestling
SHHHHH
KLINK
WANNA THUMB WRESTLE?
?!
WHERE DID THAT COME FROM?
THUMB WRESTLE?
WE'VE BEEN MEETING WEEKLY FOR SO LONG THAT OUR CONVER-SATIONS ARE BECOMING ROUTINE.
I THOUGHT A LITTLE VARIETY MIGHT BE NICE.
O-OH, I SEE.
A NEW WAY TO PRAC-TICE TOUCH-ING, I GUESS.

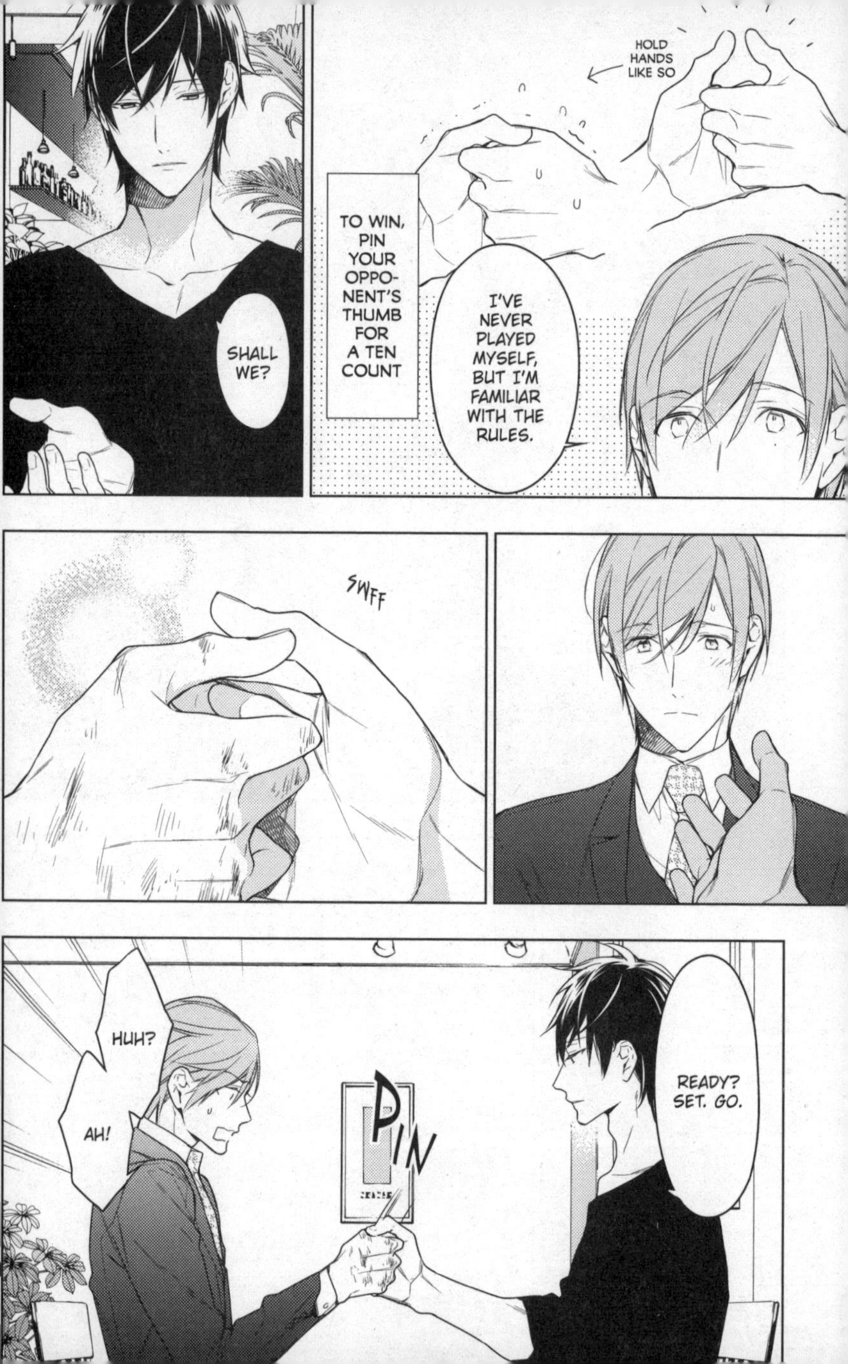
HOLD HANDS LIKE SO
TO WIN, PIN YOUR OPPONENT'S THUMB FOR A TEN COUNT
I'VE NEVER PLAYED MYSELF, BUT I'M FAMILIAR WITH THE RULES.
SHALL WE?
SWFF
READY? SET. GO.
PIN
HUH?
AH!

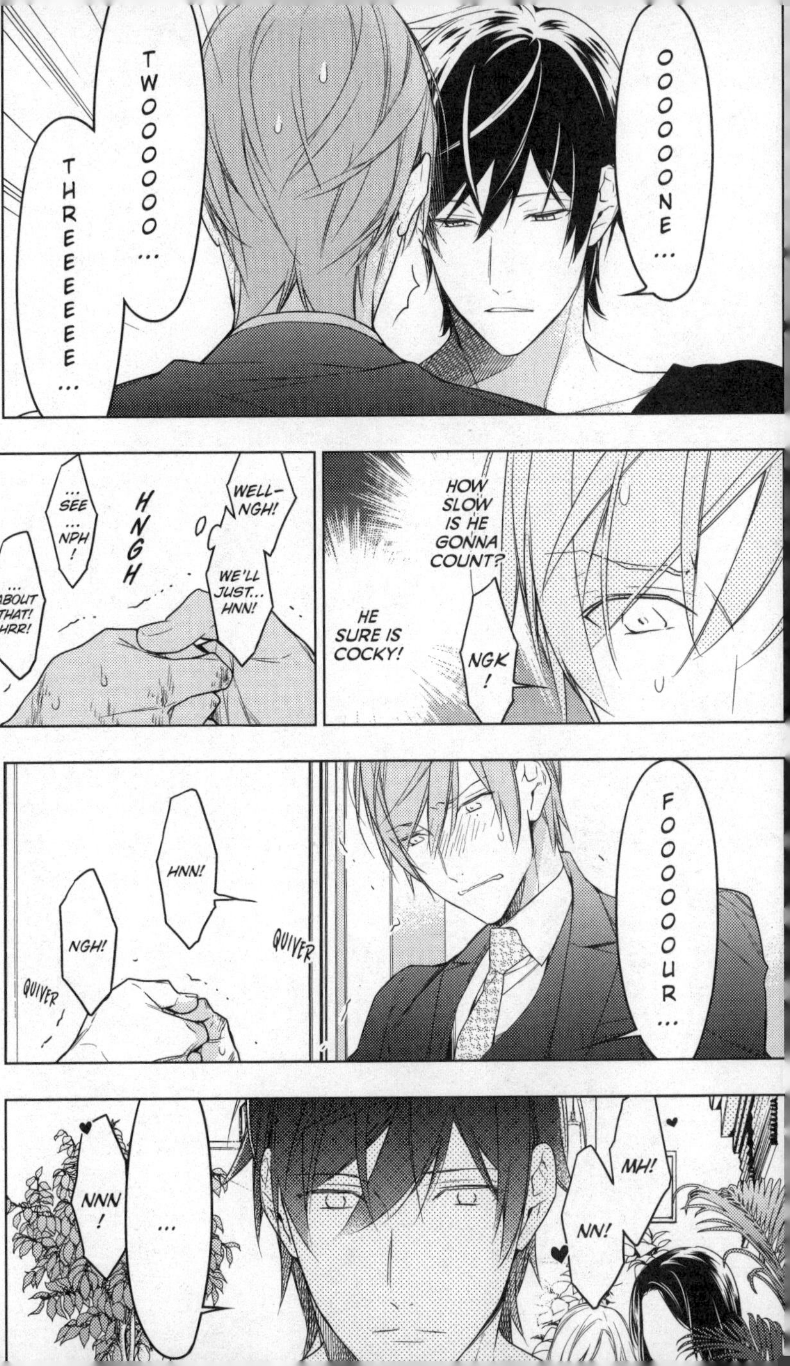
OOOOOONE...
TWOOOOOO...
THREEEEEE...
HOW SLOW IS HE GONNA COUNT?
NGK!
HE SURE IS COCKY!
WELL-NGH!
WE'LL JUST... HNN!
HNGH
...SEE...NPH!
...ABOUT THAT! HRR!
FOOOOOOUR...
QUIVER
HNN!
NGH!
QUIVER
MH!
NN!
...
NNN!

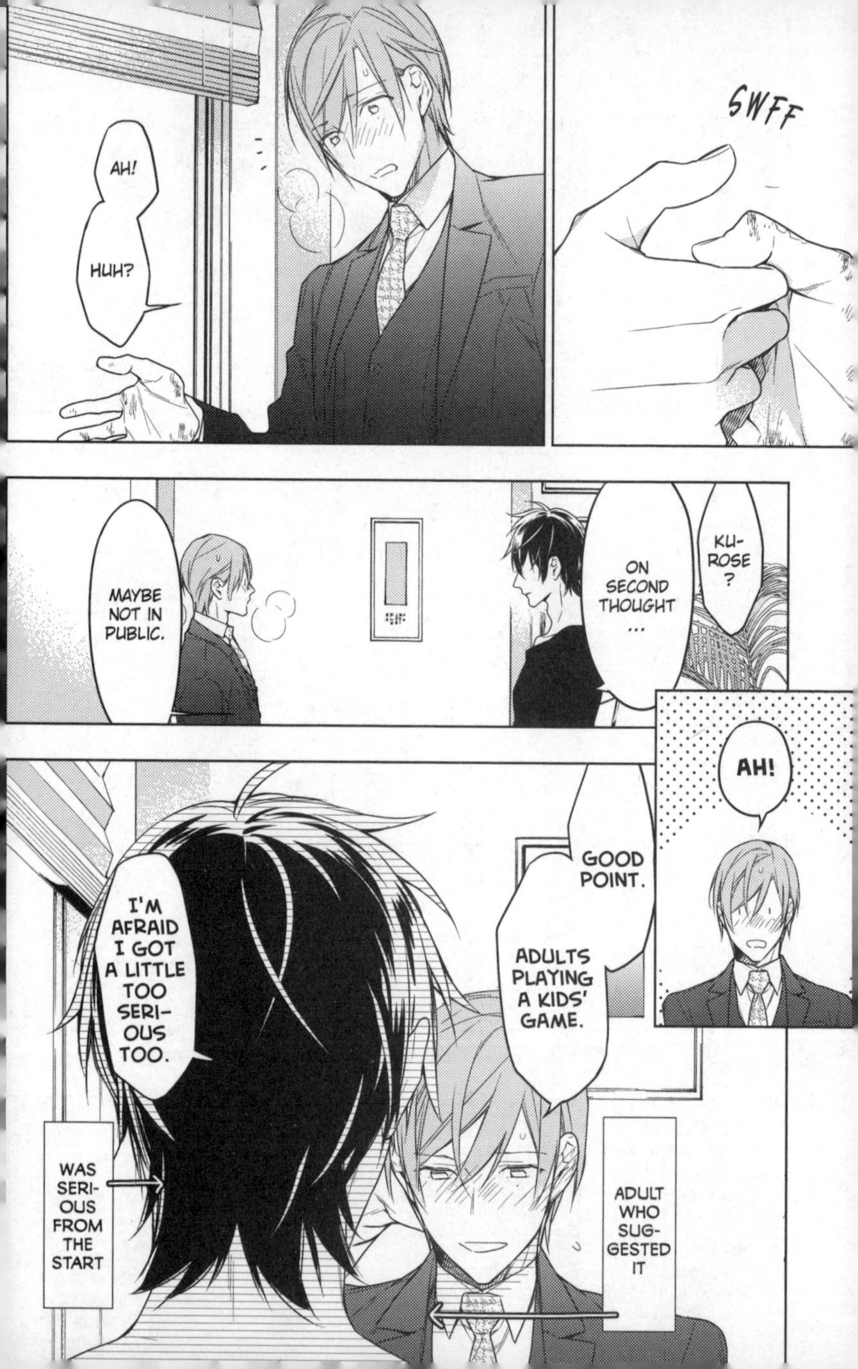
SWFF
AH!
HUH?
KU-ROSE?
ON SECOND THOUGHT...
MAYBE NOT IN PUBLIC.
AH!
GOOD POINT.
ADULTS PLAYING A KIDS' GAME.
I'M AFRAID I GOT A LITTLE TOO SERIOUS TOO.
ADULT WHO SUGGESTED IT
WAS SERIOUS FROM THE START

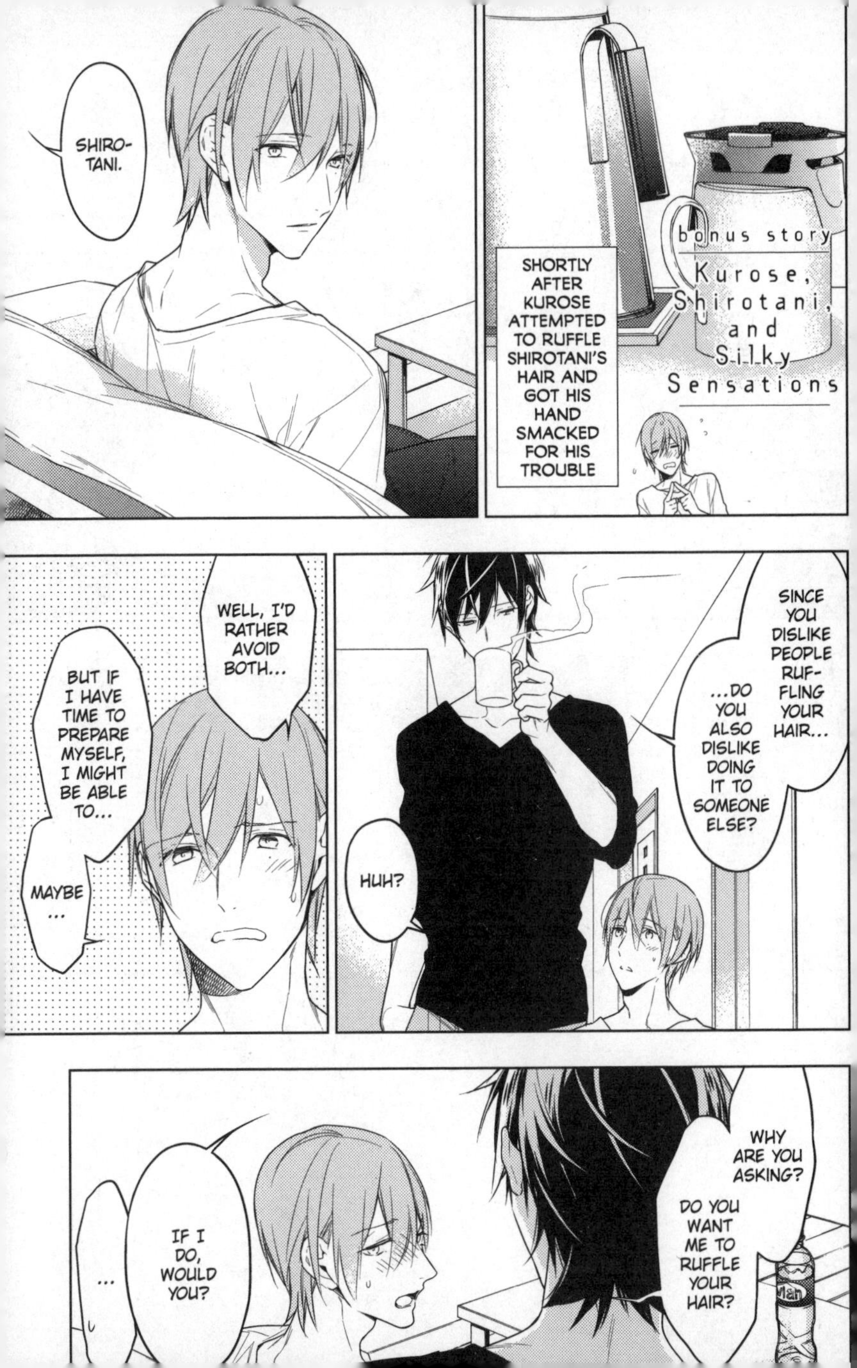
bonus story
Kurose, Shirotani, and Silky Sensations
SHORTLY AFTER KUROSE ATTEMPTED TO RUFFLE SHIROTANI'S HAIR AND GOT HIS HAND SMACKED FOR HIS TROUBLE
SHIRO-TANI.
SINCE YOU DISLIKE PEOPLE RUF-FLING YOUR HAIR...
...DO YOU ALSO DISLIKE DOING IT TO SOMEONE ELSE?
HUH?
WELL, I'D RATHER AVOID BOTH...
BUT IF I HAVE TIME TO PREPARE MYSELF, I MIGHT BE ABLE TO...
MAYBE ...
WHY ARE YOU ASKING?
DO YOU WANT ME TO RUFFLE YOUR HAIR?
IF I DO, WOULD YOU?
...

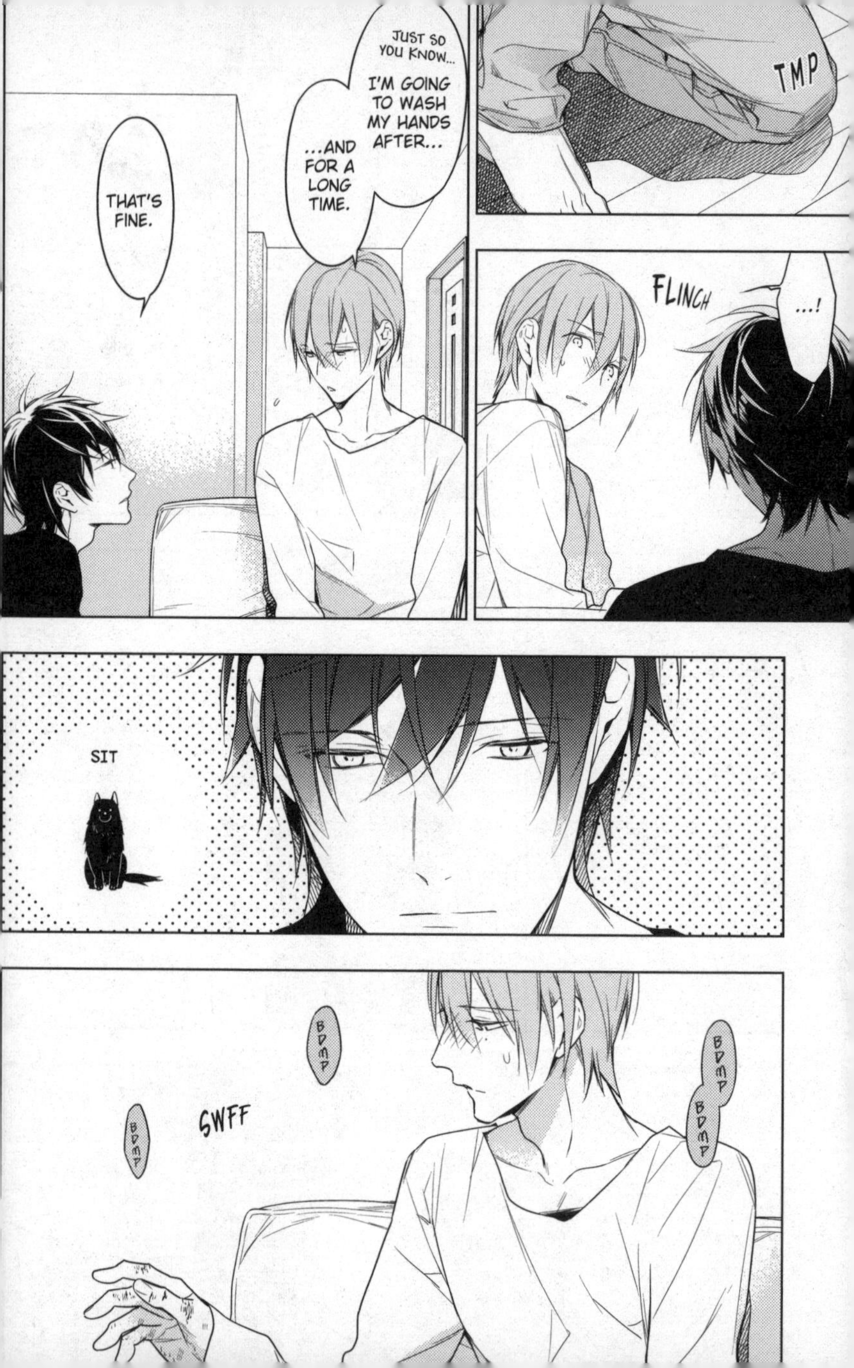
TMP
FLINCH
...!
JUST SO YOU KNOW...
I'M GOING TO WASH MY HANDS AFTER...
...AND FOR A LONG TIME.
THAT'S FINE.
SIT
BDMP
BDMP
BDMP
SWFF
BDMP

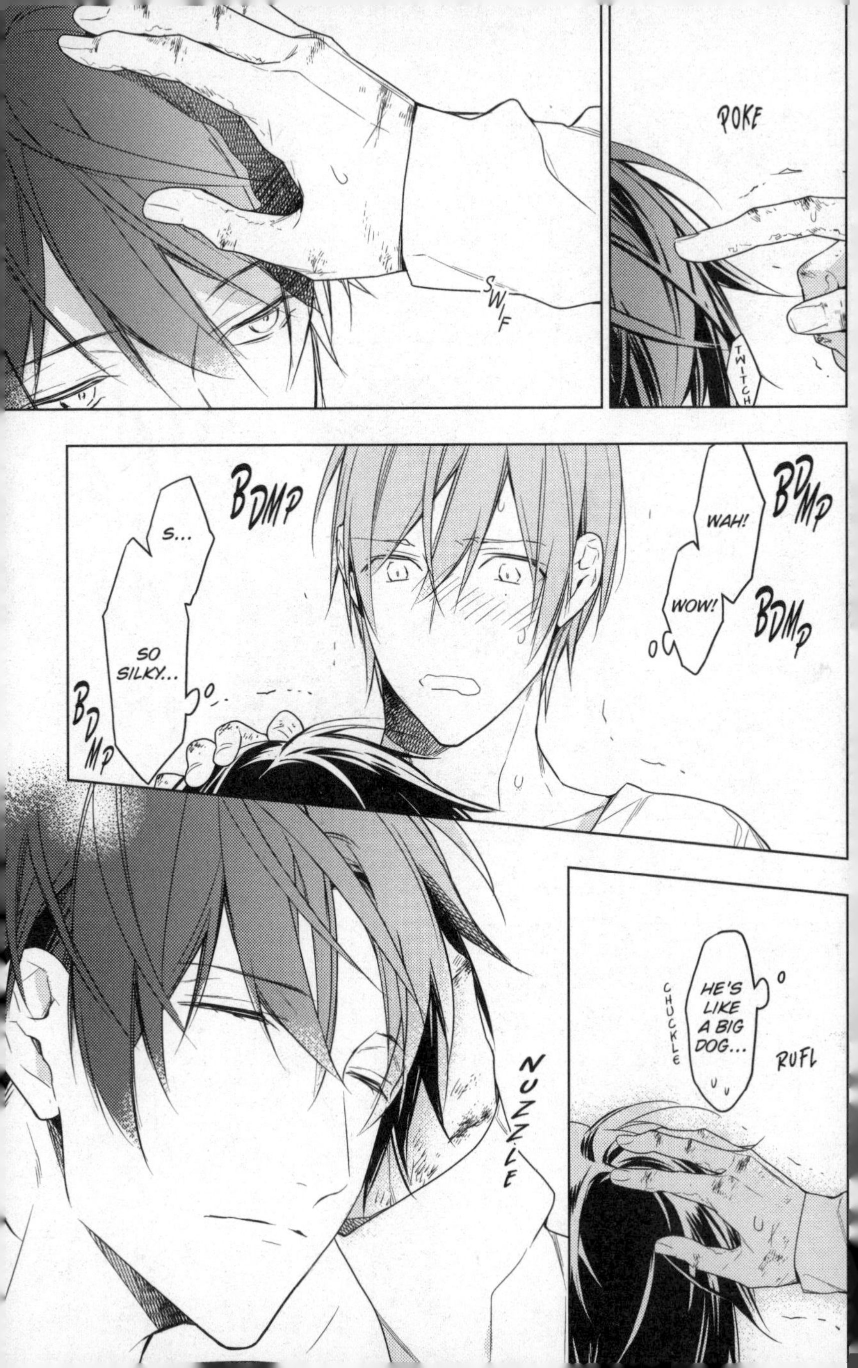

POKE
TWITCH
SWIF
BDMP
WAH!
WOW!
BDMP
BDMP
S...
SO SILKY...
BDMP
RUFL
HE'S LIKE A BIG DOG...
CHUCKLE
NUZZLE

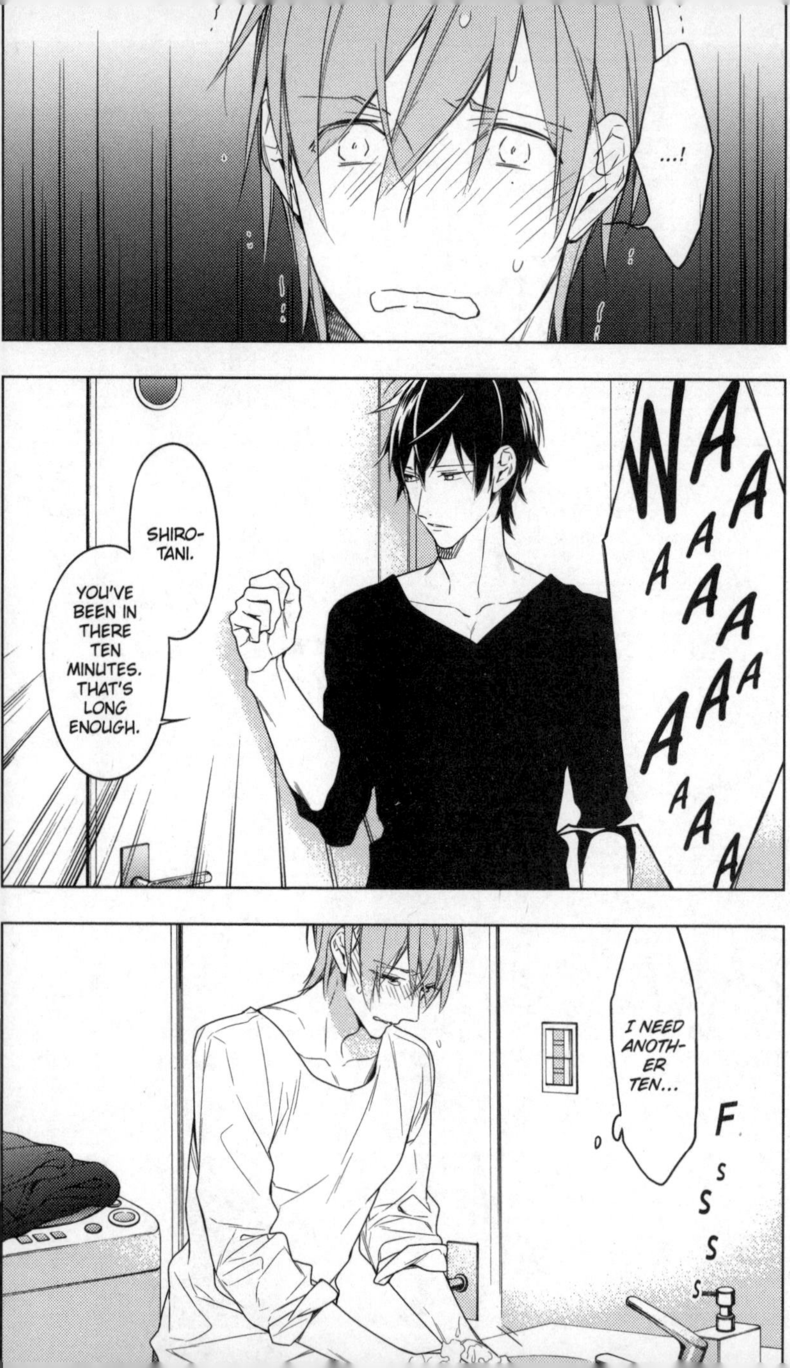
...!
WAAAAAAAAAAAAAAA
SHIRO-TANI.
YOU'VE BEEN IN THERE TEN MINUTES. THAT'S LONG ENOUGH.
I NEED ANOTH-ER TEN...
FSSSS

ten count by rihito takarai

Wow. Volume 4 is out already. Thank you so much for reading!

This year was a busy one full of autograph sessions, new character goods, and even a drama CD. I'm brimming with thankfulness for it all.

Also, this volume I tried something a little different with one of the bonus stories. I hope you enjoy it.

Rihito Takarai

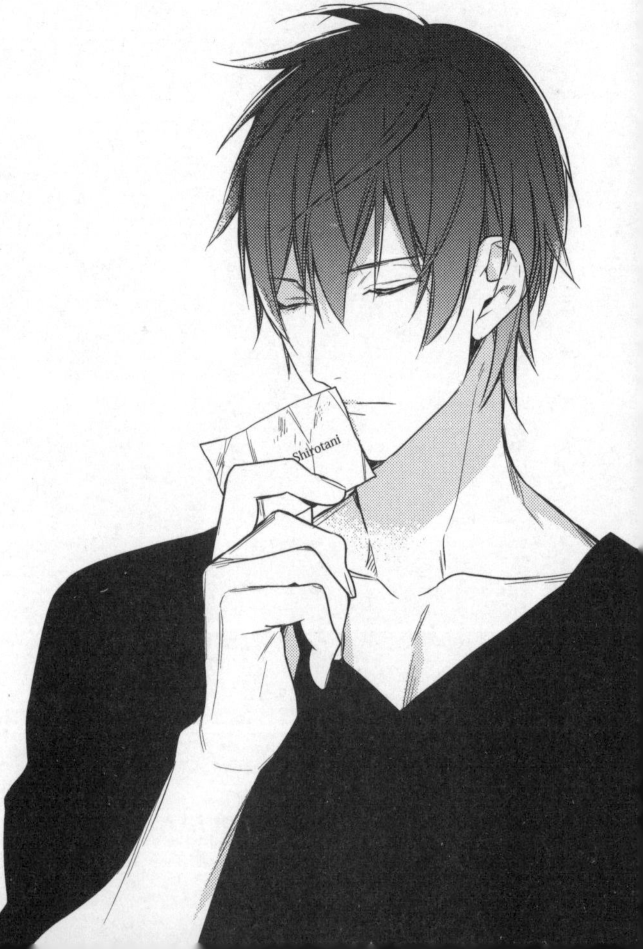
Shirotani

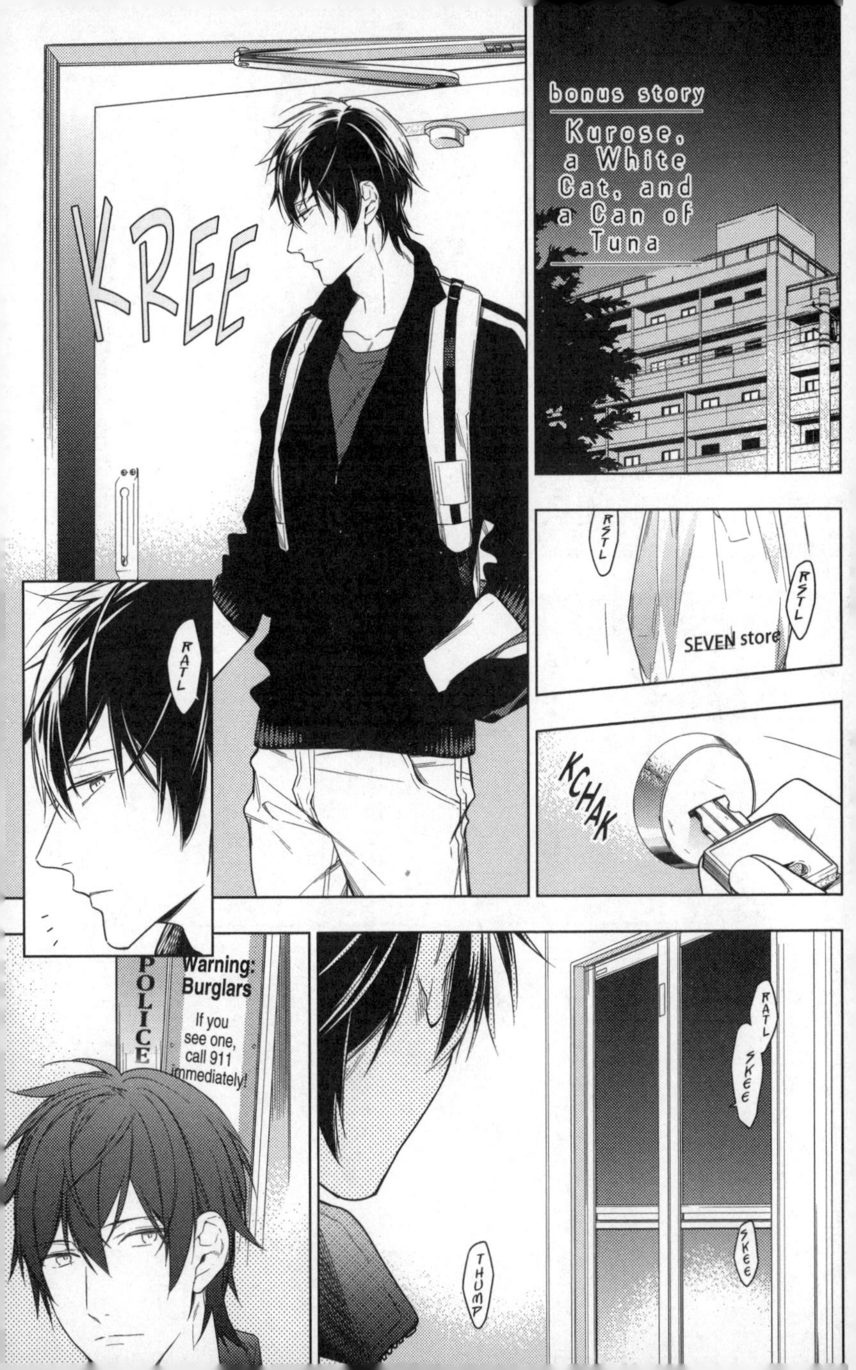
bonus story
Kurose, a White Cat, and a Can of Tuna
RSTL
RSTL
SEVEN store
KCHAK
KREE
RATL
RATL
SKEE
SKEE
THUMP
POLICE
Warning: Burglars
If you see one, call 911 immediately!

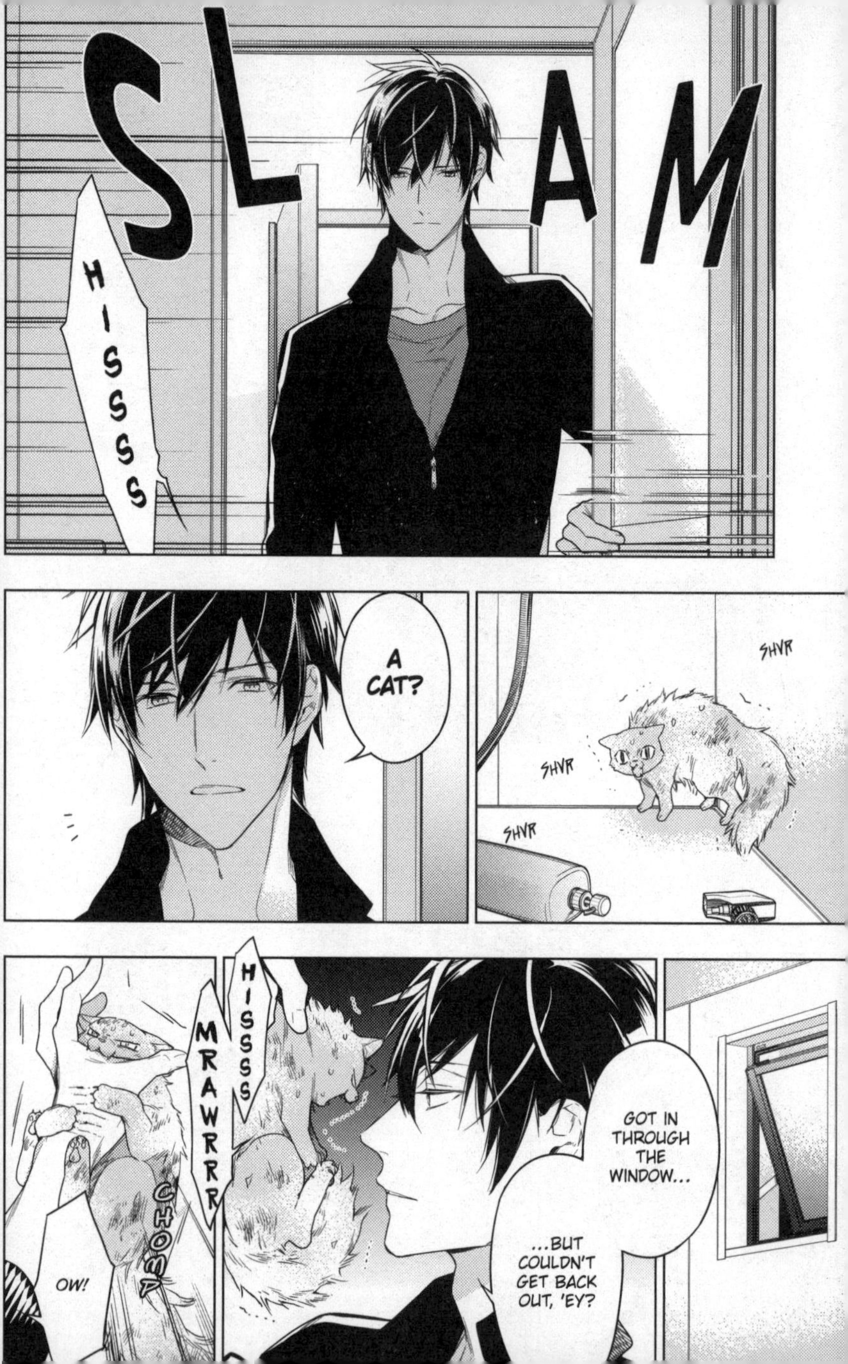
SLAM
HISSSS
SHVR
SHVR
SHVR
A CAT?
GOT IN THROUGH THE WINDOW...
...BUT COULDN'T GET BACK OUT, 'EY?
HISSS
MRAWRRR
CHOMP
OW!

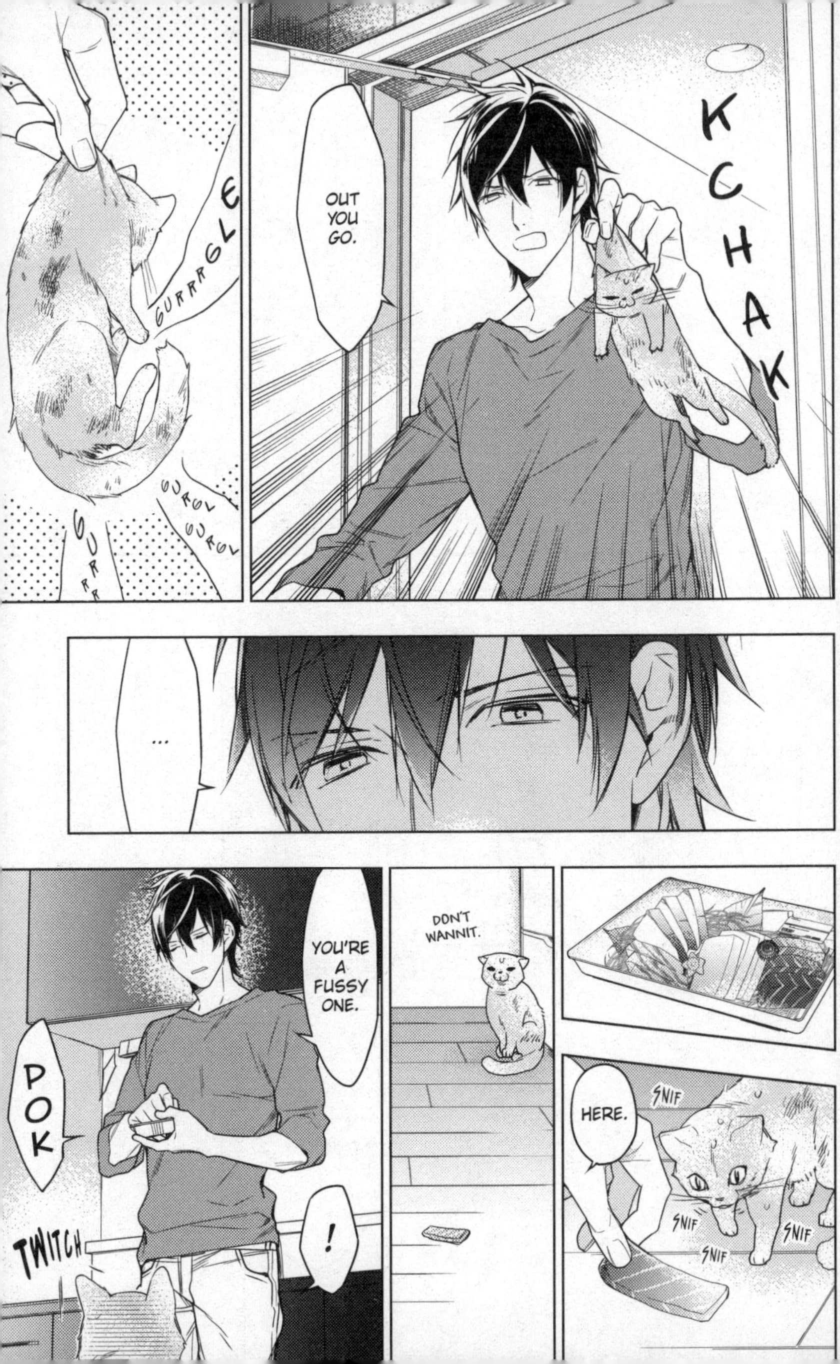
KCHAK
OUT YOU GO.
GURRRGLE
GURGL
GURGL
GURRR
...
HERE.
SNIF
SNIF
SNIF
SNIF
DON'T WANNIT.
YOU'RE A FUSSY ONE.
POK
!
TWITCH

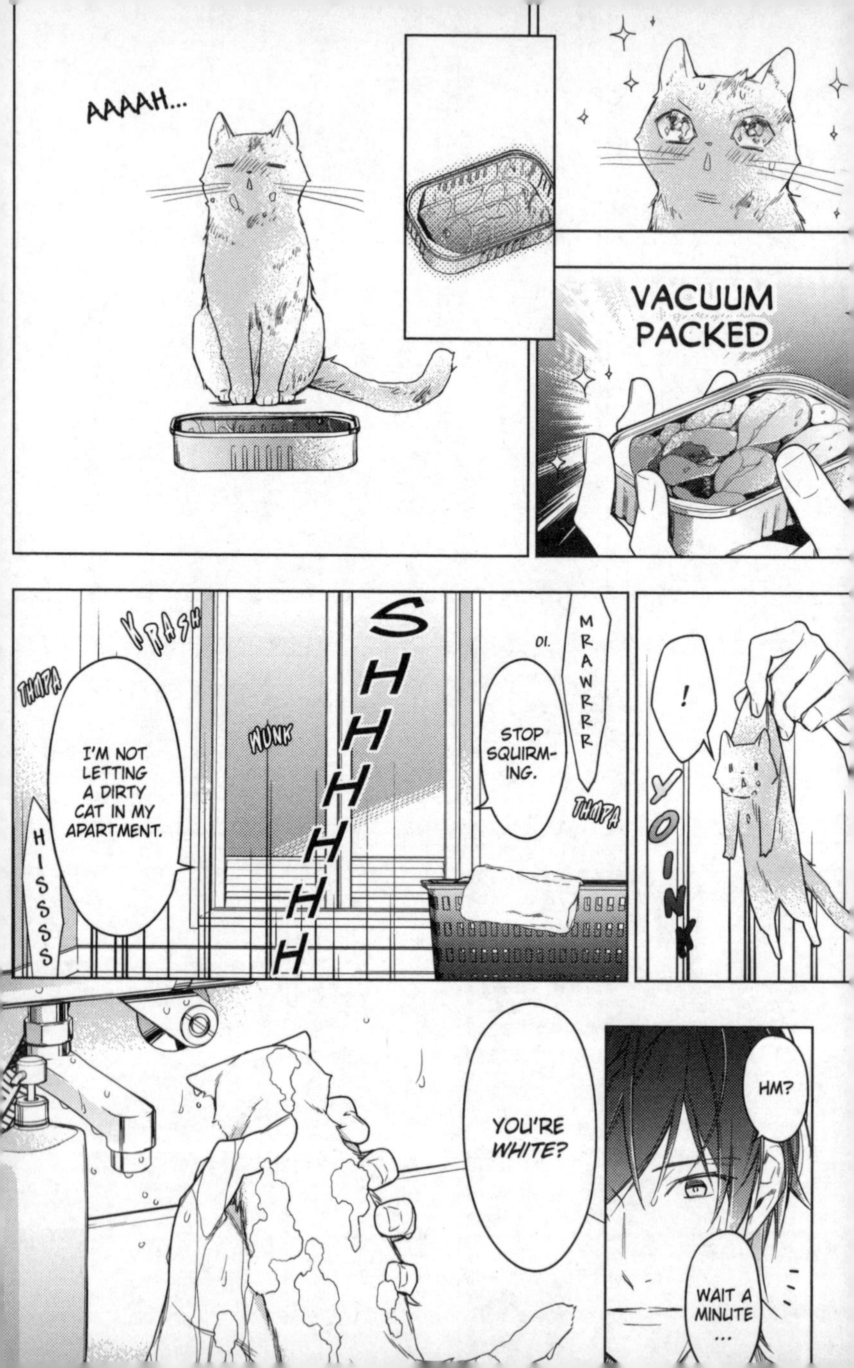
VACUUM PACKED
AAAAH...
!
YOINK
MRAWRRR
OI.
STOP SQUIRMING.
THMPA
SHHHHHHH
KRASH
WUNK
THMPA
I'M NOT LETTING A DIRTY CAT IN MY APARTMENT.
HISSSS
HM?
WAIT A MINUTE ...
YOU'RE *WHITE*?

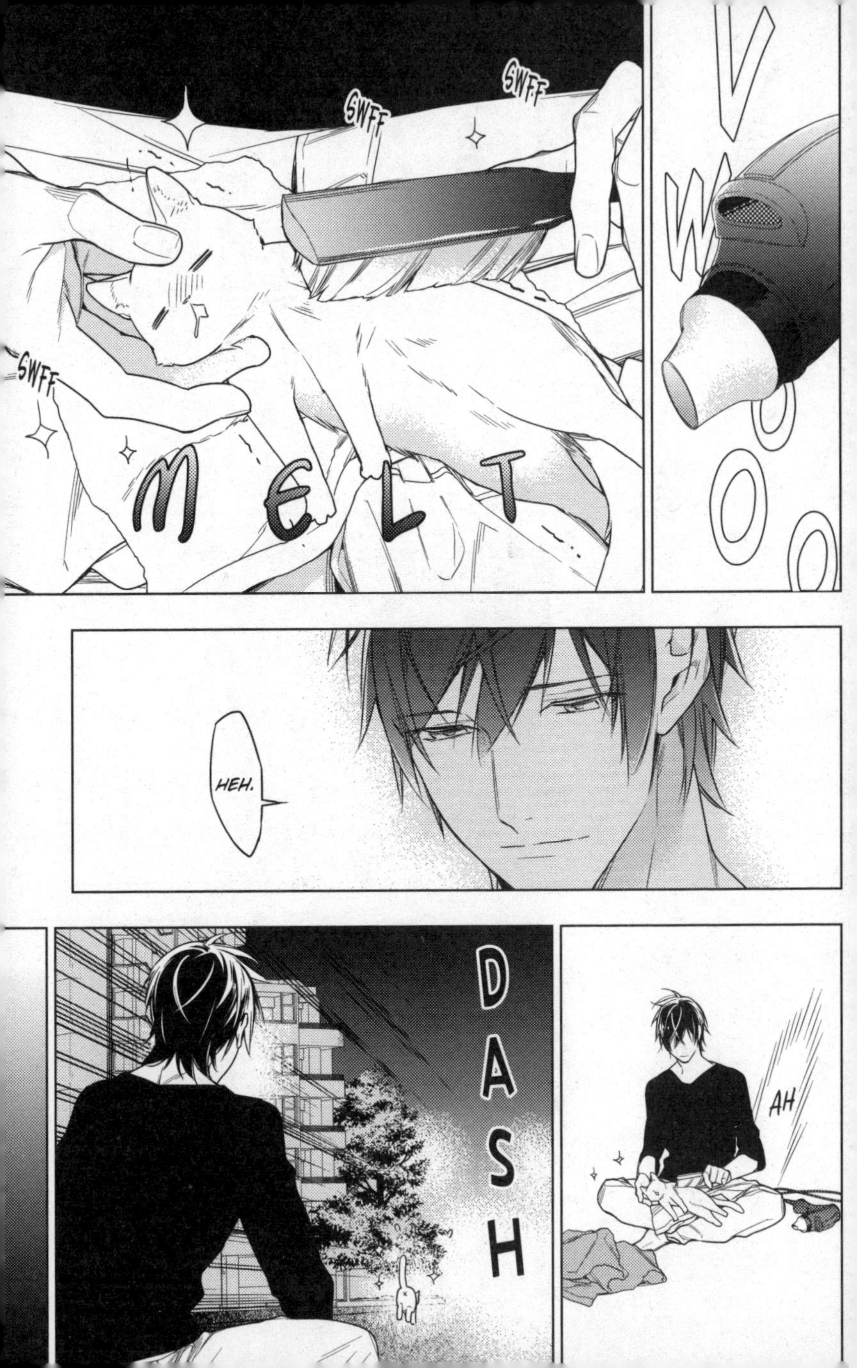
VWOOO
SWFF
SWFF
SWFF
MELT
HEH.
AH
DASH

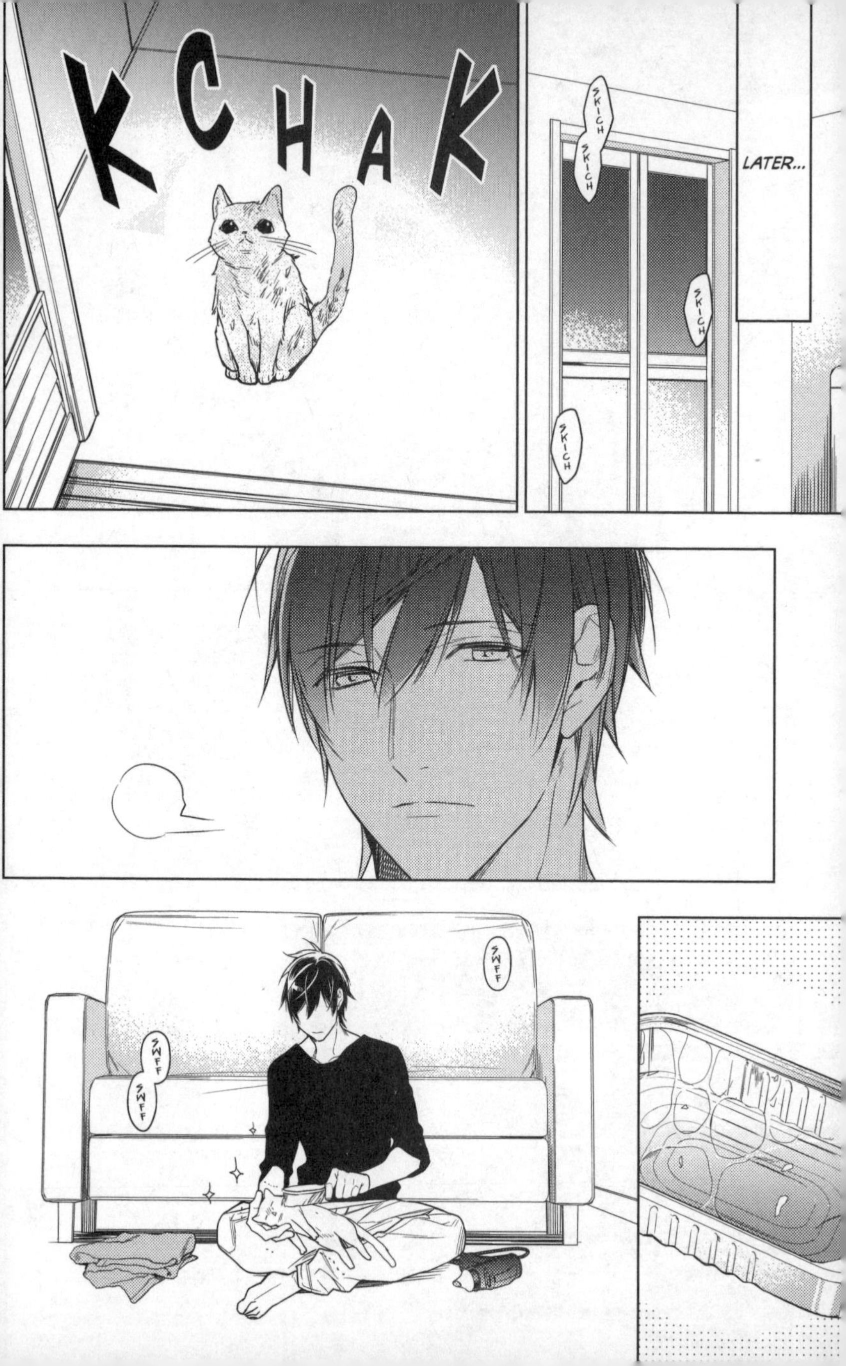
LATER...
SKICH SKICH
SKICH
SKICH
KCHAK
SWFF
SWFF SWFF

About the Author

This is **Rihito Takarai's** second English-language release, with her first being *Seven Days*. She has also been published in French, Spanish, and German. Born in Hiroshima Prefecture in October, she's a Libra with an O blood type.

Ten Count
Volume 4
SuBLime Manga Edition

Story and Art by **Rihito Takarai**

Translation—**Adrienne Beck**
Touch-Up Art and Lettering—**NRP Studios**
Cover and Graphic Design—**Jodie Shikuma**
Editor—**Jennifer LeBlanc**

© 2015 Rihito Takarai
Originally published in Japan in 2015 by Shinshokan Co., Ltd.

The stories, characters and incidents mentioned in this publication are entirely fictional.

No portion of this book may be reproduced or transmitted in any form or by any means without written permission from the copyright holders.

Printed in the U.S.A.

Published by SuBLime Manga
P.O. Box 77010
San Francisco, CA 94107

10 9 8 7 6 5 4
First printing, May 2017
Fourth printing, February 2022

 PARENTAL ADVISORY
TEN COUNT is rated M for Mature and is recommended for adults. This volume contains mature themes and frank depictions of sexuality.

www.SuBLimeManga.com

For more information

on all our products, along with the most up-to-date news on releases, series announcements, and contests, please visit us at:

 SuBLimeManga.com

 twitter.com/**SuBLimeManga**

 facebook.com/**SuBLimeManga**

 SuBLimeManga.tumblr.com

SUBLIME

MANGA

Downloading is as easy as:

1

Login/Email
Password

LOGIN
REGISTER NOW
Forgot Password

2

PAY with **PayPal**

— OR —

Pay Now with **amazon** ▶
The Simple, Trusted Way to Pay

Digital Edition includes **BOTH**
Download-to-own PDF and
online viewing option.

3

View your purchase as:

DOWNLOAD-TO-OWN **PDF**

Your Toys Love Boys' Love

Own your SuBLime book as a convenient PDF document that is downloadable to the following devices:

- ♥ Computer
- ♥ Kindle™
- ♥ NOOK™
- ♥ iPad™, iPhone™, and iPod Touch™
- ♥ Any device capable of reading a PDF document

Shizuku Hanabira Ringo no Kaori © 2009 Toko Kawai/Libre Publishing Co., Ltd. ♥ Kekkon Zenya © 2011 Kou Fujisaki/Libre Publishing Co., Ltd. ♥ Ousama no Bed © 2011 Sakae Kusama/Libre Publishing Co., Ltd. ♥ Punch↑① © 2006 Shiuko Kano/Libre Publishing Co., Ltd. ♥ Yumemusubi Koimusubi Volume 1 © Yaya SAKURAGI 2009 ♥ YEBISU Celebrities © 2004 Shinri Fuwa/Kaoru Iwamoto ♥ YEBISU Celebrities © 2005 Shinri Fuwa/Kaoru Iwamoto ♥ Hachimitsu Darling © 2011 Norikazu Akira/Libre Publishing Co., Ltd. ♥ Adult Teacher wa Osuki? © 2011 Kiu Aion/Libre Publishing Co., Ltd. ♥ Three Wolves Mountain © 2003 Bohra Naono

www.SuBLimeManga.com

More of the best digital BL manga from

SUBLIME

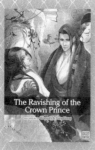

The Ravishing of the Crown Prince
by Wang Yi & Feng Nong

Sword and Mist
by Hayate Kuku

Egoistic Blue
by Mio Tennohji

{ Available **Worldwide** in Download-To-Own Format }

Boys, Be Ambitious!
by Saburo Nagai

The Match Seller
by Sakae Kusama

Lost Letters
by Sakae Kusama

Get them now for only **$5.99** each at SuBLimeManga.com!

Outaishi wa Mujihi ni Ubawareru © 2010 Wang Yi/Feng Nong ♥ Tsurugi to Kiri © 2012 Hayate Kuku/
Libre Publishing ♥ Egoistic Blue © 2012 Mio Tennohji/Libre Publishing ♥ Shonen yo Taishi toka Iroiro
Idake © 2012 Saburo Nagai/Libre Publishing ♥ Lost Letters © 2012 Sakae Kusama/Libre Publishing ♥
The Match Seller © 2010 Sakae Kusama/Libre Publishing

The highly anticipated re-release of Ayano Yamane's erotic fantasy!

Crimson Spell

Story & Art by Ayano YAMANE

Upon wielding an ancient sword that has been passed down through his royal family for generations, Prince Vald is struck by a curse that turns him into a demon! In search of guidance, Vald appeals to the powerful sorcerer Halvir for help, and the two set out on a journey to break the curse. However, there is one thing the handsome sorcerer is keeping secret from the young prince—the raging demon that Vald turns into every night can only be calmed when Halvir satisfies his lust! And so begins their epic journey in search of clues to break the young prince's curse.

MATURE

On sale now at
SuBLimeManga.com
Also available at your local
bookstore or comic book store.

SUBLIME

THE CRIMSON SPELL © AYANO YAMANE 2005/TOKUMA SHOTEN

This young master is hot for butler.

Blue Morning

Story & Art by Shoko **HIDAKA**

At only ten years of age, Akihito Kuze suddenly inherits the Kuze viscountship after his father's death. The family's capable butler, Tomoyuki Katsuragi, takes over the task of raising the boy, serving as his tutor. However, the handsome and intelligent Katsuragi, well respected even among the aristocracy, remains cool towards his charge. Akihito finds himself relentlessly drawn to Katsuragi, frustrated by the distance between them and driven to discover the reasons why.

MATURE

On sale now at
SuBLimeManga.com
Also available at your local
bookstore or comic book store.

SUBLIME

YUU–UTSU NA ASA © SHOKO HIDAKA 2009/TOKUMA SHOTEN

A romantic tale of time travel, ancient curses, and mystery!

Sleeping Moon

Story & Art by Kano MIYAMOTO

In order to solve the mystery of a rumored curse that brings early death to the male descendants in his lineage, Akihiko Odagawa goes back to stay in his family's ancestral home. One night, he experiences a time slip that lands him 100 years in the past! There he meets Eitaro, a student from the Meiji Period who is also trying to solve the same mystery. Bridging the gap between the past and the present, the two men traverse time and space as they work together to unravel the family's secret.

MATURE

On sale now at
SuBLimeManga.com
Also available at your local
bookstore or comic book store.

SUBLIME

NEMURERU TSUKI © KANO MIYAMOTO 2009/TOKUMA SHOTEN

Drawn to love.

Tableau Numéro 20

Story & Art by **est em**

Ten years ago, while still a student, Maurice stumbled across an illustration in an artist's sketchbook that instantly captivated him. A drawing of a beautiful youth with sad, gentle eyes, an expression that spoke of love and forgiveness. Now settled into his successful career as an art restoration expert, Maurice is shocked by the sudden appearance of a young man who looks exactly like the one in the drawing. Who, in fact, insists that he *is* the one in the drawing... A collection of short stories by the incomparable est em.

MATURE

On sale now at
SuBLimeManga.com
Also available at your local
bookstore or comic book store.

SUBLIME

Sakuhin Number 20 © 2009 Esutoemu/Libre Publishing